PRAISE FOR
The Sheikh's Batmobile

"Poplak's expertly researched and beautifully written book is one of the most important documents of the post-9/11 world."
—*The National Post*

"I would read Poplak if he wrote about watching paint dry. He is a gifted addition to the exploding and increasingly sloppy literary non-fiction genre. Dark, funny, self-deprecating and poetic, Poplak is a punk Graham Greene both exploiting and being exploited by the cultures he inhabits."
—*The Globe and Mail*

"A heroic feat of research, analysis, and on-the-ground reportage . . . At the very least, *The Sheikh's Batmobile* should shatter the Western stereotype of the Muslim world as repressive and stagnant."
—*Quill and Quire*

"Poplak avoids making easy connections . . . his de-embedded journalism is always open-minded and captures the uncanny perfectly."
—*Eye Weekly*

"Humorous, astute and vivid . . . *The Sheikh's Batmobile* will leave you itching to travel, giggling and glued to YouTube, looking up references. The book is less about how Muslims view Americans as it is about discovering a shared lexicon between two cultures. Poplak's view of pop culture is nuanced, as it emerges as a mutating entity crossing national and ideological boundaries."
—*The Coast*

"This is a great book and despite its lighthearted title and subject matter it's a serious book. It's an important book too, because it promotes understanding and leaves the reader with hope that at a human level, and at a creative level, the kids are all right."
—*Winnipeg Free Press*

"If . . . you're willing to join the author on his irreverent excursions to dictators' palaces, blaring Egyptian heavy metal sessions, concerts preempted by Kalashnikov fire, and secret Batmobile laboratories (yes, the book does live up to its name), then you will doubtlessly ease right into Poplak's narrative . . . The book is not a magnifying glass searching for Western brushstrokes on an Islamic canvas, but rather a kaleidoscope that bounces the reader's assumptions and expectations off the colorful mirrors of zestful narrative and impressive legwork."

—*Wiretap Magazine*

"A fast-paced and culturally savvy look at a section of the Muslim population underrepresented, if not entirely ignored, by Western media."

—*Open Book: Toronto*

"In the riotous, fearless, and very funny tradition of Hunter S. Thompson and Jon Ronson, Richard Poplak takes us through the looking glass and into an upside down, funhouse mirror pop culture universe where Homer Simpson drinks juice out of a beer can, batmobiles are custom-designed in a desert lair and Islamic children spontaneously recreate the video for Lionel Richie's 'Hello.' In the process, Poplak gives us a mantra that unites the West and the East, the secular and the sacred: 'Fuck you, Shrek, you big green motherfucker.'"

—Nathan Rabin, Head Writer,
The A.V. Club, author,
The Big Rewind and My Year of Flops

"Whether dissecting Indonesian punk bands or the eternal wisdom of *Magnum, P.I.*, Poplak is everything you want in a cultural interpreter—funny, frank and utterly incapable of spewing mass market pabulum. Poplak gets beyond the cheap, superficial observations lesser writers bring to his subject, revealing himself as a genuine thinker who delivers original insight and laughs in every chapter."

—Chuck Thompson,
author of *Smile When You're Lying: Confessions of a Rogue Travel Writer*

The Sheikh's Batmobile

RICHARD POPLAK is an award-winning writer of off-beat journalistic materials, be they for major magazines, crazed graphic novels (*Kenk: A Graphic Portrait*, 2010), or Big Important Books (the highly acclaimed *Ja, No, Man: Growing Up White in Apartheid-Era South Africa*, 2007). He races road bicycles for Toronto-based Cycle Solutions, and used to direct music videos and commercials.

www.sheikhsbatmobile.com

The Sheikh's Batmobile

In Pursuit of American
Pop Culture in the
Muslim World

Richard Poplak

First published in 2009 by Penguin Canada

Library of Congress Cataloging-in-Publication Data

Poplak, Richard, 1973–
The sheikh's batmobile : in pursuit of American pop culture in the Muslim world /
Richard Poplak.
p. cm.
Includes bibliographical references and index.
ISBN-13: 978-1-59376-292-6 (alk. paper)
ISBN-10: 1-59376-292-5
1. Islamic countries—Civilization—American influences. 2. Popular culture—Islamic
countries. 3. Popular culture—United States. 4. United States—Foreign public opinion,
Islamic. I. Title.

DS35.62.P66 2010
306.0917'67—dc22

2010019525

Cover design by John Yates
Printed in the United States of America

Soft Skull Press
An Imprint of Counterpoint LLC
1919 Fifth Street
Berkeley, CA 94710

www.softskull.com
www.counterpointpress.com

Distributed by Publishers Group West

10 9 8 7 6 5 4 3 2 1

Understanding a people's culture exposes their normalness
without reducing their particularity.

CLIFFORD GERTZ

If one cannot trust literature, one can at least trust pop culture.

UMBERTO ECO

Homer: The lesson is: Our God is vengeful!
O spiteful one, show me who to smite and they shall be smoten!!!

THE SIMPSONS

CONTENTS

AUTHOR'S NOTE

I traveled to seventeen countries in the course of my research. I mention this not to impress you, but rather to point out that while over half counted Arabic as their lingua franca, it is by no means a standardized language and regional dialects differ greatly. Even in Iran, Indonesia, Kazakhstan, Afghanistan, Pakistan and Turkey, Arabic peppers local languages, so strong is the influence of Arab/Islamic culture. This can become confusing, and there is no standardized transliteration style guide for Arabic or Bahasa or Pashtu or any of the tongues I encountered during my research. I have rendered words as they sounded to my ear. Others may, and indeed have, chosen to represent them differently.

Over two hundred people were interviewed for this book. I mention this not to astound you, but to make clear that while not all of them made it into these pages, many of them took great personal risk in speaking to me. If I did include their testimony, in some cases they asked me not to use their name; in other cases I have decided not to. I have made this obvious in the text by providing appellations. Wherever necessary, I indicate that my sources are anonymous.

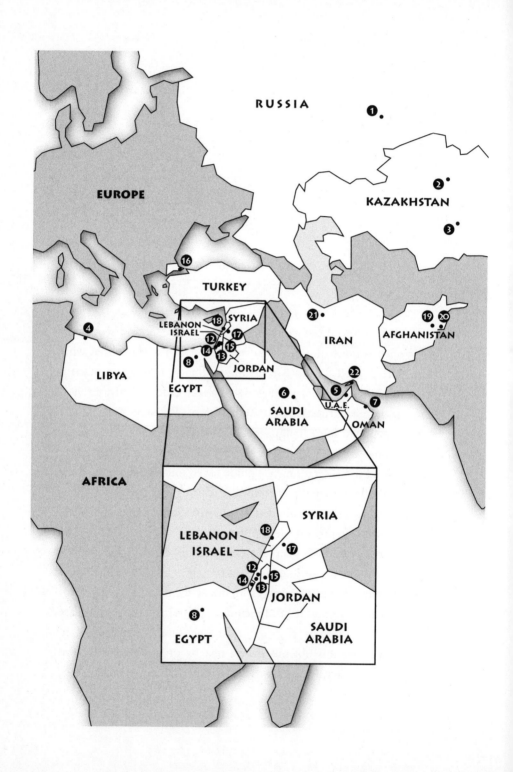

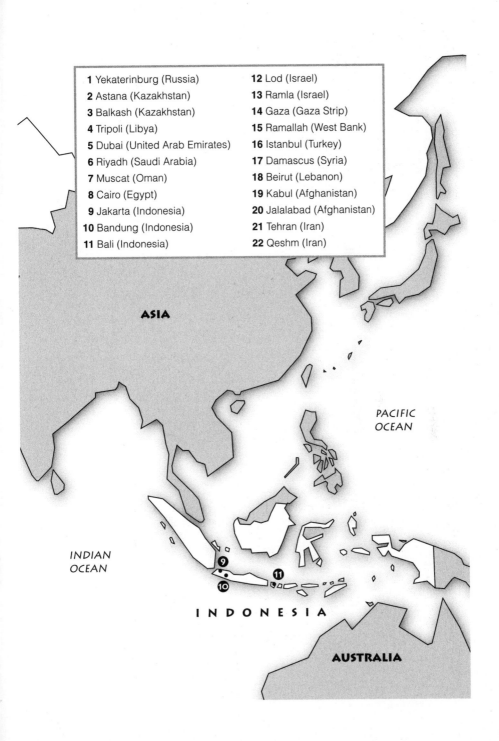

1 Yekaterinburg (Russia)
2 Astana (Kazakhstan)
3 Balkash (Kazakhstan)
4 Tripoli (Libya)
5 Dubai (United Arab Emirates)
6 Riyadh (Saudi Arabia)
7 Muscat (Oman)
8 Cairo (Egypt)
9 Jakarta (Indonesia)
10 Bandung (Indonesia)
11 Bali (Indonesia)
12 Lod (Israel)
13 Ramla (Israel)
14 Gaza (Gaza Strip)
15 Ramallah (West Bank)
16 Istanbul (Turkey)
17 Damascus (Syria)
18 Beirut (Lebanon)
19 Kabul (Afghanistan)
20 Jalalabad (Afghanistan)
21 Tehran (Iran)
22 Qeshm (Iran)

ASIA

PACIFIC
OCEAN

INDIAN
OCEAN

INDONESIA

AUSTRALIA

WaWaWeeWa: An Introduction

KAZAKHSTAN

Muslim: 47% (official)

70% (unofficial)

30% GDP

1. John Cage:
   4'33"

2. Joy Division:
   Isolation

3. Sisters of Mercy:
   This Corrosion

Pop.: 15,340,533

Avg. age: 29.3

Capital: Astana

Independence: 16 Dec 1991

The functionary leaned in. He smelled like dust and formalde-hyde, his suit jacket large enough for an adult grizzly. Outside, under a chemical-spill sunset, the brand new Kazakh city of Astana glittered like a gaggle of teenaged drag queens dressed as Tammy Faye Bakker.

"You say the question again," said the functionary through lips as thick as bicycle tires. He meant this as a warning. Grabbing another small glass of vodka—his seventh—from a passing waiter, he glared at me warily.

I was badly unhinged. For the past two days, I had sped across the northwestern steppes of Kazakhstan, cruise control set to eighty miles an hour. Time moved like stretched putty, dragging day into icy night over tremendous, Fruit Loop–hued gloamings. Decaying granaries were visible for miles, while fathoms of dead earth were interrupted only by futurist signs for what sounded like all-you-can-eat Chinatown buffets: *Happiness People's Combination* or *Togetherness Food Creation*.

Racing through a country the CIA *World Factbook* lists as "roughly four times the size of Texas," I was inadvertently following the path of Islam as it spread from Arabia into Central Asia *circa* AD 700.

Kazakhstan was now a land of chronic pollution and quiet faith, seventy percent Islamic, one hundred percent bewildering. Nursultan A. Nazarbayev, President for Life and an ally of the Bush administration, had banned the form of Islam practised by most of Kazakhstan's Sunni Muslims. Pundits eyed the region, waiting for a Red Martyrs' Wheat Brigade or an al-Qaida Socialist Workers' Collective to leap forth, bomb-belts blazing. Handshakes were proffered, weapons delivered, deals struck—anything to avoid the opening of another front along the resource-rich Caucasus.

The aforementioned functionary swayed on his feet. He seemed to blame me for the public relations debacle that had recently stricken his country, as vicious and arbitrary as an outbreak of bubonic plague. I had arrived in Kazakhstan on the unhappy eve of the North American release of Sacha Baron Cohen's *Borat: Cultural Learnings of America for Make Benefit Glorious Nation of Kazakhstan*. It was a film that no country—not even an ex-thermonuclear bomb-testing facility—would want any association with. This was bad for branding, the equivalent of discovering that a new processed meat product causes not only gastric cancer, but also halitosis, memory loss and erectile dysfunction.

From my point of view, *Borat* was an astringent comic satire, made with Dadaist glee, both mainstream money-grubbing gross-out comedy and nasty anti-art provocation. The film follows the titular Kazakh television correspondent as he undertakes a journey through America to, as the title helpfully explicates, culturally benefit the glorious nation of Kazakhstan. In this, the functionary shouldn't have felt so bad: Kazakhstan is only nominally the film's comic piñata. Borat's real target is North American white-bread xeno- and homophobia, born of suburban homogeneity. Kazakhstan was collateral damage.

Borat had nonetheless naked-wrestled his way into the upper ranks of the Kazakh regime's psyche. Blind to the basic marketing mechanics of fuel + fire = box-office smash, they issued statement after statement denouncing the movie. (That weekend, the film grossed over twenty-six million dollars in North American box-office receipts, and would go on to gross a hundred more.) Foreign Minister Kasymzhomart Tokayev, for example, managed to be both charmingly plaintive and mildly advertorial when he said, "Apart from the name of our country and our flag, [the film] has nothing to do with us. I also hope the people in your country will not laugh at us, but that the film will arouse their interest. They should come to our country and get to know the real Kazakhstan."

This I took as an invitation. It was by no means a gilded one. The drive through the Siberian emptiness from the eastern Russian city of Yekaterinburg was not endorsed by any guidebook currently in publication. I passed stand after stand of wan birch, the monotony broken only by the glimmering wings of magpies taking flight. It was as if I was driving through a one act by Beckett, translated by Chekhov, with a soundtrack by Prokofiev. The ironical grin I'd sported on the flight over had frozen into a grimace somewhere between Minsk and Moscow. Here on an unrelated journalistic errand, all I could think about was Borat Sagdiyev.

I have long been interested in what happens to one culture's pop when it meets another culture head-on. I am especially intrigued by American popular culture's forays into the Muslim world, an alternate civilization that is, according to Samuel P. Huntington, Fox News and Hezbollah, at total odds with our own (or, if one is to take President Barack Obama's famous 2009 Cairo speech as gospel, it's a world that is—give or take a few tweaks—gloriously similar to our own). It just so happened that I found myself in a country that hinted at a confluence of two of the greatest ideological forces of the last half-century: communism and radical Islam. And Borat represented an affront to both. He was capitalist and secular, craven and crass, truly popular and extraordinarily divisive. Although Baron Cohen's satirical mark was America, his film was a comic diatribe against small-minded idiocy everywhere, and it stood against regimes like Kazakhstan's merely by existing.

Certain that the functionary and I would be unable to come to any meaningful consensus on these issues, I instead said, "Can you explain to me what the official reaction to the Borat film has been within the Kazakh bureaucracy?"

He took a moment. "This film," he said eventually, after swallowing his vodka with a noisy gulp, "is *pshhhp!*—nothing. Foolish. You ask about the reaction? We have no reaction." He then went back to staring at my mouth.

With a lurch of queasy recognition, I realized that the functionary—sloping forehead, dyed moustache, eyes as dark and dead as a taxidermy partridge—reminded me of a figure from my youth, name of Pik Botha. Students of South Africa's white-ruled gerontocracy will remember Foreign Minister Botha as Apartheid's official international apologist. His obfuscations became a sort of dread poetry, and I imagined him using the same *pshhhp!* of dismissal if asked about his reaction to *Lethal Weapon 2*, in which the villains were crazed South African diplomats who, not so coincidentally, resembled Botha in dress, deed and disposition.

Like many in the Muslim world, I too was born of a quasi-religious homicidal autocracy, growing up white in Johannesburg during the waning days of the Apartheid regime, an Orthodox Jew among Dutch Reformed Calvinists. (This is, more or less, ecclesiastically equivalent to the Deobandi sect of the Taliban, but with fewer public stonings.) Our universe was small; my way into the wider world was through American television, comic books, movies, music. Freud contended that dreams are a union of "the rich material of poetry, myth, and popular idiom." It's difficult to imagine a better definition of popular culture.

I have been a pop dreamer for as long as I can remember.

As a boy, I kept a small library of scrapbooks bursting with the detritus industrial pop culture leaves in its wake: *Teen Beat* articles, carefully snipped pictures of Whitney Houston and Madonna and Michael Jackson, adverts for upcoming Hollywood features, old album sleeves, lyrics sheets, interviews. I was obsessed with American popular culture, so much so that I *viewed* myself as American. And Americans did not behave like South Africans. It's not a point in Apartheid-era South Africa's favour when I note that Hollywood, of all places, taught me that black people could become something other than domestic servants. Indeed, American pop culture—*The Cosby Show, Magnum, P.I.*, the *Back to the Future* franchise—saved me from my basic education, which was, as I've hinted, that of a racist misogynist fundamentalist religious millenarian.

Any pluralistic notions I hold today, I owe to Thomas Magnum and his sidekick TC. I found, in pop culture's irrationality, rationalism. The tenets in which I have come to believe—liberal humanism, the formation of law based on precedent, a separation of church/mosque/shul and state—I must again attribute, at least in part, to Magnum and his sidekicks. That's not to say that all of the stuff I consumed was explicitly, or even accidentally, ideological. Some of it had a social conscience—*All in the Family*, say—but most of it existed outside of such considerations—like the "Thriller" video, or *Who's the Boss?* This was *product*, but encoded into it was that glorious sense of American optimism, the understanding that within half an hour, including commercials, an individual could rise up and overcome chaos. Equally important, this stuff was fun. It melted the chunk of hardened matter in my heart. It made me human. (It's not for nothing that the Taliban, my spiritual brethren, banned kite flying along with music and television.) I suppose that this has left me with the belief—however flighty—that American pop can act as a catalyst for personal transformation, and therefore social transformation.

But what had I lost in all this? The first time I heard African music—the gumboot rhythm of the mines that ringed my hometown—was through the vector of Paul Simon's *Graceland*. And what of the garish consumerism, the me-me-me individualism, the suburban middle-class values, the skewed view of America's place in the world? I have loved American pop culture for so long that it is a part of my soul, but that doesn't mean I can watch *Two and a Half Men* without gagging. My unease moves in me like some deepwater leviathan, threatening to surface and, in a mess of roiling cultural whitewater, tear to pieces the assumptions I hold dear.

With this in mind, I skulked away from the functionary and took a slug of my own vodka—as unctuous and meaty as a hork of phlegm. I stood at an icy window and stared out at the city that the President for Life had built from scratch in less than a decade. Evocatively, "Astana" is Kazakh for "capital." There were towers of gold, blinking towers, towers capped with big gold golf balls, bent towers, twisty towers, towers that housed other towers. In a nod to Nazarbayev's Soviet roots, Astana is not futuristic but rather futurist, and therefore utopian. It is rootless, meaningless. If the city was proof of anything, it was that regional leaders no longer looked to the Prophet and the Qur'an for aesthetic inspiration, but rather to George Lucas and *Star Wars, Episode I: The Phantom Menace*.

I headed further east. It wasn't *all* muted existential Sturm und Drang, but most of it was. Concrete bus shelters, decorated with chips of mosaic, stood at the head of occasional dirt tracks that disappeared over the lip of the horizon, official roads to nowhere. Everything smelled of antifreeze. In my experience, desert landscapes quickly cease to be landscapes as such, and become the planet's formal debutante balls, in which you are, with great pomp, introduced to yourself, and stand awkwardly with nothing at all to say. I careened through the country at speeds that would ordinarily be considered unwise; the chasm I had to leap from Borat's fake Kazakhstan to Minister Tokayev's "real Kazakhstan" left me dizzy. We—all of us—are forced by popular culture to make these jumps every day. Usually they are small, barely perceptible hops. Sometimes, they are suicide leaps into the void.

In Kazakhstan, one doesn't drive with a quart of Starbucks coffee in the cup holder, but rather a fifth of sharp potato homebrew. Coffee placates; vodka agitates. Jittery, I looked outside at crushed cowboy villages—this was Kansas, but flatter and drier—and noted that from a certain angle the satellite dishes looked just like the Islamic crescents above the desert mausoleums that served as burial grounds for the local population, such as there was in this area. Advances in technology, I was reminded, have brought a tsunami of American pop to the Muslim world. So, too, has technology enabled a steely, global form of Islamic terrorism to spread across the region and beyond. The two phenomena have risen in prominence together. But were they connected? Have *Friends* reruns made young Muslims more radical? Or have Chandler, Monica and their Central Perk lattes stemmed what could otherwise have been a full turn toward the dark side?

My appreciation for the transformative aspects of American pop culture is shared by a strange coterie; we differ somewhat on the details. Sayed Qutb, modern militant Islamism's ideological poster boy, was sent to America in 1948 by the Egyptian government on a fact-finding trip. What emerged was something of an inverse, outraged Alexis de Tocqueville. When his Muslim Brotherhood (which in turn begat the Palestinian outfit Hamas and other State Department favourites) fell afoul of the Egyptian authorities, Qutb wrote from jail one of those penal tomes that are the scourge of history. In *Signposts*, he hitched Leninism to Islamic revolutionary theory, an intellectual position motivated by his utter revulsion for America. "Humanity today is living in a large brothel!" he wrote. "One has only to glance at its press, films, fashion shows, beauty contests, ballrooms, wine bars and broadcast stations!"

In this, he unconsciously echoed Theodor Adorno—crown prince of pop-cultural party-pooping—and his Frankfurt School's notion that popular culture mimics the workings of Nazi propaganda and is thus a form of fascism, a "prohibition on thinking." Industrial mass culture has commodified leisure time, enslaving us all to *American Idol*'s Simon Cowell, transforming us into zombies feasting on our own Whopper-fattened flesh.

And one need not be so radical as Qutb or Adorno to feel as they do. Indeed, it is an article of faith among the enlightened, wherever one may find them, that the spread of American pop—a steady march that began at the turn of the twentieth century, gathering in both pace and reach over the course of the ensuing hundred or so years—is a bad thing, the most obvious and garish example of encroaching globalization. In my own experience as a South African introduced to the notion of a black helicopter pilot in *Magnum, P.I.*, and as a Jew whose stereotypes of Muslims were reinforced by films like *The Delta Force* and *Navy Seals*, I couldn't help thinking that pop—that underwater sea-creature—created a fraught paradox. Let's call it a "longsighted myopia."

Is this condition more dangerous for those in the Muslim world? Historically, the treatment of Muslims in Western popular art has been somewhat less than salutary. Jack Shaheen, in his comprehensive indictment of Hollywood's racial record called *Reel Bad Arabs*, points out that the only cohort to be as cruelly treated are "red Indians"; he has identified over nine hundred films in which Arabs are depicted as either pussy-hounds in white bed sheets, terrorists, oil chuggers or some toxic combination of the three. It is a sad legacy indeed. But what of the tens of thousands of films that *don't* depict Arabs or Muslims at all? What of the hundreds of thousands of episodes of television shows, the millions of popular songs, music videos, burger restaurants, mega-malls, muscle cars: all the articles involved in the construction of American suburban space readily available in the context of, say, middle-class Cairo?

I undertook my first adventures in the Muslim world during the mid-nineties. This was a different era. Only a few years earlier, Bill Clinton grinned as Yitzchak Rabin and Yasser Arafat shook hands on the White House lawn. Terrorism was a fringe business. Eventual peace was a basic assumption. Still, arguments against Islam had changed little in one and a half millennia: This was an imposter faith, its people crushed and debased. While I could read Hebrew, Arabic seemed impenetrable, less a language than a code. In Turkey, because of the S&M soft-porn prison flick *Midnight Express*, my travel companions and I made anal rape jokes on a quarter-hourly basis. Arabs were something Chuck Norris blew up.

I was twenty years old, so these factors did not deter me; rather, they were pluses. Slowly, the veils lifted. Nonetheless, I was never fooled into thinking that there weren't very real differences between the United States of America and cultures within the Muslim world. At the most basic level, there is a divergence in sensibility: Arabic and Farsi text—from which Islam derives so much of its cultural impetus—is read right to left. The oldest level of communication technology—writing—is experienced differently, which in turn skewers our respective interpretations of the world. We look up from the page, and subjectively disagree.

Ever since those first travels, I have wondered what the great incoming pop-cultural glut meant to those who actually lived in Muslim countries, regular folks rather than those hiding out in forti- fied *madrassas* or Waziri caves. As I hammered along the deserted Kazakh highways, I wondered if Borat himself, that trickster, was being beamed from space into satellite dishes out here on the icy Siberian steppes.

That evening, I sat sandwiched in the back of a police car. The two cops on either side of me had the heft and stench of recently killed wildlife. Every time they shifted, their jackets screeched against the plastic covering the seats—protection from an excretory criminal class. The policeman to my right blew into his hands and said something, which I assumed was in reference to the weather.

"Yes, yes," I said. "Very cold."

Outside, the police car's flashing blue light illuminated the Brutalist-cum-neo-classical structure that was Balkash's town hall. I had arrived some hours earlier; this was the sort of post-Soviet town in which no two eyes looked in the same direction. Dusk was inter- minable and cheerfully toxic. Now, shortly before midnight, the firmament was oddly diaphanous, flittering as if we were trapped under the membrane of an enormous blister.

Two figures emerged—the first a hulking man in a pinstriped suit, jacket open despite the cold; the second blond and pixyish, in cargo pants and a canary yellow sweater. Chief Captain Yevgeni Kalikin opened the driver's side door and hauled his bulk behind the wheel. He looked over his shoulder and grinned, his teeth the colour of old piano keys. Beside him, Misha, his eleven-year-old daughter, wiggled over the squealing plastic and buckled up. She had her father's wide face and cartoon ears, which on her looked winsome rather than thuggish.

Misha turned to me. "My father asks what size is your shoe?"

"My *shoe*? Um, a size ten. Forty-four European. Why?"

She translated this for him, which had the effect of a well-delivered punchline. The whole car shook as he guffawed; he said something to her that, in turn, caused the two cops on either side of me to convulse, their hats, made of an abrasive material found only in post-communist republics, scraped at my temples as they rocked back and forth in unrestrained mirth.

"Uh, what did he say?" I asked Misha.

"It is a joke. He says that it is late—there will be no children, so you will be able find such a small shoe."

The Chief Captain, still laughing, reached back and patted the back of my head with a hand that, despite his size, was meant for a much larger man. He put the car in gear, drove several hundred yards, and pulled the handbrake. We parked alongside a floodlit series of monolithic concrete apartment buildings, arranged in rows, painted pastel pink—tombstones for a race of giant clowns.

"Come, come," said the Chief Captain. "Now, we bowl."

"Strike!" said the Chief Captain, ten minutes later. His roll was so substantial, concluding in a great, splintering explosion of ball and pins, that I immediately resolved never to break the law in Balkash.

The alley was lit like a military installation, painted a fading beige, a lone speaker blasting Nirvana's *Nevermind*. Between turns, I contemplated the top cop. I had met him and his daughter earlier that evening at a raucous buffet in the town hall. Foreigners who aren't mining executives or sex tourists are a rare treat in Balkash, so the Chief Captain was quick to introduce himself. We sat around a table that accumulated platters of pickled things and jellied desserts, all shimmying salaciously like booties in a hip-hop video. The Chief Captain filled non-Muslim glasses with vodka and a local plonk that made my lymph nodes throb. Others in the hall came to pay their respects. He deputized Misha as the official translator and she introduced his supplicants in turn—men in ill-fitting suits, women in worse-fitting Spandex.

"My father says this place is a good place," said Misha. "But there is no work here." The Chief Captain scrutinized my face for the appropriate reaction, and he'd lean back in his chair when his proxy's words had the desired effect. People here die young, from the metastasizing legacy of Soviet-era nuclear testing, the boredom and, of course, the vodka. Under the shadow of his broad frame, the Chief Captain was trying to protect his daughter from this fate. While Misha was precocious, she was not prematurely adult. Her English was as perfect as it could be out here on the steppes, but what surprised me was her popular culture lexicon, which was missing only one or two elements.

"No," she said, "I have never heard of Borat."

She gave a lengthy encomium on the Porsche Cayenne, spoke passionately about the work of action film stars Jean-Claude Van Damme and Vin Diesel, and ran through some Eminem lyrics. Child of an isolated ex-gulag, resident of a town populated mostly by kids in third-hand Nike tracksuits, old Manchester United swag and Michael Jordan-era Chicago Bulls T-shirts—refugees from Planet Nineties all—Misha was surprisingly erudite when it came to Western junk-culture.

Which is, perhaps, why she seemed so at home in the bowling alley.

I, on the other hand, was struggling with a particular condition of the twenty-first century. With "Smells Like Teen Spirit" blaring, I was hit with a profound disorientation, the feeling that I'd slipped through time and space and landed in the middle of a frigid purgatory. I stood at the alley, frozen, an aphasic trying to piece together the itinerary that had led me here.

The sensation passed, but it left me rattled. It then occurred to me that I hadn't seen Misha in half an hour or so. I found her nearby, in a section of the basement posing as an arcade: a paltry aggregation of pinball machines and a first-person shooter with a busted plastic Uzi hanging like a hand from a broken wrist. In the dim light, I saw her performing what resembled a spirited foxtrot, keeping time to a disco beat. She was playing a dancing arcade game—a version of what I remembered as *Bust-A-Groove*—in which the player follows the moves of a digital dancer, hitting sensors with her feet in order to rack up points.

What struck me was the expression on her face—one of fierce concentration and unmitigated joy. I knew precisely where Misha was: She existed *within* the song, inside that moment—and I knew the feeling well. I understood that her liberation—however momentary—burst forth from the range of popular culture she had borrowed from a land that was, at least ideologically, the enemy.

This, I knew, was a land of shimmering ideals, but also indomitable myths. It granted both endless vistas and shrouds of darkness; it was a place of limitless possibility and impossible limits. Buying in could be a very dangerous business. After all, hip-hop artists in Gaza or metal heads in Tehran are badly scarred with cultural marks of Cain. They are voluntary outcasts. Was it fair to dismiss their passions as frippery or the dissolution of indigenous culture under the boot of American industrial pop? Were not their choices, rather than an arbitrary act of cultural consumerism, more acts of courage? And if so, did pop not cease to be "a prohibition on thinking"?

"Come play," said Misha, who saw me staring at the game with what must have looked like jealous longing.

"That's *not* a good idea," I said, envisioning my ankle snapping halfway through Diana Ross's "I'm Coming Out." Misha shrugged. But before I could walk off, she ran up to me, flipped open her cellphone and scrolled hurriedly through her pictures with a practiced thumb. It took several seconds, but as pixels reluctantly arranged themselves, I realized that I was looking at a man in a neon green one-piece bathing suit, standing on a squalid beach. Borat. Misha winked conspiratorially; it was understood that her father would not approve.

I winked back, as if to say: Comrade.

That did it. The following morning, as the Chief Captain and his daughter drove me through streets that would have been deserted if there were anything in them to desert, I resolved that I would keep going south and east, throughout the Muslim world, chasing down my old obsessions. I wasn't so much interested in bearded *jihadis* or Kalashnikov-bearing fundamentalists—they have every mainstream news outlet in the world as a rostrum for their views. No, I wanted the Bahraini Bruckheimers, the Tehrani T-Pains, the Saudi Shakiras.

We drove in silence, and I could sense the death-calm of the steppes nipping at the eastern edge of the town. Shortly, we passed the pastel-pink estate of concrete blocks, where only a few hours ago we had concluded our bowling game. In the phantasmagorical dawn, I noticed satellite dishes by the thousands, rows upon rows of them, attached to every balcony and pointed in precisely the same direction—canted west, upward, to the heavens. That's how Misha had become Misha, I thought: Those dishes were both her prison sentence and her pardon.

When we arrived at my car, parked at the city hall, we took pictures: the Chief Captain's implausibly wide-brimmed hat butting against my head as he shuffled around arranging shots. The occasion suitably documented, the Chief Captain grabbed me by both of my shoulders and gave me one of his grins. Misha shook my hand solemnly.

"My father says to be careful."

"I'll do my best."

"Also, he says maybe you can take bowling lessons."

The Chief Captain scrutinized my face; when he saw my crestfallen look, he howled with laughter. He pumped my hand, patted me on my back again and helped me into the car as one would an invalid.

I typed the coordinates into the GPS with my aching bowling arm: due south-southeast. As I drove away, I looked in the rear-view mirror and saw Misha raise her index finger and pinkie: the sign of the devil horns, the heavy metal salutation born of the seventies. I did the same, and saw a widening smile.

Lake Balkash shimmered like a vast daub of whitewash to my left. I punched the gas and, within minutes, I was out on the plains, back at the solo debutante ball, humming "Smells Like Teen Spirit."

Part I

FAJR

1

฿ow Do You Know?

LIBYA

Muslim: 97%

Other: 3%

25% GDP

1. Lionel Richie:
   Hello

2. Lionel Richie:
   Hello

3. Lionel Richie:
   Hello

Pop.: 6,173,579

Avg. age: 23.6

Capital: Tripoli

Independence: Dec 24, 1951

Think of it as a faded music video, dimly remembered from childhood, seen at 3 A.M. on a dying TV in a shag-rug basement. The scene unfolds in one languid shot, a palette of muted greens, wan blues, bloodless reds. A man walks through the alleyways of a medina, his linen shirt fluttering in a slow-motion breeze. The sloping corrugated iron roofs shade him from the worst of the sun; still, his Jheri curls catch the light like gemstones. We see the superimposed ghosts of Romans walking these alleys, Athenians, Phoenicians and Arab warriors too. Then, we watch as Mussolini's colonial forces' leather boots creak against the worn stone. They give way to dusty Bedouin in *jallabiyas* and rail-thin teens in tight T-shirts and acid-washed jeans, the history of this alley unfolding in seconds.

We follow the man as he passes a coppersmith banging rhythmically on a jug. He presses up with the balls of his feet in a hop-step, like a dancer keeping time. He is in fact a very good dancer, and has even written a song called "Ballerina Girl" that is, in short, about a girl who is a ballerina. Behind him, he hears the unmistakable spoon-on-a-champagne-glass tinkle of children's laughter. He pretends not to notice. They follow him, these children, gathering in number as he walks on. He is, of course, used to the attention, but can't quite hide his surprise. After all, he is on the edge of North Africa, in a country that was, until recently, considered to be the undisputed ass-end of the uncivilized world.

Then something truly extraordinary happens. The laughter stops. Murmuring begins. He hears a word in English. This stops him in his tracks. The children have raised their eyes as if in prayer. They move their hands like a blind person tracing the facial features of a new lover.

"Hello," they intone, looking blankly to the heavens. *"Hello."*

Despite his fame, despite the universal reach of his music, the man cannot help but be astonished.

"How do you know?" asks Lionel Brockman Richie, Jr., of the children in the medina. *"How do you know?"*

When I first learned of Lionel Richie's close encounter in the Libyan capital of Tripoli, I initially confused it for parody. The world-famous pop star had not, according to an article in *GQ* magazine, experienced an Islamic street seance, but rather a passable re-enactment of the "Hello" video-clip (a staple on MTV in 1984, and a landmark moment in the history of the music video), in which a beautiful blind woman, who knows Richie only from his mellifluous voice, somehow sculpts a perfectly representative clay bust of his Jheri-curled visage.

"How do you know?" begged Lionel Richie of the children. I shared his bemusement. Certainly, his videos are prominent in the cultural memory of a generation of North Americans—a friend once described the "All Night Long" clip (in which Richie is followed by the denizens of a Reagan-era inner city 'hood and is *not* murdered for his leather pants) as "a profound piece of eschatological imagination." I was nonetheless taken aback by how far "Hello" had travelled. To a scion of the 1980s, the Richie songbook carries an almost oneiric weight. As with "All Night Long" and its attendant clip, the "Hello" video was an indelible piece of my childhood, a kiln-fired shard of memory somehow unearthed in the Muslim world.

On one level, the tale was a powerful, perfect metaphor: popular culture as a binding force. Hundreds of millions of people in over a hundred countries know Lionel Richie's music, and adore it. According to *GQ*, anti-Ba'athist residents of Baghdad had blasted "All Night Long" as the Shock-N-Awe™ campaign commenced. "The only thing Shiite and Sunni now share, aside from their hatred of each other and their worship of Allah and his prophet, is their abiding love for Lionel Brockman Richie Jr.," read the *GQ* article. What this rather narrow view of life in Baghdad elucidates is the surprise North Americans feel when *our* culture—*our* collective memories—are embraced by *them*.

Nonetheless, there were aspects of the "Hello" tale—little details—that troubled me. The "All Night Long" in Baghdad story went against the anecdotal evidence I'd collected about those fateful evenings in March 2003. And as much as I wanted to believe it (and for some reason, believing had become unreasonably important to me), the "Hello" re-enactment sounded, well, outlandish. Did hundreds of young Libyan children really have the "Hello" video downloaded onto their cognitive hard drives the same way a Westerner born of the 1980s did? In no way did I think that *GQ* or Lionel Richie had willfully fabricated these details. I just wondered if something had become garbled in the translation. I had to find out if that video re-enactment had happened. As *GQ* put it: "We . . . have a strategic, even moral, obligation to know: *What is the freakin' deal with Lionel Richie?*"

A year and a half after the alleged re-enactment, I sat in a battered Volkswagen Jetta and glanced across four lanes of furious Tripolitan traffic.

"These are the rules," said Eder, the Berber. He readjusted his mirrored shades and settled low in the driver's seat. "We look straight ahead. We don't stare at the guards. We play careful, careful."

I adjusted my own shades, pulled the brim of my cap low. "Roger that," I said, like a cast member of *CSI: Tripoli*.

"There, ahead," he barked. "You see it?"

I did. Behind the pell-mell tangle of traffic, a vast, fortified compound, the walls indented with the occasional Islamic tessellation. There were slats for gun barrels, turrets manned by men with machine guns.

"That's what we call *al-Qa'ida*. The Fortress. Or al-Aziziyah. Seven checkpoints you have to drive through to get to the house. A very nice place, you would not say?"

I would not: Al-Aziziyah resembled nothing so much as San Quentin on steroids. As we drove by, a gate opened to admit a small convoy of armored trucks; I glimpsed another series of gates, another contingent of armed men. We had approached the compound from the north, along a traffic-clogged ring road that changed in character from Mediterranean boulevard to desert highway in the space of a couple of miles, embracing downtown Tripoli in a languid hug. Now, at high noon, the city was stunned into torpor by the bright North African sun; men sat idly along the sidewalks on their haunches, shading their scalps with scraps of cardboard. Dozens of muezzins called the faithful to midday prayer. In response, Eder turned up Rihanna's "Umbrella."

Al-Aziziyah is one of history's punching bags. At precisely 2:00 A.M. local time, on the clear morning of April 15, 1986, the compound became the focal point of an undertaking called Operation El Dorado Canyon. Lasting all of eleven minutes, and unbeknownst to Tripolitans and those who learned of it over coffee and Frosted Flakes in the United States, El Dorado Canyon was the most intricately choreographed bombing run in the seventy-odd-year history of the art. This was the era of go-big-or-go-home: A great airborne armada was dispatched to provide a "measured response" to the extracurricular antics of a man President Ronald Reagan dubbed "the mad dog of the Middle East." This was one Muammar Abu Minyar al-Qadhafi, Brotherly Leader and Guide of the Revolution, hereafter referred to as The Colonel.

Within the fortified walls of al-Aziziyah stood The Colonel's gilded private residence, bombed mercilessly in a sort of much larger version of Castro's exploding cigar. The Colonel had read the tea leaves (as well as the newspapers, which published several leaked reports about an upcoming "surprise" raid) and had slunk off for safer climes. He nevertheless made the curious decision of leaving behind his adopted baby daughter Hanna. Along with thirty-six other Libyans, she didn't make it through the night.

Known principally for his pan-Arabic Islamofascism, a penchant for gold-plated AK-47s and his considerable bouffant, The Colonel scrambled to power in a 1969 coup and rose to subsequent infamy as the world's number one state sponsor of international terrorism. A week prior to Operation El Dorado Canyon, a suitcase bomb exploded in a Berlin discotheque called La Belle, killing two U.S. servicemen and a Turkish woman, injuring a further two hundred and twenty-nine. This was one in a long line of similar atrocities, perpetrated in an age before such things became the ubiquitous bric-a-brac of the daily news wires. With La Belle, The Colonel had finally been caught with his hand in the grenade jar.

Taken at face value, the whole business seemed like just another dance in the bitter pas de deux between America and the Muslim world, which is the fulcrum on which we now turn. And taken at face value, it was.

That is, until Lionel Richie stepped into the picture.

Eder's one muscled arm lazily guided the steering wheel, the other fiddled with his squawking PDA. At his knee, he kept a soft briefcase containing the reams of official documentation that allowed me to be in the country, all of which made me feel like a newly adopted high-end puppy.

"Keep your eyes low," he reminded me. "Careful, careful."

The tour-group operator I'd retained to organize my Libyan visa—a process that redefined my understanding of backwater bureaucracy—

had been uncharacteristically accommodating when I'd requested a guide in his mid-twenties. I'd banked on the fact that a younger man would be more open to straying from the rigid itinerary I'd been assigned. And while Eder was indeed young, I was wary when I mentioned, with exaggerated nonchalance, that I just so happened to be in the country on false pretences.

"Ex*cuse* me?" he said after a dithering attempt at explanation. He removed his mirrored shades in what I assumed was a precursor to violence. "So let me get this straight: You *don't* want to go with the Germans on a walking tour of the ruins?" he asked.

"No. I kind of lied about that on the visa application form."

Eder shook his head. "Man, people come here and ask the weirdest shit. But what you are asking is not to fuck little boys or such."

I agreed. Vigorously.

"Okay, but I warn you," he said, "the tour operator will only allow you so much freedom before you make people suspicious. And people here don't like to give information. They're afraid, and maybe they should be."

Indeed, they should be. The Colonel, while he has mellowed in his dotage, long ago wiped his enemies from Earth like so much spittle from his grizzled chin. Eder, however, was not afraid. For one thing, there was his relative size and muscle-mass. Furthermore, he was a demographically significant anomaly. His eyes, behind the mirrored shades, were the telltale hazel-green of the Berber. Although he was fluent in Arabic, he was an Amazigh—literally, "free man"—and spoke the nomad tongue of North Africa called Tamazight. It is held that almost forty percent of Tripoli was once Amazigh, until The Colonel decreed that there was no such thing. Eder thus felt more allegiance to East-Coast hip-hop than he did to Middle Eastern Arab culture. Which went a long way in explaining the Rihanna blasting from the stereo.

Eder crossed three chaotic lanes of traffic to bring the car as close to al-Aziziyah as he could without inviting an anti-tank round. His disdain for traffic regulations was an extension of his rebellion against

The Colonel's status quo. This dissension went unnoticed, largely because everyone in Libya drove like a maniac.

"You know what is the word *wasta*?" he asked.

I was familiar with the term. It translates roughly as "influence" or "pull"; it implies a connection, familial or otherwise, with the ruling strongman.

"You need big-time *wasta* to get inside there," said Eder. "Big time."

I knew al-Aziziyah was off limits, but the house was as much a symbol for me as it was for The Colonel. North Africa is, after all, where America's centuries-long relationship with the Muslim world properly began. Operation El Dorado Canyon was but another in a long line of American military engagements with the variegated rulers of Libya, a legacy that dates back over two hundred years. This linked history hinted at a lengthy cultural involvement—a mutual fascination that was tinged with both revulsion and wonder. I turned my head as we left the compound behind, looking for details, clues.

"Don't look at the guards," said Eder sharply, his shades flashing with sunlight. "You can leave any time, my friend," he said. "Me, I gotta deal with these people forever."

A year or so before I arrived in Libya, the punching bag punched back. At midnight on April 14, 2006, a convoy of late-model vehicles approached al-Aziziyah from the northwest. Armed guards opened the gates, swinging flashlights into the cabins, checking papers. Mercedes and Lexuses and Lincolns purred inside, followed by buses packed with dignitaries, foreign and otherwise. There was a festive element to the proceedings. The Colonel has a propensity for marking dates—the Libyan calendar is littered with commemorations revolutionary, religious or otherwise—and April 15 is now remembered as Hanna Peace Day. As gate after gate opened to allow revelers closer to the epicenter, spotlights flashed wildly across the night sky, a clownish aping of the anti-aircraft lights that vainly followed F-111 bombers twenty years earlier.

A crowd numbering one thousand assembled before The Colonel's decimated house. Wires dangled from the still-scarred concrete. A concert stage was set up: grand piano, electric guitars, microphones. The crowd politely applauded as Spanish tenor José Carreras took to the stage. After his brief set, Aisha Qadhafi—The Colonel's other, living, daughter—stood before them. Once considered "the Claudia Schiffer of the Middle East" for her model-like mien and hallmark blond highlights, she had of late taken the headscarf. Beneath the skeletal remains of the building in which little Hanna breathed her last, Aisha said, "Today we try to heal our wounds and shake hands with those who are here with us tonight. Yes for peace! No for destruction!"

The stage darkened. Lights swung back and forth. Then all went quiet. And twenty years to the very second after Operation El Dorado Canyon swept over this place, an icon of the 1980s—one-time member of R & B supergroup The Commodores, ninety million solo records sold, over a dozen Top 10 singles on the Billboard charts— stalked into the spotlight, a smile on his face, the velvety Mediterranean breeze fluttering his navy-blue shirt.

"Hello Libya!" said Lionel Richie. He then broke into the first of five smash hits on his set list, culminating in a rousing singalong, with forty white-clad children typical to this sort of proceeding.

"Hanna will be honored tonight because of the fact that you've attached peace to her name," Lionel Richie told the crowd. "Libya, I love you! I'll be back."

The gig was a coup of a different sort for Libya, a country only recently upgraded from pariah status, due to The Colonel's renounce-ment of WMDs, terrorist fellowships, bad hairstyles and so on. By all accounts, Richie's arrival was greeted with the rapture befitting a visiting deity; his hands were washed in rosewater, he was accorded the honorific "Brother." The take-home message was that the man who wrote "Dancing on the Ceiling" was a greater nuncio for peace—

or at least common ground—than any number of official envoys, roadmaps or summit meetings.

The obvious question was *why* did so many in the Middle East pick Lionel Richie of all the sundry American pop icons in the pantheon? The embed has become standard practice when reporting on the region; I thus decided that the only course of action was to embed myself in Lionel Richie. On my "four hours' assigned free time," I cued up "Hello" on my iPod, hit repeat and sneaked out of the hotel. I wanted to experience Tripoli infused with "Hello," like a trainee holy man wandering the New Mexican desert jacked on peyote.

This was a dangerous undertaking. It is never advisable in an unfamiliar city—especially one with traffic regulations as capricious as Tripoli's—to voluntarily erase one of your senses. After being clipped on the elbow by the rear-view mirror of a scooter, I walked with the tentativeness of the many octogenarian German cruise ship tourists bossed around by their guides. I did not want to die listening to "Hello." I have my death playlist all figured out, and "Hello" is not on it. Here I'll excerpt selectively from my notes:

Listen one: Song is pleasant. Sappy. I think the round things on the sidewalks are olives. They sure smell like olives. Olives and kerosene.

Listen two: I'm enjoying the meticulous construction, perfect in a way only a piece of pop music can be perfect. Polished. Honed. Great art is often full of mistakes. There is nothing accidental about "Hello." Those things *are* olives. I've got olive oil all over my sneakers!

Listen four: It's like the blind lady says in the "Hello" video: "too many memories, too many ghosts." This is bringing back dozens of childhood memories. Richie's music evokes a blissful naïveté I look back on with a sort of awe: me, prior to becoming fully realized as a white South African. The pang is so real that the music has become a physical thing; it hurts as bad as lost love.

Listen five: Am I *crying?* I hope that's sweat.

Listen six: Gaaaaaagh! This is a stupid idea. I feel like I'm walking around Arabia in breakdance pants and neon fishnets. This song is a relic of the 1980s. I half expect Madonna to crawl across the olives in a hijab, singing "Like a Virgin."

Listen eight: Okay, according to someone like Daniel Levitan—the music science boffin—what's happening to my brain now is a huge chemical dump of prolactin, which is the endorphin released when we are sad. Listen to a sad song when you're sad, the reasoning goes, and you're pretty much curing yourself of sadness. In other words, creating (and consuming) art—especially music—are biological imperatives. Music allowed my caveman ancestors to create social bonds, communicate with friends, identify foes, thus playing an important role in the evolution of our species. Music is hardwired into us, Muslim or Jew or Baha'i. In other words, Lionel Richie is one big-ass Prozac, and I'm about to overdose.

Listen fourteen: Helloooooooooooooow. La da dee da dee da da-ah?

Listen fifteen: Wait a second: What memory does Lionel Richie represent for those Libyans who stood before him as he sang "Say You, Say Me" along with those candle-holding urchins? "Hello" rose to the top of the charts the same year Operation El Dorado Canyon performed its morning flyover; the country was firmly in the international doghouse when Richie was at the height of his popularity. As for Iraqis, by all accounts the world's largest per capita consumers of schmaltz pop, they were caught in a protracted war with Iran during the 1980s, a period of deprivation that rivalled only the 1960s, 1970s, 1990s and 2000s for sheer misery. I suppose that the past owns its own aura: It is by definition a simpler time, and while it may have been miserable, it represented a lesser mass of cumulative misery. Therein lie the fundamentals of nostalgia.

Listen sixteen: Fuck. I wish I was a war reporter.

As one would expect, Richie has his own theories on why his music resonates so strongly with Middle Eastern audiences. "In a way," he told *GQ* magazine, "I don't know who I am," an existential state he attributes to the black American experience, yanked from the motherland, stripped of history. "Black Americans have no real concept of our origins. Whenever I show up in a country, I am *that country*." He posits that his method of songwriting—a way of grinding up his anger as if it were spice under a pestle—forms the major part of his appeal. One of his biggest smash hits, "Easy" is, according to Richie, a "Fuck You song." If so, it's the only Fuck You song played twelve times a day on Adult Contemporary radio stations, employed to sell everything from iced tea to tampons. Nonetheless, Richie contends that within his music there is a voracious anger—a *"quiet fire"*—that he has bound into a karmic knot. And it is this subsumed conflagration that appeals so to his Muslim "Brothers."

To my ear, "Easy" is about as angry as an episode of *Barney*, and as perfect an example of schmaltz pop as any. Indeed, part of Richie's appeal must arise from the fact that his solo discography is remarkably free of sexual innuendo or anything at all insalubrious. But your schmaltz ain't my schmaltz: As one critic has pointed out, "What is punk but anger schmaltz?" What did Lionel Richie's brand of schmaltz mean out here, among the squashed olives and the kerosene?

Eder was waiting for me, drinking an espresso on a downtown patio under a wide umbrella. According to the *GQ* article, the "Hello" re-enactment occurred about five hundred yards from where we sat. The plan, such as it existed, was to ask any shopkeepers Richie may have visited whether a contingent of local kids had gathered around the star, mimicking blindness, murmuring "Hello." I imagined that such an occurrence would have been hard to miss.

I was mistaken.

The Libyans I'd met so far were polite, but reticent. As for Eder, his circumspection with regard to my mission was growing by the day. Despite his disavowals of Libyan nationality, he seemed embarrassed by the local attachment to Lionel Richie. Even after I told him that Richie wrote "Brick House" for The Commodores—"the single greatest encomium to the glory of a well-built woman's ass," as I believe I put it, if not in so many words—Eder was unconvinced that there was any merit in my quest.

"I dunno, maybe you think we're backwards here," said Eder, sipping his espresso. "That in forty years—oooh!—maybe Christina Aguilera will come and rock us out."

I understood that Eder did not want his carefully managed hipness tarred with the Lionel Richie brush, but I didn't feel he was being fair. While his iPod was stocked with the latest American urban hits, and we spent our evenings haunting stores that sold bootleg DVDs of titles that had yet to be released stateside, most people in Libya existed in a very different cultural milieu. Their culture was that of North African Islam, their connections atavistic: to kith and kin, to the old codes. Eder's middle-class upbringing, and the fact that he was the eldest in a family of five kids, had allowed him semi-annual trips to Malta, where he had befriended and bedded a host of Westerners; in many respects, his world view was more nuanced than most North Americans in their mid-twenties. He was in the vanguard of a new Libyan generation, surfing the demographic wave of a massive Middle Eastern birth rate, pulled West by the accident of his tribal affiliations, plugged in because of an unprecedented technological sea change. Still, he assured me that if one of his younger sisters decided to marry outside the tribe, he'd slaughter the entire wedding party. Eder was representative of many in post-pariah Libya: He was precariously straddling two cultural realities.

"Fine. So what *is* the point of all this Lionel Richie shit?" he asked.

"If I knew that, Eder, I wouldn't be sitting here."

Across the square, the medina was starting to roil with life.

"Okay, *Mission Impossible IV*, here we come," said Eder, leaving some tattered bills for the waiter. "Follow me."

We crossed the busy street, toward the bustle of the medina, into the asphalt-paved Green Square, draped with banners of The Colonel's fusty homilies, culled selectively from *The Green Book*, his major contribution to the autocrats' literary canon. Tripoli holds a peculiar, muted dignity. The Italianate core is centered by Algeria Square, dominated by a marble cathedral retrofitted in the 1970s as a mosque. Entire sections of downtown were hidden behind the criss-cross of scaffolding, benefiting from Libya's modest bounce in fortunes, while others were still shabbily whitewashed, their green shutters shedding curls of paint onto the sidewalks below. The trunks of the trees were painted white; traffic cops stood trunk-like in their starched white uniforms. There were cars on every paved surface.

We walked past Tripoli's treasure: the rouged sandstone of the al-Saraya al-Hamra, a farrago of heavy brick buildings that formed the red castle, once the city's foremost point, now a museum. Hanging from the eastern wall was a massive banner of The Colonel, rays of light emanating from his bouffant.

"You see this?" asked Eder. He pointed to the al-Saraya al-Hamra's southeastern rampart. Sticking up behind the heavy brick, casting its spindly shadow on The Colonel's radiant likeness, was a weather-blackened ship's mast.

"That, my friend, is from the USS *Philadelphia*." He said it reflexively; it was the first piece of proper guiding he'd done in our four days together, and he sounded out of practice.

"That's the *Philadelphia*?" I asked. "They leave it out like that?"

"Where they must put it? It's tall, no?"

Tall it was. But it was still a surprise to see the relic displayed so prominently. After all, the USS *Philadelphia*'s mast represented one of the earliest martial engagements between the United States and the House of Islam. The *Philadelphia* was the great 36-gun sailing frigate captured by local pirates in 1803, shipped to the Tripoli harbor as a trophy. This was the era of Barbary, when the North African states of the Maghrib—"The Lands of the Sunset," Islam's westernmost purview—gave tacit support to privateers harassing American shipping east of the Rock of Gibraltar, justifying it under the banner of *al-jihad fil-bahr*, the holy war at sea.

The Tripoli medina has another prominent landmark, one that is definitively linked to the aged ship's mast. The Qaramanli Mosque minaret, capped with a green turret, was built in the Ottoman style by the Qaramanli pasha. Tripoli's head honcho was one of the nascent U.S.A.'s first international villains, a proto-Saddam Hussein with more chutzpah and a much bigger harem. Just like his Maghrib contemporaries, the Qaramanli pasha was a scourge to American shipping in the Mediterranean. The so-called Barbary pirates had long captured the imagination (along with the ships and the citizenry) of the Christian West. Privateering was in those days—much like the plumbing and legal professions are today—a tacitly acceptable form of extortion. In the 1780s, streaking corsairs from the Maghrib nabbed ships from a newly independent America almost at will. Ransoming sailors, ships and booty bent the nearly insolvent American states to a breaking point.

Under Thomas Jefferson, war, of a sort, was declared. In what Horatio Nelson dubbed "the most bold and daring act of the age," the dashing American lieutenant Stephen Decatur, Jr., stealthily brought the ketch Mastico alongside the *Philadelphia* and, while coming under concerted attack, burned it to driftwood in a booming firefight. Six months later, Decatur returned in force to Tripoli, lobbing as many cannonballs as time and reason would allow, thus bringing the pasha to his silk-clad knees. This is why Marines in present-day Iraq sing "To the Shores of Tripoli" at bugle call; the episode was a wacky precursor to Operation El Dorado Canyon and a reminder that, when it comes to American relations with the Muslim world, history is little more than a costume drama depicting current events.

While the Barbary Wars did not, as some revisionist historians would have us believe, directly presage everything from 9/11 to the collapse of the financial derivatives market, they did impress upon the founding fathers the importance of a federated union of the States and the need for a standing navy; they were one of the primary motivating impulses behind the formation of America as we know it. They were also the United States' first international engagement, and entrenched the "Muslim Orient" into the public consciousness.

This early fascination—which amounted to a protracted fad—was motivated also by an evangelical restorationist fervor that has slowed not at all. Evangelical Protestants sought the return of the Jewish people to the Holy Land, where their mere presence would provide the necessary celestial impetus for the third coming of Christ. It helped spur a cultural obsession that easily rivalled later innovations like the Hula Hoop and the Garbage Pail Kids. By 1870, there were more than two thousand American books on the Middle East in publication. Organized tours to the "Near Orient" were suddenly in vogue; a host of American luminaries visited (including a post-presidential Ulysses S. Grant, dubbed "The King of America"), many of whom chipped away hunks of obelisks and pyramids to bring home as souvenirs.

Although the backward, benighted Americas made almost no impression at all on the residents of North Africa (despite hundreds of captured Americans living in the region for years), the Muslim world made its way into the formative American popular culture of the late eighteen and early nineteen hundreds: Mark Twain's *The Innocents Abroad* travel memoir, the Streets of Cairo exhibit at the Chicago World's Fair, Rudolph Valentino's horny sheikh. In the few hundred yards between the Qaramanli minaret and the *Philadelphia's* mast, I was searching for the unruly offspring of this legacy. The United States is no johnny-come-lately in the Muslim world—it's been here for centuries, as foe and friend, the exploited and the exploiter—in a great sweep of conjoined history that remains, for the most part, dangerously misunderstood.

★ ★ ★

The day was fierce and bright, the sky a North African blue that pummeled the eye like a boxer on a speed bag. The medina had recently been sanitized for the cruise-ship tourists landing at the city with increasing frequency, who, like goslings, are nudged around by the peremptory beaks of their guides, prodded into stalls to purchase beachballs and ballcaps and Libyan sandglobes. Several years ago, this area was inhabited by Nigerian gangs who supplied Sicilian mafiosi with heroin and underage sex workers, but they were kicked out so that the buildings could be whitewashed, the shutters painted green, the sluices cleaned of shit. But the medina still keeps a few secrets.

"Aha!" said Eder. "There's your main man."

Tacked to the glass door of a cluttered shop, in front of a herd of miniature gazelles and trays of dusty wedding jewelry, was a series of 8 × 10 photographs. They depicted Lionel Richie posing with a stocky Libyan and browsing for trinkets. Richie wore a white linen shirt and a string of beads around his neck; the top half of his face was a puffy Botoxed death mask. The photographs were digitally dated: 14 April 2006.

We heard a polite cough behind us. I turned to see a man with an aristocratic nose, wearing a loose gray suit. He eyed me warily and handed Eder a business card.

"He's the owner," said Eder. "His name is Abdul Salem Dagdog."

Eder explained our mission; beads of sweat instantly sprang up on Mr. Abdul's upper lip, his eyes darted around for an escape route. Failing to find one, he went for the next best option.

"He will fetch us tea," explained Eder.

We sat on midget stools in front of Dagdog Jewelry and Silver Antiques, our backs to a long-closed cinema built by the Italians in the 1920s. Mr. Abdul returned, followed by a boy carrying a tray of mint tea in paper Nescafé cups.

"Your store has some great items," I said to Mr. Abdul when he was sipping tea, and thus unable to run away.

"Yes," said Mr. Abdul.

"Mr. Lionel came here?"

"Yes, he did," said Mr. Abdul.

"Did he buy anything?"

Mr. Abdul nodded, smiled. Moments earlier, I had flicked through the calendar on my phone and found that April 14, 2006, fell on a Friday. I knew from experience that the medina was shuttered on a Friday. Dead. Had Mr. Abdul opened the shop especially for Mr. Lionel?

More sweat pricked up on Mr. Abdul's forehead. He set his tea down. "It was early Friday, over one year ago. I returned from *masjid*, and there was a message from my son. I called him, and he told me that he had a message from, let us say, a friend. This friend wished for Mr. Lionel to come shop in the medina. He wished for a good shop. Antiques. Silver. So, he calls my son, Mohammed."

"Was Mr. Lionel alone?"

"With him, there was a big black man. A bodyguard. This is all I know."

"The medina—there was no one else here?"

"*Lah*—no. Very quiet," said Mr. Abdul.

"No children followed Mr. Lionel—and made like a blind person, with their fingers?" At this, Eder shook his head sadly.

"*Lah*—no. But my son knows better. He spent more of the time with him."

"And this was the only time Mr. Lionel was in the medina?"

"I think so."

"And we can speak to your son?"

It turns out Mr. Mohammed was nowhere to be found; I should come back some other time.

"But Mr. Mohammed," said Mr. Abdul, his tone changing ever so slightly, "does not much like to talk."

"Even about Mr. Lionel Richie?" I asked.

"Even about Mr. Lionel Richie," said Mr. Abdul. He drained his tea, smiled, and went back into the darkened clutter of his shop.

★ ★ ★

My investigation had taken on the nature of the Tripoli medina: a tangle of cramped alleys, a comedy of cul-de-sacs. Mr. Mohammed was now terminally "on business"; no one else knew anything. Several days later, jacked on too much espresso, I unraveled a ball of paper from my travel pants, and made a clandestine call from the hotel lobby.

I had met the man I'll call The Poet on the plane flying into Tripoli; he was resolute about the state of things: "Why does The Colonel wish to open up to the Americans? Why is this so important? He does not realize we have very different ideologies? Islam and America. They will never meet. Sometimes, I think we should fight this." The Poet was twenty years older than Eder, but in real terms they were centuries apart. He was a small man, neatly turned out, with the features and flickering red eyes of a falcon hunting jackrabbits. He said he would meet me, but only under certain criteria.

"Do not call unless you are very, very desperate," he said.

I rang his number with no compunction.

"Yes, yes," he said on answering. "I was expecting you. But first things must come first. You must read my work."

I did so that night, in translation, sitting on a plastic chair on Algeria Square, gazing occasionally at the disorienting mosque that is the city's focal point. It was originally an Italianate cathedral, plunked in the middle of this Islamic city in what must have been a calculated attempt at humiliating the local population. *Sheesha* smoke, mingling with the aroma of strong coffee, drifted across the neo-classical marble courtyard.

Even allowing for the fact that the finest Arabic poetry often translates poorly into English, The Poet was still not much of a poet. There was no iteration of death he'd failed to romanticize, no reference to God and His Prophet that wasn't repeated three times, no holding back on allusions to roses and blooms and petals: It read like the work of a suburban teen Goth-Islamist with a flower fetish.

We met the following night, in open secret, in the middle of Algeria Square. The courtyard was crowded, and echoed with conversation and the clack of backgammon pieces. Nonetheless, The Poet was nervous. I half-heartedly puffed at a burbling *sheesha* pipe, which The Poet seemed to take as an act of rank cultural appropriation. To him, I was a T. E. Lawrence wannabe, quickly going native. Next stop: camel shopping.

"We will be quick," said the Poet. "Because I confess, Mr. Richard, that I do not understand your quest."

I took a deep breath. "Basically, I'm looking to find out if children in the Tripoli medina re-enacted a Lionel Richie . . ."

"Lionel Richie!"

"You have a problem with Mr. Lionel?"

"A problem? You know I do. Now, I will admit, I of course like the *sound* of his music," said The Poet. "It *sounds* quite pleasant. But I do not like what he *means*. For us, Mr. Richard, it is as it has been for ages: Music is also about language. It is about how we use Arabic. You may recall, but Lionel Richie does not sing in Arabic."

Having recently listened to "Hello" forty times on repeat, I knew this as well as anyone.

"We don't care for new here," said The Poet, who was now sounding like a mullah at full throttle. He was engaging in a debate that has long riven Arabic culture. Popular ditties are by no means a recent innovation in the region—they have existed for centuries in the form of the *taqtuqah* (light songs), sung by women, which stood in contrast to the meatier *qasidah* (classical poetry, often set to music) that formed the male repertoire. By the 1920s, the Arabic recording industry was centered in Cairo, and boasted a number of stars in vicious competition with each other. There was a fear by conservatives that the *taqtuqah* represented a loss of Arabic tradition, a sublimation to European musical styles. It was a conversation between *al-qadim wa-al-jadid*—the old and the new—grounded in an age-old cultural suspicion of *bid'ah*, or innovation. Had not the Prophet himself warned against the newfangled when he said, "Beware of matters newly begun, for every matter newly begun is innovation, every innovation is misguidance, and every misguidance is in hell"?

In quoting this *hadith* (saying attributed to the Prophet), I knew that The Poet was playing fast and loose with his theological scholarship. But he was only just warming to his theme. "What is this *new*? We care here for *genuine* emotion. You can tell it from my own work, can you not?" I stared blankly at my coffee grounds, hoping the question would pass. "Let us call it the Big Gesture," added The Poet.

But the Big Gesture exists just as surely in America as it does here, linked firmly as it is to the tradition of both opera and parlor music, and encoded into pop music's DNA. And Arabic is uniquely suited to the Big Gesture. The Poet's poetry hinted (albeit poorly) that the language can bear an enormous amount of emotional weight, because much of the aesthetic enjoyment is derived *from the use of the language itself.*

Sophistication is by no means a cultural constant, and in Arabic song or verse, innovative content is not as important as innovative use of Arabic; the language contains an inherent power. For an American star to be huge in the Middle East, his or her work must connect with the cultural trope of Bigness. It's an accident of taste, as much as anything else, but most Arabic or Persian artists I've met consider realism or dialed-down subtlety an artistic aberration: Why go small when it's an artist's job to evoke big-canvas emotion? And what is "Hello" if not big-canvas emotion? What, then, was The Poet's problem?

"You must understand, Mr. Richard, that when we listen to music here, it is a link to the poetry of the old days. It means something. It is about *links*. What is the link with this Lionel Richie?"

In this, The Poet had a point: In Middle Eastern cultures, the great love of poetry of antiquity is still very much extant; the *qasidah* lives, set to synthesized chintz pop. Unlike American pop, it has a much better chance of crossing age, class and gender lines because it bears a formative connection to heritage, to cultural history. But this is where things get confusing: Its *primary* objective is to conjure nostalgia. Nostalgia, in other words, becomes a genuine artistic imperative.

So—given the time his oeuvre has had to steep in local cultural consciousness—why shouldn't Lionel Richie conjure the same feelings?

"Pah! It is simple," said The Poet, dismissing this with a wave. "The Americans are taking over." In this version of events, Richie meant a creeping Americanism that was sullying local culture, poisoning the well of pure Arabism that is the keystone to an Islamic way of life. But Richie was here by invitation. This could not properly be described as the beginning of a deluge from outside, because the impetus, at this early stage, was a *Libyan* impetus.

"That is a clever argument. But you do not understand the depth of the conspiracy. Don't underestimate the American wiles."

"So if this music video re-enactment were to have happened," I asked, "it was part of an American plot?"

"Perhaps. But I know nothing of this music video. But the concert? Several of my friends attended . . ."

This caught me by surprise. "Wait. You actually know someone who was there?"

"Yes, yes."

I prevailed on The Poet's hospitality, and begged him to introduce me to one such acquaintance. This was undertaken with no small measure of difficulty, and under a thick veil of secrecy. The Poet had me swear I would not tell Eder. I could not learn his friend's name, I could not describe his features.

Which is how I found myself sitting across from two Libyans on the patio of my hotel late one evening. Several zaftig Tunisian hookers kept a room on the ground floor; their perfume, wafting from their room, was so prodigious that it poisoned the taste of my tea. We kept the patio lights off—the moon was full enough to illuminate our table. The Poet's companion was, of course, sweating.

"It was a most pleasant evening," said the companion. The Poet harrumphed. "Both the wedding and the concert."

"Whoa," I said. "Was it a wedding or a concert? Or both?"

"Please, Mr. Richard, what is the difference? Both are not for peace?"

"Sure. I'm just wondering which one it was."

"First, Aisha's wedding. Then, the concert."

"Huh?"

"He played for The Colonel's daughter's wedding that same night," said The Poet. "Everything you have read is propaganda." He said this cheerfully, without a hint of bitterness. "Your facts are wrong."

Was the concert for Hanna a quick public relations exercise tacked on to a lucrative private performance, a way of maximizing a popular cultural icon in town for a massive paycheck? That seemed too perfect a metaphor for pop music: sentiment and hard cash, writhing around each other like mating snakes.

"He is wonderful man, Lionel Richie," said The Poet's companion. "Wonderful."

The hookers' perfume was burning my sinuses. I rubbed the bridge of my nose, and tried another tack.

"Did you recognize the songs he played?"

"Of course."

"Which was your favorite?"

"Such questions!" said the companion. The Poet made noises, slurped his tea.

"Any song in particular . . . ?"

"Yes, yes. The one from the video-clip. The famous one," continued the companion. "With the dead people that dance."

I looked up at the moon. The haze of the night granted it a halo, like the rings of some science fiction netherworld.

"'Thriller'?" I asked, incredulous.

"Exactly the one." From somewhere in the Tripolitan night, I was sure I could hear Vincent Price cackling.

"You have missed him," said Abdul Salem Dagdog at his store the following day. "Mr. Mohammed is on his way to Ghadames." We were not offered tea.

The time allotment on my visa was running out; I was a day away from catching a plane. Eder pushed, and Mr. Abdul reluctantly offered his son's number. Eder and I walked into a quiet alleyway to make the call. Mohammed Dagdog was, needless to say, unhappy to hear from me. The situation was made more awkward by the terrible line.

I introduced myself, and jumped right in. "Mr. Mohammed—how did Mr. Lionel come to the shop?"

"A very important friend sent me an email."

"I see. And what happened that day?"

"Excuse me?"

Over the phone, I heard gunshots, then the *KABAAM* of a huge explosion.

"Jesus! Mohammed? *Mohammed?*"

Eder snorted. "Gimme the phone. There's nothing wrong—they're watching DVDs in the car. I'll ask him."

Eder held the phone to his ear with one of his large shoulders. "There were two concerts . . . one a wedding in a compound along the water . . . the other at al-Aziziyah . . . a mix of diplomats and sheikhs and even some regular people . . . few women he could see."

There were the facts laid bare: Richie was brought in for both the Hanna Peace Concert and for Aisha's wedding at a Qadhafi compound, and paid a rumored one million dollars for his efforts. There was only one mystery left unsolved: Did the "Hello" re-enactment happen in the medina?

Eder listened for several minutes more, nodded, clicked the phone closed. He put one of his large hands on my shoulder, removed his mirrored shades and looked me in the eye.

"You know, to be honest—I was insulted when I heard about the kids following him in the street, singing 'Hello.'"

"I know you were," I said. "But that doesn't make it any less possible, Eder."

"Yes, yes. But that wouldn't happen here. There are no kids who would know who Lionel Richie was, just to see him in the street, even if they know his music. That's ridiculous. You think our kids walk around—la, la, la—and follow people in the medina. Their parents would yell at them to leave him the fuck alone." He put his shades back on.

"So Mohammed said there was no re-enactment?" My voice dinged off the tight walls of the old city, small and plaintive.

Eder shook his head. "What's the matter with you? We have been in the medina how many times?"

"Several," I said.

"I would say ten. At different time of day and night, yes? You have seen any kids around here?"

"No." He had a point. In a country where sixty percent of the population was younger than twenty, the medina was kid-free.

"Exactly. The streets were bare. *Halas*. Satisfied?"

Truth be told, I had come a long, long way to disprove that story, and now I wondered why I'd bothered. As a Middle Eastern cultural canard, did the tale not deserve to stand, perfectly harmless as it was? Should I not have left it to linger in the margins, unmolested? I felt the darkness of the abyss between Us and Them—the gaping maw of cultural difference—as keenly as a hunger pang, and it left me chilled in the Maghrib sunshine.

I looked at my reflection in Eder's mirrored shades, engulfed by the wide-angled mass of the medina. I resembled nothing so much as a melting midget.

We drove in Eder's company-issued Jetta back from the remains of the fabled Roman trading city of Leptis Magna in silence, along a smooth stretch of highway, past groves of blue gums and carobs and enormous tracts of olive trees, leaves like silver fingers waggling urgently in the heavy afternoon breeze.

I recalled some lines from Auden: "The pillar dug from the desert recorded only / The sack of the city." I loathe ruins, mostly because I have trouble thinking of them as anything other than blueprints for my own civilization one thousand years hence. What calamity shall befall us, so that future humans will walk through the wrecks of our IKEA bathrooms, digging through the remnants of our Crate and Barrel lampshades and our DVD porn collections? But I had no choice: At this point, the travel company was brooking no more of my nosing around the medina. On my final day in Libya, either I went to Leptis Magna or I went waterboarding.

The tour culminated at a shoreline shaped like a cupped palm: Leptis Magna's original harbor. To the west, the remains of the Roman-built breakwater; to the east, the piping of a desalination plant. I stumbled over a carpet of succulents, and took in the broad stretch of the Mediterranean.

Culture after culture had passed through here, spilling blood by the vat, but also depositing remnants of their brilliance, like the shards of clay that lay scattered in the Leptis Magna ruins. In one of those astonishing moments of serendipity, I had just heard Lionel Richie's "Hello," piped from tinny speakers at the outdoor tourist cafeteria. It seemed a perfect summation: an American pop song at a Roman ruin in an Islamic country. I watched the waves crash against the break-water, and imagined what Operation El Dorado Canyon must have sounded like as it swept over here.

In the car driving back, "Hello" echoed in my head as it had when I'd first heard it as a boy. Lionel Richie had enjoyed one of the most successful recording careers of the twentieth century: In short, he had nothing to prove. Yet, somehow, he *needed* this story. And I thought that I understood why. Richie's success was meaningless if his music didn't form a bridge, a structure built from the collective memory of a disparate global fan base who would otherwise call themselves enemies. The "Hello" re-enactment, although I could find no evidence of it being precisely true, was a powerful story *because* of the very fact that Richie was big in Baghdad and through-out the Muslim world. He wanted to believe that his music performed a function that music was supposed to perform: act as a unifier, between Shiite and Sunni, between Muslim and Christian, between American and Libyan. In the telling of this story, Richie wanted to invest some humanity into a discourse that had degenerated into a host of gabbling talking heads, interrupted by the occasional bombing run. If we are woven into one another's cultures, constantly intersecting, then that was at least one way to establish some common ground.

I knew that there was no implicit meaning or message in "Hello" or the video-clip, Richie's self-deconstruction notwithstanding. But from pop music's meaninglessness, all meaning can be derived. It stands as a demonstration of what popular culture does best—unite us in an indefinable, unrefined moment of merriment, sadness, sentiment, titillation. There are two great equalizers: death and pop. And that's why Lionel Richie's story meant so much.

I couldn't sleep. Before dawn, I slunk from my hotel room, past the heavily perfumed downstairs boudoir, and made my way into the cool of night. I walked toward the old city on sidewalks stained with fallen dates and olives, hoping that I would find an open espresso bar. Nothing. I passed the cathedral mosque, lit dramatically from below with spots, and waited for the call to prayer.

"*Allahu akbar. As hadu an la ilaha illa'llah* . . ." cried the muezzin, the words echoing across Mussolini's old square.

The spotlights switched off, reducing the mosque to a hulking block of dark granite. Men approached, slipping inside like shadows. Slowly, the outer walls took on the pinkish hue of morning. In a few hours, I was set to leave the Maghrib, the Land of Sunset, for Fajr, the Land of Sunrise.

Earlier that night I'd had a thought, which I'd confirmed by a quick search on the Internet Movie Database. Exactly one month and one day after the bombing of Tripoli, Tom Cruise's Navy advertainment *Top Gun* was released in theatres to a Memorial Day weekend box office bonanza. A perfect pop-cultural realization of the zeitgeist of

mid-eighties Reaganite foreign policy, the film was a celluloid rendering of the ethos of Operation El Dorado Canyon.

I also found myself wondering, given the fact that the Berlin disco
bombing took place when "Hello" was cresting the charts, whether
Richie's music was playing when The Colonel's proxy placed a suitcase
bomb next to the DJ booth in La Belle discotheque, sending
shattered Lowenbrau bottles and human remains onto a wetted
West Berlin street.

I shivered, walked toward the darkened Mediterranean, and
imagined the USS *Philadelphia* burning offshore like a lodestar.

2

The Sheikh's Batmobile

DUBAI 1.0

Muslim: 97%

6% GDP

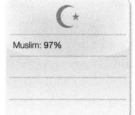

1. Lightnin' Hopkins:
   Long Way from Texas

2. George Jones:
   The One I Loved Back Then
   (The Corvette Song)

3. Tinariwen:
   Cler Achel

Pop.: 1,422,000

Breakdown:
17% UAE Nationals

GDP: $37 billion (USD)

"**Y**ou're not hearing me," said the voice on the cellphone. It was a commanding voice, with a deep Texas twang. "And the thing is: You need to listen close."

Wayne Stewart repeated the directions; they were no less indecipherable the second time. It seemed odd that he'd set up shop so far from the center of Dubaian commerce, out here in Rashidiya, south of the airport, close to the Fujairah road.

"Wait," said Claudia, who was driving, "didn't we already go that way?" Claudia is German but you wouldn't know that from her unaccented English. A longtime journalist with Bloomberg News, she anchored for them in London and New York City and now ran a bureau in Dubai. We had left an hour early; we were now an hour late. It occurred to me that perhaps Mr. Stewart did not want to be found.

Claudia yanked the wheel of the SUV and we screeched back toward the airport. Beside us, an intricate network of scaffolding sang with the wind. We crossed a great intersection and were enveloped in a mess of criss-crossed construction ticker. We hopped a sidewalk. We stopped at a food stand. A man with a mouth full of falafel flecked us with food and waved his pita in the direction he thought we should go. We followed the trajectory of his sandwich, rounded into an industrial district, drove by dark garages intermittently brightened by sparks from welding guns. We backed up, we U-turned, Claudia said I'm hungry, I said I'm beyond hungry.

"Hell's bells," said Wayne Stewart when I called him again. "You're close, son. You see the red factory building? You make a right there. Once you see the ice-cream factory, make a sharp left. Then cruise on 'til you see a blue building that says Fakon Bus Garage. There's a little something outside that should give the game away."

The sign for Fakon Bus Garage came into view. We parked outside a warehouse with double garage doors and two cars under tarps along-side Wayne Stewart's "little something," a red pickup jacked on oversized radials with a Neillsville, WI, sticker on the bumper. It was adorned with Budweiser decals and dripped condensation from the tailpipe, like slobber from the maw of a beast.

"That," said the man who emerged from the gloom of the garage, pointing to the truck, "belongs to an eclectic collector, who I shall not name. You're looking at four hundred and fifty horsepower, state-of-the-art suspension and a V8 that could tear this old earth from orbit."

I extended a hand, but Wayne Stewart pretended not to notice; his arms, the fingers of which were bejeweled with several gold rings, remained at his sides. He was so pale that he flared in the sunlight.

"Follow me," he said, receding into the darkness.

Some weeks before I met Wayne Stewart, a tall figure hunched over a bar, protecting his body from the music as from a flurry of blows, said, "Hello, Richard."

"Oh, right," said I to the British journalist. "Hello, Jack."

"Nice night for it," said Jack, straightening and disappearing into the fray.

As I stood at the bar, staring at a formidable row of sixty hookers staring sullenly back at me, and as I waved off a North African prostitute who was insistently pinching my arm, I was finding it diffi-cult to locate myself in the global maelstrom. My internal GPS had taken the night off. Possibly, it was broken for good.

"You are like me: African," said the prostitute. "So why you will never take a black woman?"

With mounting horror, I made my way to the dance floor, where a Filipino ten-piece played the hits of the eighties, the soundtrack of my boyhood. A Chinese hooker named Cherry was patient with my missteps—she winced quietly as my sneaker came down on her toes. When the chorus of Katrina and the Waves' "I'm Walking on Sunshine" kicked in, she gently guided my warring limbs away from her extremities. Shortly thereafter, I tried to ignore the absurdity of a Filipino rendition of Duran Duran's "Rio."

But really, where was I? And when? Outside the corrugated walls of the whorehouse rose the towers of a techno-city. They stood on top of Pizza Huts, Starbucks, Subways, Dunkin' Donuts, as if they required hydrogenated fat as ballast. There were billboards displaying cut-outs of new skyscraper complexes: At dusk, it was impossible to distinguish real buildings from fake ones. The Burj Khalifa punched its way into the firmament like a concrete fist, one hundred and twenty floors and counting, soon to be the tallest in the world. Everything was spectral, half-built, and therefore subject to the whims of imagination; there exists in every visitor's mind a private Dubai constructed from these adumbrations.

Underneath the towers, far beneath the fast food joints, in crepus-cular basements stinking of stale booze and sweat, there was another Dubai. It was a subterranean universe of Australia Nights with Crowded House and Midnight Oil cover bands; British Nights with Oasis and The Beatles cover bands; Swedish Nights with ABBA cover bands. These were the tacitly accepted expatriate bars, where longing, homesickness, and petulant disgust at the manners and customs of the host nation pervaded.

The youngish men and women in these bars subscribed to the old German proverb *East, west. Home's best.* But they were stuck here, wardens of their own prison, damned by financial expediency and the realities of a world that has long summoned us to foreign climes to stake our claim and find our glory. Home, in these bars, was a collective illusion.

But this wasn't the only place in Dubai where one found an obsession with some distant land that existed in the murk of memory. Since I had left Libya, the notion of a Middle Eastern nostalgia for American pop had never been far from my mind. I wanted to know how pop's halcyon past had come to be so integral a part of local culture, built into memory, part of the foundation of this spectral city along with the Pizza Huts and the Starbucks.

After a cursory review of the list of performers who had recently visited the emirate—Cliff Richard, Olivia Newton-John, Roger Waters—I was struck by how many of them were last relevant in the seventies and eighties. Of course, they bring their Botoxed acts to North American cities on a regular basis; they are part of a multi-billion-dollar business I call Nostalgia Inc. But most North American cities have other cultural outlets—art scenes, art schools, small venues for local bands. And while those scenes and schools and venues may plunder the past shamelessly, Dubai—the Gulf's great cultural hope—is becoming a waypoint for yesteryear.

I left the underworld and the following day braved the sharp Gulf light, taking an elevator ride up the Dubai Towers to meet with a gentleman named Majid Wasi. He worked for one of the region's largest public relations firms, JiWin, whose clients include the Dubai International Film Festival, which only a few months before had premiered Oliver Stone's *World Trade Center*, starring Nicholas Cage, for local audiences.

"The one thing about being here, there are invasions"—how often I heard the word *invasion*—"of all kinds. Indian, Pakistani, French, English. A lot of give and take, a platform for people to exchange ideas," Wasi told me.

"Mostly," I said, "I see American ideas."

"Yes," agreed Wasi. "Mostly."

We spoke a little about the sorts of cultural initiatives that had been undertaken in the past few years. The musical *Chicago* had its Middle East debut here some months before—thirteen nights, "and the last four were packed. We didn't know how the audience would react. You know, we're contributing to the evolution of the cultural scenario in the Middle East, and developing a platform for culture."

"Look," said Wasi, after he had run through the positives, mostly in terms of tourist dollars, that this fledgling cultural scene could mean for the city. "Dubai is trying to implement culture, much the same way that America is trying to implement democracy in Iraq—almost by force. But still, we need it. What you're seeing now is only ten years old. We need to be patient." Wasi was convinced that one day Dubai would be the region's theater capital; he knew that the Marvel Theme Park would open in 2011. (Spider-Man roller coasters! The Incredible Hulk teacups!) Down the road, in the oil-soaked emirate of Abu Dhabi, a Guggenheim and a Louvre were slated to open. Debates raged about how best to modestly obscure the naughty bits on Rodins.

"We have to be careful here," said Wasi. "We wouldn't do something that is anti-cultural or something that would cause any confusion."

So Wasi and his like sell either branded high art or the recent past to homesick expatriates, certainly, but also to tourists from Kuwait, Saudi Arabia, Abu Dhabi and even local Dubaians. Nostalgia is many things, but as a popular cultural product it is always safe—it is never "anti-cultural" or "confusing." But I wondered how Pink Floyd and their like had come to be pro-cultural. What process had occurred to render them anodyne? And could it be that the one factor conjoining the people of the Emirates (along with those of the Gulf at large) and their Western expatriate community was nostalgia for pop culture from the sixties, seventies and eighties? Was it possible that locals and Westerners shared some sort of common cultural memory?

These thoughts bubbled up into a heady froth, not unlike that of the Budweiser in front of me as I sat in the darkened confines of

Hard Rock Cafe Dubai, not half an hour after meeting with Wasi. Outside, atop a skyscraper, two vast Fender Stratocasters lay athwart each other, marking the spot for passing airline traffic. Inside, I listened to Elvis and Little Richard. It wasn't, however, until I swung open the double doors to leave—and saw her panting in the parking lot—that I had any real notion of how to make sense of it all.

There before me, steam curling from her hood, stood a beautifully rendered example of that common cultural memory: an electric centaur, a soul-mobile. She was originally built for a stuntman/actor named Henry Blight Halicki, and would appear in the extended car-chase thriller *Gone in 60 Seconds*. She remained—thirty-two years after conception—one of the most perfect expressions of automotive brawn ever forged from steel, glass and gasoline.

Those in the know called her *Eleanor*.

Wayne Stewart's vehicle enhancement workshop reeked powerfully of motor grease and paint fumes. I could at first make out nothing in the main garage, but at the far end I saw four Filipinos working under the glare of klieg lights, spraying the carcass of a seventies-era Ford Capri with paint guns. I choked on the fumes, instantly lightheaded.

"This way," said Stewart, and I followed the glint of his gold. When he clicked on a hanging lightbulb, I noticed a sheen on his pale skin, like that of some deep-sea mollusk. He had the pinched face of a Bible-belt preacher, his spectacles perched fussily on his nose. More alarmingly, his face was taut as a drum, as if the back of his head had been bunched harshly into a ponytail; his left eye lolled in a glassy, immobile stare. He wore brown slacks, a brown wool vest and a beige dress shirt. And he did not bother with pleasantries.

"You don't know me from Adam," said Stewart, "and I don't know you from a hole in the wall. So let's get briefly acquainted." He turned to look at us, squinting. I barely received a passing glance, but Claudia, who is tall, long-limbed, her hair in a strawberry blond bob, received substantially more eyeball time. I'm not sure how many women had been inside this workshop, but I knew that without her to smear axle grease on the ego, I'd have come away with bupkes.

"This," said Wayne Stewart, building rhetorical steam, "is my shop. It's where I do what I do."

"And that is?" I asked.

"Son," said Wayne Stewart, "I make American Dreams for these folks out here in the desert." Like a pup-tent predicant, he waved his hand toward the center of the garage where, on a patch of oil-stained concrete, a pristine pink 1959 Cadillac stood, missing only the chrome that would make it shimmer like a chariot of the gods. "No compromises. No shortcuts. Perfection."

The paint job on the Cadillac was lustrous and thick, like candy coating on an M&M. The seats were expertly sewn in a brown cross-weave, the leather as luscious as freshly churned country butter. The dark oak of the steering wheel and the trim on the inside doors and dashboard were stained jet-black—the work of an artisan cabinet-maker. With so many converging points of supreme craftsmanship, the car seemed, in the low light of Wayne Stewart's workshop, as if it had rolled out from a dream version of the 1950s and that the essential lie of that decade was rather an enduring reality.

"Things you should know about me," said Stewart, whipping back a stained tarp, and revealing a partially built vehicle underneath. "I'm a Corvette man. I own sixteen. My favorite is a 1972 LT1 called Lady—chrome front bumper, same again rear, manual transmission."

He was moving fast now, displaying a surprising strength as he ripped off tarps with a sharp crack. Dust motes sparkled around him, catching light from the bulb.

"Now, how about this?" asked Stewart.

I knew what it was immediately: sensual, rounded headlamps, a smooth wave of metal rising up on its haunches like a sprinter set to leap from the blocks. Built across the space/time continuum in St. Louis, Missouri, in 1954, costing $2,774 and change, this example was a rich luster Chevrolet once called "pennant blue." It remains a vision of the future, even though it is a relic of the past.

"Corvette. First year of production," said Stewart. "Bought this sucker twenty years ago, and it still ain't quite done." He stopped a minute to look over it, his chin touching his chest. "Isn't easy getting parts for her. Especially not out here."

He turned sharply, whipped off another tarp. What lay beneath was barely recognizable as a car. The top had been scraped away, as if a giant potato peeler had sheared the cabin off. Stewart turned to face us. His right thumb worried a chunk of heavy bling on his index finger.

"There are occurrences," he said, sounding like Billy Graham doing Cormac McCarthy doing Faulkner, "and then there are occurrences." This felt like an unmasking, as if Claudia and I were about to learn something fundamental about the price of passion. He raised a flap of gray hair, revealing a filigree of white scars. His forehead looked sculpted from delicate marble; his glass eye was refulgent under the bulb.

"See here?" said Stewart.

"I do." I swallowed dryly. I was becoming simultaneously high and hungover from the paint fumes, and I wasn't entirely sure I wanted to know the origins of those scars. So I was unhappy to hear myself ask, "What happened?"

Wayne Stewart hitched his slacks, sat on the edge of the busted chassis and told us a story.

It's early on a Gulf morning. The heat is not yet properly up. The asphalt streaking beneath the Corvette doesn't pave a desert highway so much as open a pinhole in time. This isn't Proust's dainty madeleine, but rather a catalyst for memory traveling at one hundred miles an hour. Electricity poles flit by as the car gathers velocity. On one side, the desert. On the other, the Persian Gulf.

The light here in the mornings is thick, almost greasy. Shadows stretch across the highway, mingling with the haze, while the rising sun shimmers like a just-cracked quail's egg. At 6 A.M., it is ninety-five degrees, which means the tarmac does funny things to the rubber. The desert seethes. Wayne Stewart has always felt that he must fend it off with one hand, and steer with the other.

A sudden glint in the side mirror. A truck merges at the wrong angle, listing like a sinking ship. There is no time for an escape maneuver: It slams into the Corvette broadside, fender connecting hard, shattering the windows outward. Stewart's world lurches sickeningly. The front bumper grabs the tarmac, sending up a shower of sparks like Fourth of July fireworks. He sees the barrier separating the other side of the highway coming toward him. The last thing he realizes is that the car won't go into it. It will go *under* it. He hears the crunch. Then the desert darkens.

Emergency crews arrive and survey the mess. It takes them a few minutes to figure out how in the name of God and His Prophet the Corvette came to have its roof sheared clean off the chassis.

And a few minutes more to find the top of Wayne Stewart's head.

The accident caved in Stewart's chest, collapsed a lung and removed a goodly portion of his skull, exposing the mulch of his brain to the humid Dubai morning. It threatened to erase experiences he'd accumulated over a lifetime spent in shops similar to Fakon Bus Garage, on the other side of the world, in another era.

Born in hardscrabble Oklahoma during the war, he grew up a farm boy when the South was modernizing and farming belonged to the likes of John Deere. He learned to fix those machines, and fix them well. By the time he was thirteen he was sweeping floors for a couple of fellows named Jim Hall and Hap Sharp. They formed the legendary American marquee Chaparral, in Midland, Texas, and their cars went on to win a host of racing titles, including the 12 Hours of Sebring. They were true American originals, relics of the can-do spirit of the sixties, and heroes to any car nut who came of age during the period. For Stewart, it was like learning how to be a Catholic directly from the Pope.

When he wasn't building cars, Stewart was teaching himself to fly crop-dusters over Texan farmland. He became an airline pilot in the glory years of international air travel, and during the many days off that are the prerequisite of the intercontinental captain, he customized cars for a select list of clientele. When he moved from the States to the Emirates, flying one of a fleet of four super-sized 747-400s for the ruling Sheikh Maktoum's VIP and cargo airline outfit, he assumed that his Texan side business would suffer. He was mistaken. In 2000, Stewart hung up his wings and made the Fakon Bus Garage his primary place of business.

Claudia, Stewart and I had by now walked a loose circle back to the '59 Caddy. It flared out like a glorious winged creature, a mythic Yankee angel.

"So who buys this stuff? You have a catalog?" Claudia wanted to know.

Wayne Stewart almost smiled. "It's a lot more complicated than that. See, this isn't a regular car lot. The rules are different. Let's think of it as something of a dance."

There is a specific protocol: A quiet Emirati arrives at Fakon Bus Garage in a beat-up econo-car. He wears shabby clothing, a ratty dish-dash or the slacks and button-up of a poor foreigner, and waits outside under the furious sun. He watches. Then he leaves. Some weeks later he will return to ask some deferential questions. Some months later he will return for a third visit, this time in a late-model sedan with tinted windows and a single-digit licence plate, driven by his chauffeur. He wears a fresh white dish-dash, and subtle emblems of his royalty.

And he tells Wayne Stewart—like a man describing a fever dream— exactly what it is he wants.

"It's a heck of a task. And an enormous responsibility, building someone's fantasy," Stewart told us. "You see, there's a way of doing business here. I work with people who must become my friends before we get started. I need to know that I'm building *their* car, the car they always wanted." He pulled the crease mark in his slacks straight. "I'm a little bit arrogant. I don't take people off the street. You want something in a rush, you go somewhere else."

As with so many things in the Emirates, discretion is everything. Stewart would not reveal his client list. "They would not like that, and I'd lose their friendship and their trust." He did concede that he's "done some work for the extended family of Sheikh Maktoum, and I'll be doing a lot more."

"Show him the thing," said a voice behind us, in an accent that central casting would dub "Cowboy Movie Sidekick." I turned to see a portly, bowlegged man handing Stewart a can of A&W Root Beer. "You can't get root beer here in Dubai," explained the man, pronouncing Dubai as Doo-bay. "Can you believe that?"

"Leon is the root-beer supplier," said Stewart. "Can't get work done without root beer." Leon, I learned, flew for Sheikh Maktoum, and had known Stewart for close on forty years. He took a long, noisy slurp of his beverage.

"Show him the thing," said Leon again.

"Sheesh. Hold on to your pants," said Stewart. "Now remember this," he instructed us. "Things worth doing come in five flavours: fattening, immoral, illegal, dangerous and expensive." He looked at Claudia. "There just ain't any getting around that."

Leon sputtered into his root beer. "Amen."

"Follow me," said Stewart. "I don't bring many people up into the sancta sanctorum, but I guess it's your lucky day."

We bent double to negotiate the cramped stairwell and assembled in a small office overlooking the chop-shop floor, surrounded by lesser examples of Stewart's extensive model car collection. There were several framed Garfield cartoons, a desk cluttered with files and drawings.

"I'm not entirely sure," I said once we had settled, "if I fully under-stand the attraction to your work, especially out here in Dubai or the

Gulf, where luxury cars are cheap to buy and cheap to run. Why would a local sheikh bother earning the trust of a bespoke car builder?"

"Show him the thing," said Leon for a third time.

Stewart turned his glass eye on me. "I'm gonna make you privy to something I'm working on right now." He sat back into a chair and scooted in front of his computer, clicking his mouse insistently. The hard drive groaned and clacked, reluctantly coughing several images up on screen. "Know what that is?" he asked, scrutinizing my face. "That should explain things for you."

I was not sure how the pictures before me were supposed to count as explication. The vehicle in the first picture looked like an insect, mandibles clasping the turbine of a jet engine. Jet-black, it swept into a glistening, fissile crouch. The next image depicted a second black vehicle, this one a modification of Ford's abandoned Futura concept. It was a fantasy rendition of a fifties-era Caddy, black with red trim, two pod-like windows instead of a windscreen, with pipes like those from a church organ bristling from the trunk.

"What are they?" asked Claudia, squinting at the screen. How, I wondered, had she been able to maintain her extraordinary level of pop-cultural naïveté?

"Tell her, son," said Stewart, his specs low on his nose.

"Those," I said, "are Batmobiles."

"Bingo," said Stewart.

"Right you are," said Leon.

"*Bat*mobiles?" asked Claudia. They don't go on assignments like these at Bloomberg. "You're *making* them?"

"Yup," said Stewart.

"I don't understand why someone would want Batman's car," said Claudia. "And those other cars downstairs. It seems silly."

Stewart stiffened, bringing his knees together like a prissy debutante in a roughhouse saloon. "Silly? How so? It goes back to the movies, like every darn thing. A lot of the TV shows and movies had muscle cars in the seventies and eighties—don't need to tell you that."

"Yeah, but what TV shows and movies were the sheikhs watching here?"

"Thing is," said Stewart, "they weren't necessarily watching them here. They watched 'em in Cairo, Beirut, London, Dallas, Miami, New York. They watched 'em wherever they damn well felt like it."

Wayne Stewart was, in his obtuse way, referring to one of the more astonishing, if misunderstood, geopolitical and cultural transformations of the twentieth century. He was talking about the Gulf's post-oil boom—a *sahwa*, or awakening, that sent thousands of young Arabs from the middle and upper classes out into the wide world to bring a little slice of the West back to their own countries.

In this, Osama bin Laden's Saudi Arabian family proves to be a representative, if extreme, example of the phenomenon. Mohammed bin Laden, the family patriarch, came to Saudi from Yemen in the mid-1920s. His early life followed the ebb and flow of fortunes in the Gulf state, which was run jealously by the Saudi royal family. When oil was discovered, Saudi Arabia became rich in a way that was previously unfathomable. Those who had the royal family's patronage became outrageously wealthy alongside them. Mohammed bin Laden fathered fifty-four children and, as was fashionable in the Kingdom at the time, educated them all over the world: Beirut, Cairo, Houston, Los Angeles, Miami, London and—in Osama's case—staid Jeddah.

The family, like so many of their contemporaries, was steeped in Islam. When they went forth into the world, their faith slammed into a popular culture of desire, but desire manufactured perfectly. The sixties and early seventies—a golden age of pop—served as the backdrop for what was essentially a one-way cultural conversation. Many of the bin Ladens wore bell-bottoms, caroused at parties, sang along to rock tunes. (Osama's older brother, Salem, once started a rock band called The Echoes.) Because there were television channels throughout the region playing Western fare for expatriate oil workers, Osama himself grew up watching *Bonanza*. Given their appetites, their means and their mobility, this generation of Gulf Arabs was perhaps the most cosmopolitan cohort of all time, equally at home—at least on the surface—in Paris, New York and Mecca.

The age of petroleum changed the Gulf at a punishing pace. Mohammed bin Laden's generation grew up on the backs of camels; their sons drove versions of the cars Wayne Stewart modified on the shop floor below us. Conservatism and progressivism pummeled each other like drunks in a brawl, with conservatism coming out on top every time. Thus, a hard-line, inflexible version of Islamist was born, one with a paradoxical soft spot for all things American, which in those days stood in for a utopian vision of all that was possible in the Gulf. But as successive rulers relentlessly pursued modernization without secularization, history shattered and, for many, an idealized past became the future.

"So you're saying there's an appreciation for American popular culture among your clients?" asked Claudia.

"Appreciation?" Stewart chuckled dryly. "Girl, I'd term it reverence. But it's reverence for a culture that is quickly disappearing. It's the same way with folks who are interested in rock 'n' roll of the sixties and seventies—folks that go to the Hard Rock Cafe to get a burger and stare at Elvis's jockey shorts. It's like sand disappearing beneath their feet. They're hanging on. They need it. I suppose you'd call it nostalgia."

Indeed. When the term was first coined, nostalgia was considered a disease, a "mania of longing." It was born and diagnosed on the great European battlefields of the seventeenth century and it spread, virus-like, through entire armies posted far from home, reaching epidemic proportions during the Napoleonic Wars.

Something happened to nostalgia as the centuries wore on and time accelerated, spurred ever faster by technological advancement. The ailment was less a result of physical displacement and more one of temporal disorientation. In other words, time became place. Idealized memory of a utopian homeland that once plagued Napoleon's legions now ran roughshod over entire cultures brutalized by relentless change. We weren't wallowing in the misremembered comforts of home, but the misremembered consolations of yesterday.

No longer do we pretend that there is a cure for nostalgia; it is an indelible part of the modern condition. American popular culture is powered—at least in part—by the "mania of longing." But what had nostalgia come to mean in the Arab world, in the Gulf especially, where progress has occurred so quickly that it has all but annihilated history? Longing, nostalgia's handmaiden, has always been at the heart of Arabic culture. But the longing in Wayne Stewart's workshop was for an imagined *America*. This chimerical place was defined by unbridled power, leavened by uncomplicated fun, heightened by the perfection of its products.

But the nostalgia I saw here had an ominous corollary. Weren't the shadowy figures posting beheading videos on TerrorTube also subject to utopian visions of the past? Weren't they also pining for Shangri-Las lost in the maelstrom of progress? If Osama bin Laden hadn't chosen to use his father's wealth to finance a return to the glory days of the fourteenth century caliphate, would he not be in Wayne Stewart's garage scratching the same nostalgic itch with a pimped, four hundred horsepower Ford Capri?

What's more, the contrast between the notion of America offered to outsiders via pop nostalgia and how the "real" America was currently behaving around the regional corner in, say, Iraq was so vast that it was becoming harder to swallow the former. This I knew because I suffered in kind. I couldn't help wondering if Wayne Stewart's clientele felt betrayed, and had thus become entirely ambivalent toward the American Idea. Were they bitter cuckolds, looking over scented photographs of a lover in better times, trying to stop the ache in their hearts? American pop construct vs. *realpolitik*. Never pretty.

Claudia contemplatively tapped the Batmobiles on the screen. This got me thinking superheroes, and how hard their originators work on their backstories, their histories. Without it, they are just men in tights. Likewise, without a proper history, the people of the Gulf can too easily be summed up as dudes in bedsheets either aping Americans, or trying to blow them to pieces. We must therefore look into the sands of the ancient desert, if you'll excuse a moment of mytho-poeticism, for meaning.

In the long-ago winter of 1921, if the Bedouin of the al-Dahna Desert had crossed the path of a caravan en route from Bahrain, they would have witnessed an incongruous sight: a box-like metal carriage, seemingly smoke-blackened, being pulled by a camel train, its wheels either disappearing in the sand or traversing a grass-weave carpet so they would not become mired. The contraption was being transported through the Nejd from Bahrain to Riyadh, where the warrior King Saud would take ownership of it, the first of what would become a fleet of such contraptions. This unlikely looking carriage was made in a faraway place named Detroit, Michigan, and it worked—under very specific circumstances—without the assistance of a horse or a camel. It was called a Model T Ford.

It was something of a homecoming. Five thousand and four hundred years before this strange procession, the Sumerians, in what is now southern Iraq, invented the wheel. (They also invented writing, so it's fair to say that without their dual contributions, this book, and others like it, would not be possible.) By 1926, Model T Fords were regularly making the *hajj*, transporting pilgrims from Medina to Mecca in the path of the Prophet's stately caravans. These cars were conferred a mystical ability in the desert; they were almost hallowed. "Seen by a stranger," wrote the poet Baq'r, "it seems more like a vehicle exhaling fire . . . covering the deserted territories and vales . . . challenging birds to a race above the steppes and the deserts."

The first reported car in the region was a French Dion-Bouton, a 187cc trouper belonging to the Egyptian Khedive's adventuresome grandson, Prince Aziz Hassan. In 1904, he piloted the vehicle across a hundred-mile swath from Cairo to Alexandria in an astonishing ten hours. There were few formal road paths, so it was incumbent on the prince to steer through the land of the unfortunate *fellaheen*, whom he was obliged to compensate for ruined fields and felled livestock. Indeed, cars were at first either the playthings of royalty or emblems of foreign power. In 1929, using language that is now distressingly familiar, the Palestinian newspaper *Al-Zouhour* warned, "Do not be surprised, dear reader, if we describe the introduction of automobiles to our country as [an] 'occupation' . . . impoverishing our people who are spending their money buying automobiles, thus benefiting the plundering Western countries without equal return."

The voices of dissent were, however, in the minority, especially as the car began to establish itself as a means of traversing treacherous desert territory long regarded as impassable. László Ede Almásy de Zsadány et Törökszentmiklós—Hungarian aristocrat and model for the title character in Michael Ondaatje's *The English Patient*—earned the honorific Abu Ramla (father of the desert) by finding the legendary Zerzura, or Oasis of the Birds, in a Model T truck. The Damascus to Baghdad desert route was forged by Buicks, Cadillacs and Oldsmobiles that left pillar-like dust clouds as ephemeral monuments to the future.

This transformative technology was definitively linked to America, and quickly worked its way into local culture. The father of populist pan-Arabism, Egypt's President Gamal Abdel Nasser, traveled in an iconic jet-black 1948 Cadillac convertible. King Saud favored Imperials. The singer Um Kalthoum, incontestably the Arab world's most revered personality, drove a Buick. Her male counterpart, Mohammed Abdel Wahab, drove a Dodge. Big American cars consistently found their way into Egyptian cinema; in *Jawhara* (1942), ingénue Nour al-Huda, in one of the more famous songs of the era, rode in a convertible Cadillac singing *Oh you beautiful automobile, how sweet you are!* And then, of course, there was Hollywood's love affair with the car.

The car in the Gulf has become a locus of cultural energy. In societies where everyone is expected to dress and act the same, the car, and how one drives it, becomes a means of conveying individuality and status.

"You are what you drive," Richard Whitehead, editor of *Middle East Car*, once wrote. "When you roar down a highway, cameras flashing as you break the land speed record, your foot on the dash of your SUV, you're the man." (Or the woman: There's a definite *Sopranos*-ish female obsession with the high-end SUV in the Gulf.) In middle-class clans, cars are accepted as gifts from wealthier families. They are business incentives, wedding presents, a vital fixture of local life and the only place where, in big families that live twenty to a compound, one can find even a hint of privacy.

And there is a definite desert driving culture—an old and venerable one that started with the likes of the English Patient and continued with the first imported GMC trucks hitting these sandy shores. "The wealthy, in those early days, could explore the desert like no one ever had before," writes Whitehead. "This is a means of status as well—those with skills have been driving high-end 4×4s in the desert since they were children. It's almost like they're born in those things they're so good at it. Trucks is where the love for American car culture comes full circle," adds Whitehead. "The muscle car is more of a dream of America. An idea."

While Wayne Stewart might be an anomaly, what he *represents* is part of something much, much larger. Often, a cultural obsession is defined by its extreme edges. Stewart defines the obsession.

The Batmobiles flickered on Wayne Stewart's computer monitor. They were Bruce Wayne's favored modes of transportation *and* philosophical constructs: Within those slender fuselages existed a mélange of history, cultural complicity and enmity. Stewart pointed a pale finger at his computer screen, leaving a smudge in the dust.

"I've been commissioned to build three of these," he said. His client wanted one from each of the successive Batman eras: the sixties TV show starring Adam West, the Anton Furst–designed Tim Burton Batman Gothic, and the tank-like 2004 version from Christopher Nolan's do-over *Batman Begins*. The fiberglass bodies alone would run his client $10,000 apiece.

"Oh, and he wants the suits. I gotta get him the suits, too."

"You're kidding me," I said.

Stewart raised a razor-sharp eyebrow as if to say that even if he did possess a sense of humor, he wouldn't waste it on me. Some months later, I noticed an item online that made me think back to that gesture. A firm called Profiles in History organized an auction in which Val Kilmer's Batsuit from *Batman Forever* sold for $63,250. I'm not suggesting that Stewart made the winning bid, and obviously he wouldn't tell me if he had, but it's worth a speculative "hmmm." Other items on the block included Christopher Reeve's Superman suit, which sold for $115,000 to an undisclosed buyer, the H.R. Giger creature suit from *Alien* for $126,500 and the Golden headpiece from the Staff of Ra from *Raiders of the Lost Ark* for $69,000.

When there is no cap on spending, indulgence in nostalgia can seem insane. Boomers are buying up their pop-cultural history, literally piece by piece. Ghastly as this may initially seem, there is something poignant about the need to own flits of memory, these wisps of pop-culture ephemera. Indeed, Profiles in History suggests that pop culture may not be so ephemeral after all. Memory has become matter: In this case, a $63,250 Batsuit.

This new desire to own pop-cultural artifacts is one of nostalgia's late-stage manifestations: the need to transform our invented memories into hard reality. And Wayne Stewart is a Sandman with a toolbox. In the Gulf, it's not *culture* itself that acts as a bridge between cultures, but rather the nostalgia for American pop that acts as a binding force. Like Boomers everywhere, the Petro-Boomer elite are buying up their memories. Worlds away from each other, two oppositional cultures dream the same fading dreams.

Stewart leaned back in his chair, and brought his glasses down to the tip of his nose. "In the Emirates, you can live the American Dream like nowhere else in the world. It just depends on how much *wasta* you have. Now if you'll excuse me," said Stewart, his body tightening. "There's a Caddy downstairs I have to finish."

★ ★ ★

"Now *that*," said a booming voice, "was a fucking movie." Mohammed bin Suleyman swept in wearing a splendid white dishdash, lithe and athletic even though he no longer bore the frame of an athlete. He swung his paunch like a man proud of every illicit calorie that went into its creation. "Do they make them like that anymore? The answer is *No. Fucking. Way.*" Bin Suleyman shook my hand with a large, hirsute paw; his publicist, Tony, introduced us with a formality that didn't fit the occasion.

Bin Suleyman turned to the widescreen television in his gilded *majlis*, which was playing, for reasons known only to the gods of irony, David Lean's *Lawrence of Arabia*, and said, "Look at this movie." The sound was up so loud that it felt as if the bullets were tearing through my brain stem. "I have driven all this desert. I have seen all the history in these places. I can find for you on a map where John the Baptist was born, all the places he lived in his life, where he had his head chopped off. And I can fucking drive you there. My friend, I have read the Old Testament, the New Testament—and I have seen where they take place. You do not know this, but it is from those books that the Qur'an comes."

I said that that was very interesting.

"The desert," said bin Suleyman, shaking his head. "You see the fucker on the Discovery Channel, but you cannot see what I see, feel what I feel. It is exactly like the Highlands to a Scotsman. But maybe less whiskey." Bin Suleyman guffawed, I laughed politely, Tony looked up from his laptop. "My friend," said bin Suleyman, "I am the desert."

This was not mere poetic hyperbole. Bin Suleyman was the most gifted sand driver in the history of competitive rally racing. He intuitively understood the sweep of a dune, read it like text, understood how the vehicle would move across its surface. He could read the desert too, was not intimidated by its vastness. Like T. E. Lawrence, he mastered it, made it a domain he could manage. But he was a hard sell to a local culture not used to Yankee-style dash and panache.

If the United Arab Emirates has an icon—a face that sums up the Petro-Boomer generation—it must be the caddish bin Suleyman. From an incredibly wealthy and influential family, bin Suleyman took to rally driving in his twenties, after completing his education in America. He was the quintessential over-rich Arabian prince, dismissed as a dilettante by the international community, his ostentation similarly abhorred at home—incapable as he was of abiding by Emirati codes of discretion. Bin Suleyman helped define the stereotype of the Gulf playboy. But when he was behind the wheel of a car, in his red Marlboro jumpsuit peppered with Western brands, his enormous nose askew on his face, Mohammed bin Suleyman was unbeatable.

If there was anyone in the United Arab Emirates capable of unironically donning a Batsuit and driving a black rocket safely down Sheikh Zayed Road, it had to be the man I had come to see. I was almost sure that I stood above an under-construction Batcave. It was, after all, bin Suleyman who had hosted the late Michael Jackson's post–molestation indictment, when the King of Pop managed to embroil himself in an international controversy by applying makeup in the women's washroom of a Dubai mall, transgressing about one thousand major and minor rules of Sunni Islam, and several dozen rules of universal etiquette beside.

I wanted to speak with bin Suleyman partly because of his representative status for a generation of sixties-era Arabs, but also because he so clearly shared Boomer obsessions with his North American contemporaries. But *so what* if we shared these obsessions? I was beginning to wonder. In the ultimate reckoning, what did it mean if the ideas within them didn't transfer, ideas that had meant so much to me growing up at the bottom of Africa? Bin Suleyman *was* the American Idea in a dish-dash. And it didn't seem like he cared anymore.

We turned once again to the movie. "This film," said bin Suleyman, "it is classic. It is legend. Look at us!" Peter O'Toole as

Lawrence debated with an Arab. "Oh, we were the savages!" he said happily. "Oh my! Now, how things have changed."

"How so?"

"The movies, the music. Coming from there: It is a fever, not a culture. In the sixties and early seventies, when I was the first time in America—what a time! They were good at everything, because they were *trying*."

"Virginia! I would go back to that era if I could—I love it, the movies, Eddie Cochran, the great cars, the beautiful cars. Then the late seventies and the early eighties came, and everything went bad. The oil crisis, terrorism—they started to look at me with suspicion. The beautiful concept of America—the optimism—it went missing. I would like to forget about it."

Bin Suleyman leaned forward, his dark eyes flickering with the reflected panorama of *Lawrence of Arabia*. "Remember—the culture there in those days was more conservative than it was here. It was strict. You could not go naked, you could not have long hair. And if you were a communist? My God! Maybe that's why we loved them so much. They were conservative, like us. But now, you can have long hair, but in their hearts they are still conservative. The best and the worst. They want to shove their culture up my ass? Fine. But make it the culture of the sixties. Any day. But not this new shit."

We took a walk to bin Suleyman's garages and gazed over limited edition cars that cost a million dollars apiece: metal twisted and stretched and pulled into sleek lines, perfect interpretations of speed and power, with great scoops to cool coiled engines, and big swaths of rubber to hold them to the ground.

Something bin Suleyman said hit me as hard as a truck once hit Wayne Stewart on an open stretch of desert highway. *They were conservative, like us.* I recalled some lines from music critic Amanda Petrusich's study of musical Americana, *It Still Moves:* "We are ostensibly a devout country—one of the most religious in the world—that is also preoccupied with temptation. We are a nation of hell-fearers and heaven-hopers who still like to have a good time, and that tension seeps into nearly every cultural artifact we produce." I couldn't pretend to understand the precise nuances of Gulf culture in the 1960s, but what bin Suleyman was saying was really just a confirmation of what existed in Wayne Stewart's chop-shop: There was, for a resident of the Gulf states in the 1960s, a definitive link, a deeper cultural connection with the United States than mere exposure would allow for. And the link appeared to come from the tension between the devout and the deleterious.

"Who is more religious: USA or UAE? USA or KSA?" asked my host, referring to the Kingdom of Saudi Arabia.

Reflexively, that's a laughable question. But what bin Suleyman was saying was that the Gulf—while deeply devout—is arguably more *traditional* than it is religious. The lines blur, of course, but while a Gulf Muslim will subvert the tenets of Islam—a Scotch here and there, some loud Led Zeppelin in his SUV—he would never, *ever* subvert traditional values. In other words, he's not taking his wife to a key party any time soon. Nonetheless, the pull toward iniquity is hardwired into the culture. It's the inevitable result of religious conservatism putting a bottle stop on more insalubrious impulses.

"With the old American pop, it was always this mixture," said bin Suleyman. "There were values. Strong, hard values. Ideas. And underneath? This titillation, this sale of objects. The shininess. Money. *We* in the Gulf are this way. *We* are Texans. On one side, family, God, the *ummah*. On this other side, in the secret *majlis*, dancing girls and flighty songs."

If one is to agree with Suleyman's version of things—and that's a safe bet, considering his status as a representative of his generation—then Gulf Arabs who came of age in the 1960s, steeped in the American culture of the time, were as intimately involved in the cultural chasm that opened up during the Vietnam War era. Gulf Arabs, like so many conservative Americans, could not relate to the Woodstock set. What's more, they became both geopolitical victims and accomplices in the vicious pragmatism of the Cold War. The beneficiaries of the Persian Gulf oil boom rode the unbridled optimism of the late fifties and the sixties, only to slam up against the cynicism of the Vietnam era and the libidinous culture of the seventies. Like many in America, they had lost their compass. They gave an ear to the religious hardliners among them, and donned their faith and their own culture like a thick desert cloak, coming to believe that we are opposites, while Steve McQueen raced his Mustang through their dreams.

"It is a large joke," said bin Suleyman. "I am nostalgic for an America that only half existed. I'm not a big fan of boxing, but there is a man named Muhammad Ali. He did what he did with a lot of people against him. He believed. He win. He lose. And after ten years, he comes back in the Rumble in the Jungle. That was America. It is America no more. But what problem now belongs to us all? It is that no one believes in the future any longer. When I was in Virginia, *all* we believed in was the future."

"Let me show you something." The Gulf's driving superstar guided me over to a Mitsubishi Pajero that he had modified himself, installing an eight hundred horsepower engine, thereby turning it into something Hans Blix and his fellow U.N. weapons inspectors would have confiscated back when they had the mandate. "You see here, how we had to modify, to change the engine block. We basically reinvent the piping, the wiring. And they say the Arab is a backward monkey." He paused. "Optimism never dies. Only, it is in hiding." Then, "My friend, I can say only this: *insha'allah*. It is in God's hands."

Courtesy of the Texan Sandman, I needed to know what it felt like to travel the desert in an iconic American machine. Some weeks later, I rented from an obsequious Singaporean with a harelip a 1200cc Harley-Davidson Sport, midnight-blue tank and tail. It was early in the morning on a Friday—not yet 7 A.M.—and I familiarized myself with the machine, running through the clutch, waiting for my convoy.

It was as if a ten-pound weight was attached to every molecule in the air, so heavy was the atmosphere. The heat from the Harley's shuddering tank rose up, meeting the heat from the new sun. Ahead, the metal intestines of the Mall of the Emirates; behind me, the nascent towers of south Dubai, rising up from the desert like a sun-bleached ribcage.

I kept my eyes on the highway.

They appeared, heading north on Sheikh Zayed Road at a stately speed: a young Kuwaiti on his cherry-red Harley at the front of six other motorcycles. I clicked down into first gear, feeling the power rumble through the meat of my inner thighs, and pulled out of the slip-road, nodding as I joined their number. We sped up to cruising speed, the road empty for the holy day, a streak of dawn trapped in the haze over the Persian Gulf.

I felt the power of the machine beneath me, popped down from fifth to fourth gear, pulled the throttle low and surged ahead. As I gained speed, I glanced at my rear-view mirror: five vehicles gaining on us, their hoods low to the tarmac, moving almost twice as fast as our fifty miles an hour. Corvettes. Mint condition. One of their number a gorgeous lime-green Stingray.

For an instant, there were, on the desert road to Abu Dhabi, eleven icons of American power on one strip of tarmac. The Corvettes tore past us, the whine of their engines audible above the roar of the motorcycles. They stayed in sight for about five minutes. Then they disappeared.

Part II

DHUHR

3

So You Can Watch What They Watch

DUBAI 2.0, FEATURING SAUDI ARABIA*

Muslim: Everybody

45% GDP

1. Jefferson Airplane:
   We Built This City
2. Gary Portnoy and Judy Hart Angelo:
   Where Everybody Knows Your Name
3. Zita Swoon:
   TV Song

Pop.: 28,146,656
(550,000 non-nationals)

Avg. age: 21.5

Capital: Riyadh

*Stats on this page are for Saudi Arabia.

I

Saudi Arabia, the port city of Jeddah, October 2005: If Abdullah bin Mahrabi had a gun, he would have shot up his plasma screen. And he loved his plasma screen, a new fifty-four-inch job he'd purchased in Dubai during the shopping festival. As is the case with most acts of near violence against televisions, it wasn't the TV itself that was the problem, but what was on it.

"What the hell *is* this nonsense?" thought bin Mahrabi. "Is there no end to the idiocy?"

This was not, of course, the first time in the history of televised entertainment that such questions had been asked, but it was the first time Abdullah bin Mahrabi had asked them. In the main, bin Mahrabi is not the sort of man who shoots so much as a basketball. He is thirty-two years old, rotund, with a soft mien and softer hands; in his white dish-dash, he looks like the Pillsbury Doughboy with a tan. Nonetheless, he was never in the best of moods after the first fast of the holy month of Ramadan. All he asked was to sit, for an hour or so, and watch something engaging on TV. This was a wish he shared with a significant number of his fellow twenty-two million

Saudi Arabians, many of whom had also tuned in to the region's most celebrated station—the Middle East Broadcasting Corporation, or MBC—in order to watch a show that a furious promotional blitz had promised was unmissable. In the dullest, grimmest, most spirit-crushingly boring theocracy on earth, if one promises fun, one had best deliver.

The program was the tale of a family of orange people ("Yellow, papa, yellow," said his youngest son, reminding bin Mahrabi that he was color-blind) called *Al Shamshoon*. The hero—and bin Mahrabi used the term loosely—was a family man named Omar who worked at a nuclear power plant in small-town America. Although he occasionally choked his rambunctious son, Badr, he was at heart a loyal father and husband; every time he did something daft—which was often—he let fly with a *D'oh!* that has become something of an international catchphrase.

Bin Mahrabi wanted to laugh. Badly. A man with decided ambassadorial tendencies, he constantly informed foreigners that, despite all, Saudi Arabians are funny people: "Our sense of humor is along with American comedy—the sarcasm, what the French say is 'repartee.' But religion, sex and politics are off-limits, and the problem is that this is all Americans laugh about. We are very much the same, but also very much different."

The gap, it seemed, was both widening and closing. There was no way for bin Mahrabi to know this, but he was watching the first salvo in an intended bombardment of the region, not with incendiary ordnance but rather repurposed American cultural product. With sixty percent of the population in the Arab world under the age of twenty, and forty percent of that under the age of fifteen, "Arabization [of American animated television] is going to boom in these next few years," Sherine El-Hakim, head of Arabic content at VSI Ltd., a London-based dubbing service, promised *The Wall Street Journal*. "We're such an impressionable people and we aspire so much to be like the West, that we take on anything that we believe is a symbol or a manifestation of Western culture. The Americans are taking over."

This put a whole new spin on the American relationship with the Muslim under-thirty demographic: young Muslims viewed not so much as a tidal wave of screeching jihadis trained in *madrassas*, murder thumping in their breasts, but rather as a huge, growing cultural market waiting to be tapped. If Abdullah bin Mahrabi was anything to go by, this first volley had gone way wide.

To calm himself, bin Mahrabi removed his sandals and placed the soles of his feet on the cool ceramic floor. "Ahmed," he said to his youngest, "change the damn channel." Across Saudi Arabia and beyond, untold numbers of viewers were doing the same.

Were Arabs unrelentingly dour, bin Mahrabi wondered, cursed to a lifetime of weeping to sappy synthesized pop songs and ancient poetry? Was the sitcom—that most American of things—doomed to flounder as it crossed the cultural moat into the deserts of Arabia? But had he not just yesterday laughed his ass off to a subtitled episode of *Friends*? As far as he was concerned, everybody really *did* love Raymond.

No—it was different with this Omar Shamshoon. Something, somewhere had gone horribly awry. As the idiot himself would say: D'oh!

Dubai, one and a half years later: If I had a gun, I would have shot up my Nokia. As is the case with most acts of near violence against cellular phones, it wasn't the phone itself that was the problem, but what was coming out of it.

"We are *all* new," insisted the man on the phone, who said his name was Basra.

The comforter on my bed at the Sun Int'l Hotel (abbreviation theirs) in Bur Dubai district was more like a discomforter—scratchy, patterned like Skittles throw-up at a kid's birthday party. I squirmed in frustration and said, "Basra, please. All I'm looking for is someone who can help me with *Al Shamshoon . . .*"

"Please sir," said Basra, "I am new."

"Well, can you get me someone who is old?"

"Sir, everyone here is new. There is no one."

And with that, the line went dead.

For the past two days, the pan-Arabic TV channel MBC's telephonic shock troops had kept me from any edification regarding Omar Shamshoon. According to a slew of "ain't-this-nutty" Western media news reports, *Al Shamshoon* debuted in 2005 on the first day of Ramadan for the pleasure of a potential one hundred and thirty million Arabic-speaking viewers. American fans of *The Simpsons* were encouraged. "[This] signifies something absolutely incredible," wrote a reader to *The National Review*, after ABC and other major networks ran the story. "It means that we have won the culture war. It's over, and the West has won. Ten years from now, we'll be looking at this as a turning point in Arab culture."

The Simpsons has a tendency to elicit such overreaching Internet blather from the Cheetos-stained fingers of its fanboys. In their minds—and here I should add: in mine too—*The Simpsons* was, among other things, a societal corrective, a paddle dipped into the rapids to keep us from going too far off course. Surely, after a couple of seasons of Springfield-based shenanigans, the Middle East would foreswear authoritarianism, cast off fundamentalism and don instead the velvety gowns of liberal humanism, free speech and franchise for all. Homer—a modern-day fool, nuggets of truth so easily panned from the silt of his idiocy—is as universal a figure as exists in the global cultural pantheon. The Saudi royals best start packing their luxury 747-400s. Eat my shorts, Colonel Qadhafi.

However, without the aid of historical hindsight, cultural turning points are not so easy to identify. American sitcoms—bad and good— are not a new phenomenon in the region. Bin Mahrabi in Jeddah, much like bin Suleyman in Dubai, had grown up watching the TV shows broadcast throughout the Gulf for Western expatriates. MBC 4, one of the most popular channels in the Arab world, plays everything from *3rd Rock from the Sun* to *Seinfeld* with Arabic subtitles; the morning lineup includes CBS's *The Early Show, Jeopardy* and *Days of Our Lives*. Indeed, the station's tagline is *So You Can Watch What They Watch*. (Who *they* are, MBC leaves tantalizingly unsaid.) In other words, local viewers—sheikhs, jihadis and everyone in between—were more or less familiar with the concept of the sitcom. Nonetheless, *The Simpsons* Arabization made the news, mostly because it seemed to herald a cultural shift in the making.

Yet the general consensus amounted to a big fat "Meh." "Do'h! Arabized Simpsons Aren't Getting Many Laughs" ran a *Wall Street Journal* headline. According to ABC news, MBC had made some significant changes to the show, removing anything that could fall afoul of a touchy Islamic fundamentalist: no beer, no bacon, no Rabbi Krustofski. Homer Simpson without Duff Beer is like Pamela Anderson in an A-cup, which is to say a pop-cultural figure shorn of signature adornment. "I drink, therefore I am!" is Homer's Cartesian battle cry. To consider the problem existentially, who does Homer become when he no longer behaves like Homer? Al Jean, *The Simpsons* executive producer, was resolute: "It's not Homer."

If the blogs were anything to go by, MBC had stripped *Al Shamshoon* down to mere situation: fat man does dumb things. "They've ruined it! Oh yes they have, sob. . . . Why? Why, why . . . oh why?!!!!" wrote blogger Noors from Oman. Did Noors form part of a coherent, identifiable demographic—a phenomenon I called Generation *Al Shamshoon*: young, savvy Muslims like my Libyan guide Eder—tapped into Western popular culture, swept along in its tide, but subject to their own geographical, geopolitical and cultural realities? What, I wondered, did *The Simpsons* mean to Noors? Was it fun to watch Great Satanists act like overfed buffoons, tripping over the tails of their own avarice and stupidity? Or did the show resonate with Noors's *own* culture?

I hadn't expected Basra from MBC to clarify *all* of this, but neither had I expected to be so thoroughly stonewalled. In the heartland of the conspiracy theory, I was formulating one of my own: MBC had buried *Al Shamshoon* and didn't want it exhumed. And while this may have been true, there was also the fact that MBC is a Saudi Arabian company, and if Saudi Arabian companies share one attribute, it is a paranoid discretion that made Libyans seem gushy.

Meanwhile, Dr. Phil's Zamboni-waxed cranium glinted at me from the television set. Fortified by tubs of Diet Pepsi purchased from a nearby KFC, I had for the past two days been flicking through a three-hundred-channel cathode-ray universe, a pursuit I have long believed is akin to traveling a culture's subconscious. I lay on the discomforter with the Pepsi bucket balanced on my sternum. And I watched.

Tweaked on caffeine and aspartame, I saw endless text message tickers running under incomprehensible talk shows; I saw men in white robes fulminating about football; I saw the swirl of the Al Jazeera logo, the sweep of the Fox logo, a polar bear lunging from the jungle in an episode of *Lost*; I saw channel after channel of Qur'anic exegesis; I saw *Looney Tunes*, I saw *SpongeBob SquarePants*; I saw Oprah; I saw Springer. I saw housewives in acts of great desperation.

Was I clicking back and forth *between* cultures, or was I clicking my way *through* a culture? My days surfing those hundreds of channels felt like a stroll through a meta-version of *Al Shamshoon*—an unholy cultural amalgamation that was borderline unnavigable. But of one thing I was certain: a culture that had to leap so constantly from universe to universe was a culture under pressure, a culture that would have to fight to formulate a coherent idea of itself.

"Oh yes, culture is a dangerous business," said the man in the glass tower. I could not make out his features; he was backlit against a bright smear of the Persian Gulf. Behind him, I watched skyscrapers being born. The Sun Int'l comforter had given me a rash on my leg. I scratched it.

"You must understand," said the man, "that Dubai is a very different world. It may look the same, but that's where comparisons stop."

Look the same as what? I wanted to ask, but he didn't seem to be in the mood. He pushed a card across the table toward me, along with a DVD, with the word *Freej* scrawled across the disc in black marker.

"You wish to find out about *The Simpsons*—about those who turned it into an Arab program. And I tell you: They are unlikely to talk. Here, mistakes of that magnitude are not acknowledged."

The man raised a slender finger and answered a call on his vibrating mobile. He spoke in rapid Hindi, clicked his phone closed, tapped the card.

"I urge you to contact this man. I think he will talk to you."

"Who is he?" I asked.

"He is the person who beat your friend Homer." I could hear, from the change in tone of the man's voice, that he was smiling. "He is the one who defeated *The Simpsons*."

Some minutes later, I stood under a three-story banner rippling in the desert's heaving breath: four elderly women, the stuff of crisp 3-D animation, posing alongside each other, patterned *abeyas* and golden *niqabs* obscuring everything except pudgy hands and boinging cartoon eyes. This was a first for me: Islamically correct female cartoon characters. Beneath them, in cheerful bubble script, both in English and in Arabic: *Freej. Dubai TV. Daily.*

I was in Dubai Media City, a conglomeration of very tall buildings housing companies that fall, in one way or another, under the banner of media. It stands alongside Internet City, which in turn borders Knowledge Village. These "cities" are meant as conduits for the smooth flow of ideas—nodal points of concentration and connection. What they are concentrating on and connecting to is a veritable revolution in Arab media, spurred on by the technological changes of the past decade, shifting desert sands in which power games with real stakes are being played.

This place has risen from an ancient cultural imperative: only twelve percent of the world's 1.3 billion Muslims are Arab, but Arab elites have always believed that they should form the *ummah*'s cultural driving force. Islam was born of their region and their language, and it must continue to grow thereof. Dubai Media City, an initiative fully backed by Dubai's ruling Maktoum clan, is a means to define media—and therefore culture—in the Islamic world. Still, there is no unified Arab front. Sheikh Maktoum was trying to counter Saudi hegemony, balance the weight of Qatar's Al Jazeera, fend off the glut of Syrian and Egyptian television programming. I'd recently read of a prediction from Sheikh Maktoum himself: Dubai Media City will become the major regional drama production center within the next five years.

The good sheikh has a tendency to follow such pronouncements by writing checks with a dizzying number of zeroes. But culture is only partially responsive to twelve-figure endowments; it moves according to its own complex economics. For instance: *Al Shamshoon* had the backing of the largest satellite station in the region. *Freej* did not.

I looked down at the card. Mohammed Saeed Harib. *The one who defeated* The Simpsons.

"You have five minutes," said the brusque assistant, sitting me down on an icy leather couch. "He will be up in a moment." The studio was stainless steel, frosted glass, sharp edges, whispers.

A moment passed, and I heard the robes before I saw him: a great susurration of fabric against the spiral staircase. I leaned forward, and Mohammed Harib appeared like a diminutive, unmasked Darth Vader, splendid in a shiny black dish-dash. His hair was meticulously gelled, his beard precisely sculpted. This careful studio, I now realized, was an expression of his laser-eyed focus. I could smell ambition on him, like premium cologne.

"We must have water," he called, and water appeared, placed carefully alongside his two phones and a packet of Winstons on the glass coffee table before us. He swept onto the couch and sat beside me in one neat movement, like a bat at bedtime.

"What do you think of my show?" he asked. No salaams, no nice-to-meet-yous. All business.

What did I think of his show? The previous day, I'd carefully arranged my tub of Pepsi and my laptop on the bed in Sun Int'l, slipped in the DVD, and beheld Harib's meticulously assembled world.

Freej, I knew, was slang for "neighborhood": *With the elderly*, reads the tagline, *anything can happen.* (Incontinence, disease, and death, mostly, but I hoped the show skirted these.) It opens on a swell of choral synths, the *doomp-a-doomp* of *doumbeks*. We are in the heavens: wispy clouds part. (The *Simpsons* fan instantly gets the reference to that show's opening credits.) Zooming along, we maniacally dodge sailing *dhows*. A Lisa Simpsonesque sax riff. Then, Arabic script intro-duces the first character, Um Saeed, rangy and wizened in a red *abeya*, pouring coffee from an urn. Cut to bespectacled Um Allawi, waving a cellphone by way of indicating her tech-geek prowess. Side wipe: the stout Um Saloom, tapped on her back to wake her from an aphasic stupor. Another wipe: Um Khammas, holding a microphone in her fat hands. She turns, shimmies, spreads her hands as if to say, "What *you* looking at?"

A burst of blue and we whip through the mock arch of Dubai's World Trade Center. A flash of white and we tear along the cobbled alleys of a ramshackle walled village: wind towers, curls of smoke, flurried activity. We pull back into the Gulf for an establishing shot. I recognize this place as Bastakia, not a few minutes from the Sun Int'l, an old pearl-diving compound built on the Dubai Creek by a wealthy Persian merchant at the turn of the previous century, back when this was little more than a fetid beach camp. Welcome to *Freej*.

The signature character—call her the show's Homer Simpson—is the fat, declamatory widow Um Khammas. She waddles—lime green abeya, chubby digits splotched with henna—and sits at the privileged position in the *majlis* she shares with the other ladies. Um Khammas speaks in a deep rasp—sandpaper on brick—in an accent tinged with what locals would notice as the *khamsim* grit of North Africa. Her signature line, her *D'oh!*, her *Yabba-Dabba-Doo!*, is a shrieked *YewwwHeeewww!* She eats with appetite. She throws things. She brooks no shit.

The animation is hyper-jacked, supersaturated. Our heroines nosh, kibbitz and get into all manner of awkward shenanigans in the madhouse outside the coral and gypsum walls of their cozy 'hood. But mostly, they kibbitz. If I didn't know exactly what was going to happen next, I knew how it would all unfold, because the narratives were drawn directly from the sitcom playbook. The show did not feel culturally exotic in the same way that some Japanese animé does. It travelled along an arc I knew as well as the rhythm of my own breath: normalcy, followed by chaos, followed by normalcy restored, the beautiful aria of American optimism packed into every episode of every sitcom ever made.

Freej was, without a doubt, one of the most skillfully executed pieces of Arab popular culture on television, not counting the video-clip channel Rotana or the big *American Idol*–style reality shows, all of which blow more dinars per minute than Suha Arafat on a Harrods shopping spree. Contrast this with your average show on, say, Nile TV, where the makeup is shoddy, the costume jewelry looks cheap, the outfits are gaudy (and that's just the male characters), and *Freej* was Pixar as compared to one of those Sunday school animated Jesus movies.

Nonetheless, the show felt strangely outside my purview. It hinted at something I couldn't fathom, because I did not yet posses the cultural vocabulary. I was both too far inside the frame of reference to garner any perspective, and too far outside to get a clear view. Why had Harib chosen elderly characters? Why were they female, especially in a society in which women were purportedly voiceless? Was the show radically progressive, or hyper-conservative? As far as I under-stood it, *Freej* was a metaphor for the battle between tradition and modernity, a comedy of manners in a world that has forsaken them, and a plaintive cry for sanity inside a city that has grown at a pace that is not just astonishing, but also brutal. *Freej* is, however, as much a product of Dubai as it is a comment on it: a global, high-tech, cross-border effort made on the sheikh's dime.

"Very impressive," I said to Mohammed Harib. I meant it.

"You are not alone in thinking this way," said Harib. "As a Westerner. Most think of Arab animation as garbage. I have hoped to change this."

"I think you may have done that."

He nodded, and looked at me with an unblinking gaze before flicking open a Zippo and firing up a Winston, the cigarette brand for which Fred Flintstone was once—coincidentally?—a pitchman.

"I'm wondering," I said, "where the inspiration for the show came from."

He waved his arm, the smoke of his cigarette forming an expansive O.

"Part of the inspiration comes from here," he said. "This place."

"Dubai, you mean?"

"Yes. To be from Dubai—a native Emirati, like me—is to be in a strange position. We are only twenty percent of the population, and less every day. *Freej* is what you would call a fish-out-of-water tale, but here, the fish are out of water in their own pond. My characters are strangers in their own land. Part of the inspiration is to make us less strangers. You see, what Walt Disney did was not just invent characters, he invented history. I will do the same. Americans, they have Mickey Mouse. They have a history around Mickey Mouse. We do not have this. We do not have an idea of ourself that doesn't come from a Hollywood version of the Arab. It is my job to provide it."

"So I'm sitting across from the Arabic Walt Disney?" I asked.

Harib shrugged, took a long drag, and leaned forward on the couch. "I should say that there is one other major inspiration for *Freej*. One that you might perhaps find surprising."

"Oh yes?" I said.

Harib butted out his cigarette. The meeting was over. "You have, of course, heard of *The Golden Girls*?"

★ ★ ★

Oh, I had heard of *The Golden Girls* all right. For seven glorious years of my childhood, I was intermittently ensconced in a fictional Miami retirement community, watching acid-tongued Dorothy, her sarcastic octogenarian mother, Sophia, ditzy Rose and slutty Southern belle Blanche hurl Borsch Belt yuks at one another like pitches at a seniors' league softball tourney. I remembered one exchange in particular:

> Blanche [gushing]: Oh girls . . . I'm just in ecstasy! My body is tingling all over! You'll never guess what just happened!
> Sophia [deadpan]: We know what happened. Let's just guess what part of the Middle East he's from.

How this resonated with Mohammed Harib, I couldn't say.

A muggy dark fell as the taxi left the maze of Dubai Media City only to be trapped in traffic at a construction project worked on by what appeared to be the male inhabitants of a mid-sized Bangladeshi village. The site was illuminated by banks of halogen work lights steaming with humidity; above all loomed a vast *Desperate Housewives* lightbox. I sat for fifteen minutes looking up at the fluorescent mugs of the ladies of Wisteria Lane and wondered whether, and in what way, the housewives of Dubai were desperate.

The cab, a Korean-made bug caught in a vast web of concrete and asphalt interchanges, crawled onto Sheikh Zayed Road toward a mess of towers that are the temporary homes for workers from almost every nation on this great earth: the city's great expat engine. Their eyes are dark with exhaustion, they walk with the rolling stumble of the horror-flick undead.

Gazing at the skeletal Burj Khalifa tower as the cries of the *ad'han* echoed against the buildings, I thought that Dubai, or the idea of Dubai, confuses one as to what era we're in. Is this the End of Days, or just some odd midpoint, a lethargic blip in history? Is this city a précis of our dreams and our desires, another of those Astana-like odes to a future envisioned by Lucasfilm? Mohammed Harib, no doubt, was plagued by the same questions.

Dubai's strangest attribute, however, is that it feels like a summation. It is a gargantuan sculptural hunk of post-postmodern pop. But what, or where, one asks, is the context? Mohammed Harib had taken it upon himself to provide Dubai with one. He had come up with his own Mickey Mouse, this one clad in a patterned *abeya*. *We do not have an idea of ourself,* Harib had told me. But what does it take, I wondered, to create such an idea? Where does one turn for the Lego blocks of national self? As far as Harib was concerned, one turned— at least in part—to 1980s American prime-time television.

Ramadan: September 22, 2006. Even if it weren't the most important moment of Mohammed Harib's life, he would still have been excited, much as he had been since he was a boy. Religious significance aside, anyone who loves TV loves Ramadan: This is when the stations have always rolled out their big-name productions, the equivalent of sweeps week in the United States. In the old days, there would be thirty-episode serials from Egypt or Syria, the anticipation for the next installment making the day's fast seem less of a trial.

It's just that this year, Mohammed Harib had a million bucks riding on the Ramadan sweeps.

The money was invested in fifteen fifteen-minute episodes of *Freej*. Call this a gamble, but Harib felt he had taken no chances. Eight years of work, eight years of development. When he decided it was time to finally undertake the production, he knew he was going to do it the American way, with a level of competence and professionalism that few associated with television production in the Gulf. He'd trained in America, in "cartoon school" at Boston's Northeastern, and had watched animators all over the U.S. practice their craft. He knew what it took to produce great work.

Harib's Lammtara Productions designed extensive market surveys and handed out six thousand questionnaires at a variety of Dubaian educational institutions. They found that Emirati women at the American University were downloading *South Park*, kids were downloading Japanese manga, and that reality shows were the most popular thing on television. They collated the data, and arrived at a rough mandate of what locals wanted from homegrown pop: Nothing educational or religious. Nothing *ir*religious. They craved culture. Their *own* culture. They wanted a Mickey Mouse.

Harib started to assemble a team. He needed voices. His most important hire in this regard was a young man named Salem Jassim. (The actor Ashjan, who voices Um Allawi, is the only woman in the cast.) When Jassim stepped forward to the microphone in a Dubai Media City sound studio and started yelling, it was like a scene from *Frankenstein*: great jolts of electricity, and Um Khammas was suddenly alive . . .

This thing could work, thought Harib.

Still, the suras tell us that only God knows what is manifest and what is hidden: Ramadan approached and Harib found himself increasingly nervous. The show employed a crew of five hundred; the million bucks were disappearing faster than Um Khammas's husbands. (*Freej* represented an enormous risk for its main investor, Mohammed Bin Rashid Establishment for Young Business Leaders, which tends to finance Internet ventures or engineering endeavors, steering well clear of the culture minefield.) The operation was split between the UAE and India: pre- and post-production in Dubai, animation rendered in Bangalore. Harib shuttled back and forth every couple of weeks. There were cultural specifics that the Indian animators could not be aware of: The ladies must drink tea with their right hands, the detail of the henna work, the way the characters walked in their abeyas.

Harib's attention to detail was obsessive: Plugged into every frame were references to his culture, his religion, his traditions. There were in-jokes within in-jokes. Nothing was arbitrary, no image slapdash, the show thoroughly self-aware. He would even tip the odd sacred cow, as in the now-legendary Ramadan episode:

The four Ums sit around the *majlis*. They are starving, grouchy.

Um Khammas: Um Allawi, turn on the TV!

TV Presenter: And now! "Islamic Treasures."

Groans. *Click!* Another channel.

"Islamic morals."

Click!

"Islamic teachings."

More groans.

Click!

TV Presenter: "Exotic dishes!"

Tongues hang out. Eyes droop.

Click!

TV Presenter: And now! The new sitcom, *Pain*.

By demanding something relevant, Harib was *creating* something relevant. And he was building relevance from an assemblage of seemingly disparate parts: *The Golden Girls* hinted at his bossy grandmother, his snide great-aunt, the daft family friend; women whose *abeyas* he had flitted under as a boy, listening to the back and forth of their badinage in the days before he became a man and was no longer allowed among them. He absorbed the rhythm of their dialogue, the acid on their tongues, the sharpness of their wit. *Freej* was also a love letter to his mother, who passed away when he was eighteen, a way to imagine her as she might have been had she lived into her dotage.

Thus, *Freej* would filter *The Golden Girls* through his passion—animation—and his culture, which was that of the Persian Gulf. It is a confluence of what Harib knew, a mash-up of his cultural experiences, a product of being Emirati. And for those who believe that American television, like all American low culture, is a form of cultural imperialism, Harib was comfortably wearing the mantle of his enemy.

"He is very clever. I suppose he is what you'd call the exception that may prove the new rules," a producer for the Dubai-based Showtime channel said to me. He chuckled, adding, "You have no doubt heard this: *They cannot represent themselves. They must be represented.* Mr. Karl Marx. That is what Harib is doing. Representing himself."

I had indeed heard Mr. Marx's famous maxim: It had provided literary theorist and cultural commentator Edward Said with both the intellectual starting point and the epigraph for his most famous work, *Orientalism*. Said insisted that the body of Western scholarship, literature and popular culture concerning the "Orient" (in this context the Middle East) was in service of, and created the foundation for, the imperial aspirations of successive Western powers. According to Said, this corpus created a mythology of the East, inventing its narrative, subsuming its voice. The Eastern story was folded into the Western canon, local self-representation crushed in the process, laying the groundwork for exploitation.

Whether or not one believes that a tsunami of Western monoculture has submerged the indigenous Eastern landscape and refashioned it as islands of foreign representation, it quickly becomes obvious, as the Showtime producer put it, "that Dubai Media City is one of the places where Arabs are currently representing themselves. It is a schizophrenic space: both Arab and American in thinking. Harib brings us a sitcom. And while there is a long history of televised Arabic drama, there are very few examples of sitcoms—that most American of things. It is an intriguing choice."

It was a choice that in 2006 came down to Day One of Ramadan. The Mohammed Bin Rashid Establishment for Young Business Leaders, the show's primary investors, had seen the first episode and hated it. Harib knew he wasn't leading with his best foot—the series heated up by episode four—but he had tested demos among his university focus groups, and it had played like gangbusters.

By the fourth day of Ramadan, young Emiratis were text-messaging each other *Freej* jokes. By day eight, the show was a cultural phenomenon. Halfway through Ramadan, it was broadcast five times a day. It is now a television staple.

★ ★ ★

I lay on the discomforter in the Sun Int'l, laptop on my belly, breathing in the pong of stale smoke and fried chicken. Outside, mugginess wafted off the nearby creek that disfigures the city like a scar from a knife fight. I watched *Freej*. Then I watched *Al Shamshoon*. Then I watched *Freej*. Then I drank Pepsi.

In a whiz-bang city of the future, I used a machine to leap between versions of cultural interpretation, a dizzying game of Frogger with the pop references I had grown up with as a boy—references I shared with Mohammed Harib, despite the fact that I watched *The Golden Girls* in Johannesburg and *The Simpsons* in Toronto, Montreal, London, everywhere. *Al Shamshoon* seemed tragically stillborn: the voice-work leaden, the jokes lumpy, the editing enervating. *Freej* was imbued with life. Vital. It was, as Marxists and hip-hoppers say, *reprezentin'*.

I rode the Sun Int'l elevator to the ground floor. Outside, neon flashed uselessly, blunted by the thick air. Despite the fact that it was almost midnight, traffic was at a standstill. Within minutes I was in Bastakia.

The creek smelled of kerosene from the *dhows*, mud and seagull shit. Bastakia was closed for business: the high-end art gallery-cum-hotel, the high-end boutique hotel, the high-end coffee shop, the low-end stamp museum. The cobblestones were scrubbed, the walls gleamed with fresh stucco, spots lit the wind towers. There was no life in Bastakia at night, and only marginally more in the day. Yet this was the vessel into which Harib had poured *Freej*, the pumping heart of his imagined universe. This was his Springfield: a walled 'hood surrounded by encroaching skyscrapers. I tried to imagine the day in 1998 when Mohammed Harib walked through here and first heard, in his mind's ear, the *YewwwHeeewww!* of Um Khammas. I had to admire the guy: He had dredged an alternate world—an entire history—from a place where all I'd managed was a seven-dollar coffee.

★ ★ ★

Some days later, I followed Mohammed Harib up the spiral staircase toward his darkened sound studio. He looked back at me and said, "As an artist with my ambitions, I must be willing to consider the following: As Arabs, *who are we?*"

The room was dark. On this second meeting, Harib was almost garrulous. He'd recently seen tapes of the second season; he'd been in talks for merchandising soft toys, pen cases, backpacks. His movements were expansive; he was generous with his insights. And they came down to the following:

The Arab story—like the story of all cultures over time—is a tragedy. From desert-dwelling nomadic tribe, to loosely connected civilization constantly at war with itself, to a comprehensive world-beating monotheistic faith, to a period of high culture and imperial glory, to dissolution and contraction and centuries of darkness, to the present age: an in-between purgatory where the confluence of Islamic and Arabic culture struggles to find a place in a world that no longer accommodates so many of their defining values. It was a dangerous history to parse, because at this moment in its continuum, it was a losing history. An invalid history. Mohammed Harib had to reinvent it.

"So, I decide that I must give us history in a different way. The same way Americans give history: a version with dignity. I go to America to study. And what do I find?"

He found ignorance—an ignorance he considered dangerous, indicative of the racism against Arabs that has always been prevalent in Hollywood cinema. "Even my professors would say, 'When you go to see your king, do you wear a golden rope—what we call an *agal*—over your bed sheet?' They knew nothing about my world, and I knew everything about theirs. But I wasn't interested in teaching Americans about me," he said. "I was interested in teaching *my* culture about *ourselves.* So why should we not have a commercial for our own way of life? Something that we can buy, that we can touch? Kids were not exposed to what we ideally are as a culture. They lose a sense of themselves. So I must do something. What model should I use? Of course, the one that works. But there is a darkness to this thinking. I do not use the American model wholesale. You must understand this."

He stared at the flat screen above the soundboard.

"In many respects," I said, "your show seems like an answer to the Arabic *The Simpsons*, a retort."

Production on *Freej* was well underway by the time *Al Shamshoon* debuted, but in the final year of *Freej*'s development it was clear that Harib had the show in mind. "I love *The Simpsons*, but in the language it's supposed to be in. Also, there is our idea of what's morally right and wrong—our ideas on this are different. Morally, *The Simpsons* was not accepted in that sense—hence, when it was released, many people started attacking it. And hence, season two was not Arabized. I think *South Park* is very funny; it all depends on who you're showing it to. But it's never meant to be for this audience in this region."

"You mean because of Islam?"

"Let's not put it this way. Is *South Park* against Islam? No. Or should I say—it is against everything equally. But we are very protective of our customs here. Some of the things are just not meant for this region. I'll tune in, and I think it's funny. But you really need to be educated about American culture. I'll give an example: the first kiss in American TV. We have our own version of the first kiss, of courting. But for an uneducated person to see an American first kiss, this will perhaps cause him to rape someone, to make him become out of control. These alien ideas, they need to be balanced. And this is where Um Khammas comes in. And maybe why she beats Homer Simpson."

So, was *Freej* a way of maintaining and validating traditional behavior? The ladies are powerful personalities—and seemingly free agents—but they are literally walled in, captives of a highly conservative and incredibly restrictive Gulf culture battling an encroaching modernity. Harib was apparently using *The Golden Girls* to contain the damage done by the Emirati cultural obsession with America, building a blast wall against American culture *from* American culture. But the paradox was that while his audience, many of whom were female Emirati teenagers, were downloading *South Park* and animé, *Freej*, his weapon against those "alien ideas," was rife with alien ideas itself.

Where, after all, were the men? (Um Khammas's first deceased husband occasionally shows up, Casper-style, but other than that, it's slim pickings on the testicular front.) Although the ladies occasionally waddle off to the mosque, where was their Reverend Lovejoy, their imam? Indeed, *Freej*'s second season would turn out to be extraordinarily controversial when Um Saeed—the tech-geek—has a two-episode fallout with Islam, insisting that there are other ways to enlightenment, mainly through her laptop. Although she relocates God and gets re-jazzed by the words of the Prophet, this story arc was blogged about furiously. The powers-that-be noisily tut-tutted. For a show that had become something of a national project, this was a bold move: Harib had shot a popgun across the bow of the status quo. He risked all that he had built to at least suggest the unthinkable. Millions watched him do so. Perhaps they questioned along with him.

Whether this sort of subtle subversion was to become a defining factor of the show, Harib would not say. *Freej* is, after all, now a major corporate brand, and Harib spoke like a responsible CEO rather than a nutty cartoonist. Tatweer, the massive Dubaian construction firm (with links to the ruling Maktoum clan), has purchased a thirty percent stake in Harib's production company, Lammtara, and intends to build a four-million-square-foot *Freej* theme park by 2014. This will stand alongside DreamWorks Animation Theme Park, Marvel Theme Park and Universal Studios Dubailand. Um Khammas and Shrek, Um Saeed and The Incredible Hulk, Um Allawi and Indiana Jones—finally together in one convenient location!

"Why have tourists come here?" Harib asked me. "To see America? No. Now they can come and I can tell them our story, about *Freej*, about Arabia. It's good, we're giving an alternative to the American brand."

The *Freej* theme park will, according to the press materials, "focus on Arab culture and creativity, heritage and achievement, seen through the eyes of the ladies from *Freej*." I didn't doubt, backed by billions of dollars, that Mohammed Harib would invent a very plausible Arab brand.

"The question—this 'who are we?'—is not resolved. But I leave you with one thing," said Harib. "I know Disney well. I have studied almost every frame of many of his films. And I know that he invents American childhood, he invents American history. It is a theme-park history. This is both good and bad. It is my job to do the same. You fight fire how?" he asked.

He stood. Six months after our last meeting, Mohammed Saeed Harib—a middle-class Emirati of relatively humble means—would be ranked thirty-third on *Arabian Business* magazine's Power 100 chart, right behind men who count their wealth in the tens of billions.

II

"Basra," I said into my cellphone, "you'll never guess where I am."

"Sir?"

We'd been at it again, Basra and I, dancing the MBC telephonic two-step. I watched four workmen wade through a fountain, clearing the filter of silt with their hands. Beyond them, atop a boxy glass building, the MBC logo glowed in the overcast afternoon like a beacon. I walked toward the building, my reflection wobbling in the polished blue panes.

"I'm standing in Dubai Media City, right outside MBC, and I'm going to go in. And I'm going to start screaming." This was a George Costanza move; I was surprised to learn that it worked.

"Sir!" Basra was alarmed, but I imagined the standard operating procedures for just such an emergency were posted on the wall of his cubicle in bright-red lettering. "Sir, please hold. I'm going to connect you with Zena from Programming."

I strolled through the sliding doors, into the chilled, pale wood interior. A bank of five plasma screens played, respectively, a re-run of *The X-Files*, a report from Al Arabiya (MBC's news channel), a football game, a movie with that kid from *Malcolm in the Middle* and a Dove soap commercial. The MBC headquarters, which stands in a hunched row with the identical Reuters and CNN buildings, may aspire to slick, elevated cool, but the three suited thugs at the reception desk—stock villains who could easily play as background extras in an MBC Action show—somewhat undermined the pretension.

MBC was established in London in 1991 as a 24-hour free-to-air satellite television station beaming to Arab audiences the world over. Most media observers took little notice; this was an age when pan-Arab media was left to severe men with mustaches who read five-day-old news in classical Arabic to an audience of none. But MBC was different, couching the news between popular Arabic programming and a slate of high-profile, subtitled Western shows.

Sixteen years later, under the stewardship of Sheikh Waleed bin Ibrahim al-Brahim, MBC, now headquartered in Dubai Media City, is a thriving multi-platform popular-culture delivery system, bankrolled by . . . well, whom exactly? The shareholders remain a mystery. Few observers believe that anyone other than the Saudi royal family has the wherewithal to back the enterprise, which costs billions to operate and is not designed to make money. (Total advertising spending in the entire Gulf Cooperation Council, or GCC, across all media was $5 billion in 2007. By way of comparison, ad revenue for Fox's 2010 Super Bowl broadcast was over a quarter of a billion.) But why would the world's dourest Wahhabist theocracy want its twenty-two million Saudi-born subjects watching re-runs of *Friends*? Or, for that matter, an Arabized version of *The Simpsons*?

Dating back to the founding of the kingdom in 1926, Saudi Arabia has existed as an uneasy alliance between the pragmatism of the ruling family and the ultra-conservative, semi-independent clergy. The Saud's grim circus act is a centuries-long juggle between the unerringly severe conservatism of those who help keep them in power, and the extremism that this interpretation of Islam engenders. It isn't good business, after all, having one's citizens down skyscrapers in the very zip code that funnels trillions of dollars into the national treasury. Funding Wahhabist *madrassas* the world over is one thing—the Saudis enjoy the idea of Islamist extremism in, say, Indonesia—but they do not like it linked so definitively to home.

In the early nineties, the circus act was becoming increasingly tenuous. After the Saudi regime allowed American coalition forces to use the kingdom as a forward base for the attack on Iraq during the first Gulf War, there was general outrage among hardline Saudi Arabians: The infidel had his feet up on the table in the holiest room of the House of Islam. A number of prominent conservative Saudis—including Osama bin Laden, flush with the thrill of battling the Soviets in Afghanistan—issued a declaration called *Khitab al-malalib*, or letter of demands, a series of requests for mild democratic reform in the context of a not-so-mild radical Islamist state. (How Saudi Arabia could get more Islamic is anyone's guess.) A wave of young imams used the *medium* of American pop—cassette tapes, VHS tapes—to market their inviolable views. (Here, Marshall McLuhan's famous aphorism seems tragically quaint: the message was the message, the medium a mere vector to be discarded when recordable CDs and YouTube came along.)

The so-called Awakening Sheikhs were the undisputed stars of the show, two imams who perfected the spittle-flecked Wahhabist invective. They were, in spirit, Tupac Shakur crossed with Rush Limbaugh meets a fundamentalist Islamic Oral Roberts; a bestselling tape called "America as I Saw It" posited a pop-cultural netherworld in which a "nation of beasts . . . fornicate and eat rotten food." The duo was such a threat to the regime that they *weren't* summarily tried and beheaded, but gingerly placed under house arrest. In their preternatural understanding of the pop-cultural seesaw among their subjects, the Saudi regime needed a moderate cultural venue. And while by no means as rabidly conservative as the Awakening Sheikhs of the world, the royal family and their retinue should never be confused with the hippy libertines they shared spliffs with at NYU in the sixties. Satellite television was becoming a reality, which meant that the regime needed to play the "message-is-the-message" game with new equipment. But what were the rules?

My phone clicked off hold. I heard a sharp "Yes?"

"Hello? Is this Zena from Programming?" I asked.

"Who is this, please?"

I stumbled through an explanation of my interest in MBC, and told Zena that I was looking to speak with anyone—even the lowliest of production coordinators—in order to make some sense of Omar Shamshoon's Arabian adventures. This earned me ten seconds of icy silence.

"You should not just have shown up," said Zena from Programming. "Hold."

I didn't fancy being Tasered by the glaring guards, so I walked back through the sliding doors toward the fountain, past it, and on toward the parking lot draped with the vast *Freej* banner. Um Khammas looked down with accusatory eyes, as if warning me against consorting with the enemy. After all, she had so thoroughly vanquished Omar Shamshoon that she could afford to gloat.

My phone clicked off hold. "Mr. Richard?" said Zena.

"Yes ma'am?"

"This is very irregular."

"Yes ma'am."

"I'll forward your request up the line," said Zena, adding, in a voice dripping with horror-movie menace, "I hope you enjoy your stay at MBC."

"My *stay?*" I asked, in genuine alarm. I involuntarily hunched over, bracing for 10,000 volts of electricity administered by one of MBC's martinets.

And with that, the line went dead.

★ ★ ★

A week later, traveling in a bus near the Western Hajar mountain range, I received a phone call.

"Say again," I said.

"Mr. Richard, this is Poula from MBC. Your name has been forwarded to me by Zena from Programming."

I leaned forward in the rickety bus seat and peered out an impenetrably dust-caked window. I was, I guessed, halfway between Oman's Muscat and Dubai, approaching the UAE border.

"Wow. Thank you for getting in touch with me," I said.

"Yes. You will be seen by Mr. Baddih Fattouh."

How had this happened? How had my name slipped through the booby traps, the razor wire, the natives with poisoned arrows?

"And Mr. Baddih had something to do with *Al Shamshoon*?" I asked.

"Mr. Baddih is head of acquisitions and drama commissioner. He *made Al Shamshoon*," said Poula.

For two scorching weeks, I'd been chasing Omar Shamshoon around the region like Lawrence of Arabia on an ephedrine drip. I'd spoken to production executives ("TV mullahs," as one dubbed himself), journalists, commentators, regular people. It took me close to a week to track down Noors—he of the "they've ruined it . . . why, oh why . . . etc." blog post. I took the five-hour bus ride to Oman, met him and four of his younger cousins in Oman City Center Mall. We watched *Al Shamshoon* on YouTube in the room Noors shared with his brother in Muscat's Ruwi neighbourhood.

"Listen to this shit," said Noors, a wisp of a twenty-year-old who had spent enough time in the U.K. to speak with a perfect American accent. "You call this funny?"

Nope. Part of the problem, at least according to Noors, was Mohamed Henedi, the Egyptian comedian who played Homer. "Does he *understand* Homer?" asked Noors. "Does he *get* it at all?"

We watched an exchange between Omar and Mona (Marge to you) that was about as exciting as listening to two technocrats jaw about municipal tax policy.

"This is shit," said one of Noors's cousins, and sauntered off.

"Ohh, Arabs are idiots?" spat Noors. "Give us any old crap in our language and we'll accept it?

"Your cousins, they know the original *The Simpsons*?" I asked. "Do they like it?"

"It's the same as everywhere: some like it, some don't. These later seasons, many are bad. You compare to *South Park*—which they love—or *Family Guy*—which I love—and what can you say? We see this stuff. We know. So we understand *The Simpsons*. Maybe I don't understand everything, but I know the spirit."

"And *Freej*?" I asked Noors.

"Yeah, I've watched. It's cool. We can watch with the whole family. It's fine."

This was Generation *Al Shamshoon*. Mohammed Harib understood them. It seemed that MBC did not. Nonetheless, I was now speaking to one of their representatives over the telephone, which counted as a minor miracle.

"Mr. Richard," said Poula. "Three in the afternoon tomorrow."

That was that. I fished for pistachios from the bag of mixed nuts on my lap, and mused on the mystery that was Zena from Programming. After six weeks or so in the Gulf region—a place I visited for the specific purpose of tracking down Omar Shamshoon— I was finally meeting his maker. I closed my phone, and looked out the bus window.

"Please," asked the young man seated next to me, "memenem?"

"Pardon, what?" I asked, and then noticed the proffered bag of candy-covered peanuts. Bus trips in Arab countries are like being locked accidentally in a 7-Eleven after hours.

I nodded thank you, and grabbed a handful.

I stood before the suited thugs at the MBC reception desk and offered my credentials; with an ease that felt criminal, the automatic security doors swung open. The wide, glassed-in lobby housed two makeshift live-to-air studios backing onto a typical Dubai Media City vista: a man-made pond and a man-made mess of construction-in-progress. I traversed the lobby and waited for an elevator alongside young women wearing expensive denim. Except for the odd dish-dash, this could have been the BBC.

Whisked upward in a box of brushed metal and cherrywood, I pondered the extraordinary case of *Al Shamshoon* and the *abeya* of secrecy so effectively cosseting it. Here's what I'd learned: Commencing on the first day of Ramadan 2005, the channel aired thirty-four episodes of the freshly Arabized *Al Shamshoon*. (On Arab stations there is a culture of running shows daily rather than weekly, a nod to the Egyptian serials that were once the mainstay of Arab television.) Carefully picking shows from the storied fourth season and on, a slate of fifty-two episodes had been Arabized; the show was unceremoniously cancelled several days after *Eid al-Fitr*, the feast day that marks the close of the fasting month. That left sixteen episodes unaired. "In Saudi companies, there is no culture of analyzing failure," a British MBC public relations representative told me. "You just move on. We know that has to change. But here, bombs are swept under the carpet." I assumed she was being figurative, but nonetheless stepped gingerly.

By all accounts, the show was also a contractual disaster: Gracie Films, the de facto owner of *The Simpsons* copyright (which is otherwise broadcast and distributed by News Corp's Fox Broadcasting Company), was mysteriously silent on what should have been a watershed moment in the life cycle of the show. Where was all the Hollywood "we're building bridges" bluster? It did not seem that MBC had the rights to alter the show so radically.

The elevator doors slid open at the third floor. "This way please, sir," said a veiled woman, inviting me into the open-concept office where MBC's Dubai-based administrative department inhabits desk after desk. I was waved along toward that most TV-ish of status markers, the corner office.

"Mr. Richard," said a woman with acne scars peppering her jawline, "I am Poula."

"Ah, Poula," I said. "My savior."

"Please wait for several minutes. Mr. Baddih is on the phone." I pictured him—rail thin, wolfish overbite, liver-spotted—bending over his vast desk, a Smithers-like minion at his side, finger on the release-the-hounds button. Moments later, bidden by a curt smile and a nod, I made for the office of Mr. Baddih Fattouh, the man I assumed was the Charles Montgomery Burns of MBC.

Baddih Fattouh was indeed a small man drowned by the heft of his desk, but that's where the parallels stopped. In his left hand he worked a stress ball; his right thumb whirred over the keyboard of a Nokia PDA. He looked up at me with eyes that seemed too soulful for a television executive. His face was soft and kind, with a large nose and a fading sweep of hair. He wore a cream blazer and a dress shirt tucked into MBC regulation premium denim.

"Welcome," said Mr. Baddih. "Let me offer you a tea or coffee."

He spoke quietly into his intercom; I could tell from his English that Mr. Baddih was Lebanese, as are many of the Arabic media caste working in Dubai. Beirut, even during the civil war, boasted a number of journalism and communications programs; many of the Lebanese media students from the seventies and eighties did time abroad in the U.K. or the U.S. and, armed with this experience, formed the core of MBC and other Arabic satellite channels. What's more, Lebanon was always an Arabic media center, running a close second to Egypt in terms of film and television production.

In this, Mr. Baddih's backstory was typical: He graduated with a B.A. in Communication Arts from Lebanese American University and, thanks to the civil war, had to move on. He started out in television broadcasting in London, and then settled in with MBC. He married an Egyptian woman in London. "I joke that we are a pan-Arab family," he said.

It's precisely his pan-Arabism that made me initially uneasy about Mr. Baddih. He spoke a little too confidently of the Arab "mind" and about Arab "needs" and "requirements." However, it didn't take long before I realized that, given his position as chief of acquisitions and drama commissioner for one of the largest and most successful pan-Arab media initiatives since the days of Egypt's Gamal Abdel Nasser (more on him in the following chapter), he was one of the few people in the world qualified to speak this way.

Shifting in his plush office chair, staring at his phone, Mr. Baddih said, "I would say that *Al Shamshoon* was not a big success. Otherwise, of course, we would have continued to do another season. I would say it was fairly received, but average. This made us reconsider."

"Fairly received?" I asked, with a tone of mild incredulity.

"Why, what feedback have you heard?" asked Mr. Baddih, feigning nonchalance.

"I'll be frank—most have suggested to me that the show didn't work. Especially the online chit-chat."

Mr. Baddih smiled. "Ah, yes—online chit-chat." He squeezed his stress ball.

"I take it you thought the results would be different?"

Mr. Baddih's eyes dipped down at the edges. "It is a big international brand. It could have been a very easy product for us. We cater it for our audience, we run it year after year—voila. You must understand that we did not simply dub, but we Arabized the concept. We toned it down in the cultural sense. Perhaps I could say we softened it? All the characters' actions have been brought more to what we here consider acceptable." Mr. Baddih looked up; a young Filipina brought in a tray of coffees. We augmented them to our tastes in silence, teaspoons dinging against china.

"What of the Jewish Krusty the Clown?" I asked. "The good Reverend Lovejoy?" I knew from several other television executives that Arab programmers would go to any lengths to excise clearly Christian—but especially Jewish—characters from licensed American television shows. It's taken as a matter of, well, faith that Jews are so reviled by Saudis that even animated portrayals are enough to cause riots.

Mr. Baddih found several pencils on his desk very interesting. "These things . . ." he trailed off. "Complicated."

"As for the strong women characters?" I asked. "Was there a mandate to tone Lisa down?"

Mr. Baddih stiffened. "No, no, no—why? We kept this stuff. You want to know who is calling the shots in this society? The women."

I refilled my coffee. There was something tugging at my thoughts, some notion working at the edge of this conundrum that I couldn't quite parse.

"Given that the show wasn't as successful as you'd hoped, is Arabization the problem here?" I asked. "That's obviously what bothered some of the show's local fans. What if you'd left it as is? Simply dubbed it, and left it."

"No, I don't think so. The masses who don't speak English don't know how the show was in America. But culturally it didn't cross very well. Maybe the sense of humor is too North American. Comedy is especially a culturally sensitive matter. Drama is one thing—but with comedy, it is black and white. Deep inside, either you laugh, or you say, no, this is not funny."

"So would you consider the *Al Shamshoon* saga a mistake?"

"No, no—in television you try a lot of things—trial and error. I accept this as part of the job. The mistake is when you really go out and majorly offend people. But it was not a mistake—out of such experiments, you take such adventures and learn."

But learn what? How to Arabize American television more successfully? The nature of this problem began to take shape. The elephant in Baddih Fattouh's office, it seemed to me, was his core audience of twenty-two million conservative Saudi Arabians.

"MBC calls itself pan-Arabic," I said. "But can pan-Arabism work in this context? Doesn't a territory like Saudi—or, more generally, the Gulf—tip the scales toward a more conservative programming slate?" If all television in the region was intrinsically attracted toward the magnetic pole of a Saudi Arabian audience, then how could any daring television be made? In a free market, exciting programming means more viewers and higher ad revenues. But MBC didn't need advertising revenue to survive, because it isn't subject to market forces. Its bankrollers have unfathomably deep pockets. So why were they bothering with pan-Arabism, unless there was something more at stake here? Did it have something to do with the long-running smack-down between the likes of the Awakening Sheikhs and the Saudi royal family?

"Listen, we pride ourselves on being a family channel," said Mr. Baddih. "We do push the boundaries within certain limits. We would never go to the extent of some of the Lebanese channels and the amount of flesh they show. But we are moderate and liberal. Even when we are targeting the Gulf, which can be difficult, it doesn't push us back from being reasonable and liberal and open-minded. We have an intention—and that is to be the number one satellite station in the Arab world.

"The whole region has gone through huge changes in the last two to three years," continued Mr. Baddih. "We are putting on things that five years ago I would never have *dreamed* of broadcasting. Even *Sex and the City* played on MBC—which never even played on network television in the States. You have a strange mix in this part of the world. You have contradictory ways of thinking. MBC2, 3 and Action are for those who enjoy Western entertainment—these channels could be viewed by certain groups in the Arab world as blasphemous, poisonous. But 9/11 has put the spotlight on conservatism and fundamentalism. It's made us ask what is acceptable and what is not."

"But I was under the impression that things were becoming *more* restrictive," I said. "Aren't we constantly being told that in the wake of the Iraq war there has been a hardening of the position against American-style reform, especially in entertainment? Who has been telling us such things? Are they wrong?"

"The media say these things, and they are right and they are wrong. No one loves American policy; most do not mind American entertainment, regardless of what they say. And through entertainment, we are shown different ways to live—more modern, more relaxed, less restrictive. A different social milieu."

"So TV pushes this forward in the Gulf?" I asked.

"Well, two things. TV can be an indication of what is happening in a society—it shows how things are turning. Like it once was in America." If one were to look at the broad sweep of network television in the States, Mr. Baddih pointed out, one would see a societal sea change from *I Love Lucy* to *Friends*, a journey through two generations of liberalization taking a parallel track alongside core conservative or religious values that have only hardened. This is mirrored by the journey from Petro-Boomer to Generation *Al Shamshoon* in the Muslim World—that strange mix of burgeoning middle-class values tacking alongside a closed social conservatism and hammer-fisted religiosity. It is not a precise analogy, but the overlapping pattern is worth noting.

"While TV can definitely influence society," said Mr. Baddih, "it cannot do so if the society is not ready. If you're not ready for positive social change, nothing will change your mind. If you're ready, art will push it forward."

I leaned forward in my chair. There was a vast paradox at work here: A Wahhabist Kingdom trying to turn its subjects into middle-class Americans. "Is MBC using all this programming—this American stuff—as a means of weaning Saudis onto Americanized thinking?" It seemed as if the Saudis were counting on the fact that the American Idea had long been rejected, and what audiences would adopt was the mindlessness, the consumerism. Homer as Omar, stripped of satire, denuded of social commentary: a fat, bald, indolent cretin whose every mistake is solved by wacky circumstance.

"I cannot answer this question," said Mr. Baddih. But this one thing was clear: By controlling the influx of Western entertainment— a flood that MBC's backers both foresaw and presaged back in the early 1990s—by Arabizing it and parsing it out in a measured manner, the Saudi ruling elite meant to manage the growth of the very extremism that is such an existential threat. After all, if there is anything a soft-bellied bourgeoisie is not, it's extremist. It was an astonishing notion: a societal transformation to a more Western way of life imposed from above. Like a California peach that travels across an ocean in a container to end up in a Dubai convenience store, American popular culture, when Arabized, was steadily leached of its nutrients. All that remained was mulch.

A professor at the American University of Beirut would later crystallize things for me: "MBC is seen as the realization on the part of Saudi investors and royal family [that] if they did not define the market parameters, then others would. MBC would provide Saudis with the kind of entertainment they were seeking elsewhere, but *they* would set the limits, particularly in politics. A preemptive move."

According to this theory, MBC would reverse-engineer a society, managing that inherent push/pull between deeply conservative sensibilities and Saudi Arabia's patented version of American-style suburban neo-liberalism. This was Baddih Fattouh's job. He had earned his stress ball.

"We are done," said Mr. Baddih. "But there is more you can find here." He scrawled something on a slip of paper for me: an address that was, not so conveniently, quite some way from where we sat.

"Cairo?" I asked.

"Cairo," said Mr. Baddih. "My assistant will see you out."

4

The Genie Leaves the Bottle

EGYPT 1.0

Muslim: 90%

Coptic: 9%

7% GDP

1. Snow White Soundtrack:
   Heigh-Ho

2. Pointer Sisters:
   Fairytale

3. Colby O'Donis:
   Mouse in the House

Pop.: 81,713,520

Avg. age: 24.5

Capital: Cairo

Independence: Feb 28,1922

After his third volcanic outburst, Amro Hosny, the celebrated poet, quieted down and spoke of love.

"I am a man who has been married. It was a disaster, of course—these things always are—but we were passionate. I have children. I have been enamored with women for sometimes an hour, or for days, or for years. But I cannot say anything more about the subject of *amore*," he concluded, "than was said by Homer and Marge, of Springfield, U.S.A."

Hosny took a violent slug of beer, foam sizzling on his goatee like a breaker dying on a beach. Even when deep in thought, there was an aspect of crazed gesticulation about him. In full rhetorical flight, his chopping hands would articulate vast cabinets in the air, and he'd madly open drawers, proffering insights like glinting baubles. His salt-and-pepper hair bristled at odd intervals on his head: along his chin, above his lip, in random Krusty the Clown tufts on his head. Like any lifelong joker, his eyes were dark with melancholy, but the face surrounding them was rumpled with laugh lines.

Many hours earlier, I had taken the train to meet Amro Hosny, crushed among rush-hour commuters heading home to the western fringe of Cairo, a city that crawls out along the Nile in an endless chain of human settlement, all the way back in time to an age of treacherous kohl-eyed queens and gilded palaces. Where *belle époque* Cairo frays at the edges of the downtown core, there is the vast Cairo of the slums, where too many of Egypt's eighty million citizens move in by the hundreds of thousands every year, slowly changing the tenor of the city. Cairo is Egypt and Egypt is riven. It always has been; there are many who believe it is hurtling toward terminal velocity, picking up enough speed to burn out like a meteor entering the earth's atmosphere.

Amro Hosny is one of those people.

He is a poet, but poetry—like crime—doesn't pay. So for the past ten years Hosny has been the go-to Arabizer for a host of high-profile American entertainment brands. He's the guy Arab producers turn to when they need something completely, impossibly American transmogrified into the Arabic idiom. It's not enough simply to translate. No, this is something else entirely. It's more like *reculturating*.

Sesame Street? Hosny worked on dozens of episodes of the Arabic *Alam Simsim* that, because of its huggy love-thy-neighbor pluralism, was so culturally perilous it required the backing of Suzanne Mubarak, Egypt's First Lady, to shelter it from hardline opprobrium. *The Simpsons?* Baddih Fattouh agreed instantly when the Egyptian production company suggested Hosny. But his main gig—and indeed, his greatest success—has come courtesy of one of the most maligned cultural brands in human history. Amro Hosny made his name Arabizing Disney's Pixar titles. In doing so, there are those who believe that he has written some of the finest Arab comedy of all time.

But that night, Hosny wasn't interested in funny. "When writing *Al Shamshoon*, I used a reference to a wonderful sense of Egypt in the sixties—a singer named Abdel Halim Itafez—and I used him whenever we flash back to Omar and Mona in college. Abdel Halim was a symbol for the sentimental and the platonic love. He became the shorthand for the sixties, for an era. Every Arab of that time knows him. The scenes are very touching, very beautiful scenes. But *they* didn't fucking like them. *They* sneered. Against *them*," said Hosny, trembling like a tectonic plate moments before an earthquake, "we are always fighting for our lives."

By *they*, Amro Hosny does not mean America.

A week earlier, I was awakened by a phone call at 4:30 in the morning. "Mr. Richard, please come join us at the Odeon, the tenth floor," said an acquaintance. "We are enjoying some beers, and would further enjoy the pleasure of your company. Perhaps some things will be made clear to you."

I cursed in six languages, washed my face, and made my way through the darkened lobby of the Berlin Hotel, passing the slumped bellhop in his faded red livery. The Berlin is splendidly located on the fourth floor of a dying *belle époque* masterpiece. The roof has in places caved in; patches of moonlight dappled the thick balustrades. I negotiated stairs so worn by foot traffic they curved like the lips of stone fountains; a shadowy bestiary inhabited an elevator shaft hanging with stalactites of muck. The Berlin Hotel is like a sundial after dark: It speaks voluminously of time without telling one what time it is.

I walked the block to the Odeon through wet alleyways, past the occasional small boy bundled under rags and soggy newsprint. I rode a rickety elevator up as far as it would go. My acquaintance sat at a patio table bathed in moonlight with several men drinking bottles of beer. They were hunched over the table discussing, with a theatricality that suggested it was somewhat for my benefit, Gamal Abdel Nasser, once the Arab world's great strongman, now a divisive historical figure apparently due for a revisionist whitewash.

"He was a buffoon, a fool—a Saddam with a bigger nose," said my acquaintance, a lugubrious soul who slept through the day and worked at night, and was thus as pallid as a fish's belly. "The West laughed at us with his silly bluster."

"Fuck the West," said another, a filmmaker, nodding at me apologetically. In his mid-thirties, thoroughly Westernized and thoroughly drunk, he waved his supersized bottle of Stella as he spoke. "He was strong. He was powerful—a *man*. He had ideas. When was the last time you heard an idea in this country?"

Ah, Nasser! Where have the likes of you gone? To Latin America, actually: Venezuela's Hugo Chavez is from the same mold—a blowhard populist with a histrionic streak. From 1956 until his death in 1970 Nasser was the president of Egypt: He was one of the first developing-world leaders to stoke the fires of nationalism, lighting the conflagration of pan-Arabism that others have fanned, in one form or another, since. But he was also brutal, small-minded and myopic, undone in 1967 by the calamity (from an Arab point of view) of the Six Day War, in which any idea of a consolidated Arab political/military entity was thoroughly scuttled. The defeat was a shot in the gut to Arab pride, a weeping historical wound that still requires dressing. Give Gamal Abdel Nasser this much: He attempted the Sisyphean task of politically and culturally unifying the Arab people, even if his intentions were shortsighted to the last. And with his sophisticated state-run propaganda machine that railed against Arab nations out of step with his vision with as much vitriol as it did against Israel, along with his tacit support of secular popular art—which he used as a bulwark against the popularity of the Islamist Muslim Brotherhood—he redefined (or rather, defined) the Arab media landscape.

"I despair of us," said my acquaintance. "See what is left to discuss? Foolish men from the sixties. Here, everything is in the past, the past, the past," to which The Filmmaker gave a dismissive sweep of his beer bottle.

I strolled with my own beer to the edge of the Odeon's patio, where dawn slowly revealed a farrago of garbage-strewn rooftops, everything covered with a thick layer of uniform grime. On a streak of asphalt brilliant with morning sunlight rode a lone cyclist, trays of bread balanced on his head. Otherwise, all was still.

"We continue to hide from the Saudis, and we hide from ourselves," said The Filmmaker softly. "There is no courage any more." He had a point: Egyptian television and cinema were once the envy of the region, producing some of the finest Arabic drama of the past century. But the twin tentacles of the Ministry of Information and of al-Azhar—a mosque (and later a university) established in tenth-century Cairo and for eons the vanguard of traditionalist Sunni Islamic thinking—have between them kept television, and other Egyptian media, in an impressively tenacious wrestling hold. Their influence is everywhere; financing and air time are contingent upon their approval. The government's main domestic concern is keeping Islamism in check. Al-Azhar's intentions, besides ensuring that Islam and the Prophet remain unsullied, are murkier. This keeps artists like The Filmmaker between a rock and the Dome of the Rock.

He took a long pull from his bottle. "You are here why?" he asked.

I told him the long story. At one particular proper noun, he raised an incredulous eyebrow.

"Disney? *Disney?*" said The Filmmaker with an emphysemic chuckle. "Hah! Good luck. You shall go—how do you say?—down the rabbit hole."

Consider the image: The lion, lithe and bony, stands high on a rocky outpost. His dark mane flows like a mullah's beard. Call him Scar. He is framed against a sky that—but for a sliver of a crescent moon above him—is as black as his soul. Like Claudius, he has engineered his brother's murder. He has sent the rightful heir to the throne, the plucky cub Simba, into exile. Like Jesus, Simba will enjoy a lesson-packed Second Coming.

Consider the message: "What you see," says Mohammed Harib, creator of *Freej*, "is a subtle statement against Islam. The link is clear—the evil of Scar with the crescent of Islam. Every frame of

Disney holds a message—they leave nothing to chance. They are exact, exact—precise to the last line. I know this. I have studied with their people." This represented my first, but by no means my last, encounter with *The Lion King*/Scar/anti-Islam algorithm. The Great Arab Conspiracy Theory: Mouseketeer Edition.

Like most people born in the latter half of the twentieth century, I've never had to search for Disney. Disney found me. My first experience in a movie theater involved my grandfather—a man of infinite love and patience—repeatedly pulling me up from under my seat in Johannesburg's Seven Arts Theatre during a matinee of *The Rescuers*. That tenebrous space contained all matter of magic.

It is magic with a dark flipside. When Harib and I spoke about Scar, I was at the time rereading an Everyman compendium of the *Cairo Trilogy*, the novelist Naguib Mahfouz's tragic story of three generations of a Caireen family during the first half of the twentieth century. Mahfouz chose to model his classic on the nineteenth-century psychological novel, not only for aesthetic reasons but also for intellectual ones: how else to convey, and to implicitly criticize, the workings of his society without seeming to judge it?

There seemed to be a link between how Mahfouz wrote his novels and how Harib read the Disney image: Many in the Muslim world are used to scouring popular art for codes because so much of their art has existed in disguise—written or filmed or sung in what amounts to an analogical style. (The convention in Arabic popular songs sung by men is to address them to other men, because singing to a woman one hasn't seen or met would be an obvious impropriety, as well as impossible.) Culture—high, low or in-between—is not received passively; the hidden message must be deciphered.

It is where a *covert* message is identified that the trouble starts. *The Lion King* is indeed a massaging of the Christ myth; the film works hard for its portentous Judeo-Christian overtones. Muslims reading the "text" of such American pop, hunting for signifiers, have little trouble locating a deeper meaning and drawing further conclusions.

With Disney, one need not dig so deep for trouble. No other American brand—*pace* Coca-Cola or McDonald's—has come in for such blanket condemnation. If one were to summarize the gazillions of words of denunciation with just a few, we could conclude that Disney is one creepy man's interpretation of white suburban American values, in which an invented innocence reigns supreme by confirming gender stereotypes, ransacking other cultures for ideas that are then leached of authenticity and churned into a cutesy, if rigid, formula, further packaged and sold for enormous profit. Disney created a company that laid claim to childhood, and helped turn that childhood into an ATM spewing out endless *dineros*.

If we take Carl Hiaasen's observation that "the [Disney] message, never stated but avuncularly implied, is that America's values ought to reflect those of the Walt Disney Company, and not the other way around," and apply it to the Muslim world, then we arrive at an interesting—and rather perilous—cultural intersection.

A plane lands at Cairo International Airport on an afternoon in 1975 and discharges the tanned, slim figure of Blake Todd. He walks across the tarmac, sideburns bristling. Todd is here—the epicenter of the Arabic movie industry—to build a veritable Magic Castle alongside the pyramids. But it's bad timing. The OPEC oil crisis rages, there is a boycott of Coca-Cola and about eight thousand other American companies by Egypt and the Arab League. But Blake Todd—late of Burbank, California, and an executive at the Walt Disney Company—is undaunted. He brings with him five heavy reels of 35mm film, amounting to eighty-three minutes of celluloid genius. *Snow White and the Seven Dwarfs*. Adjusted for inflation, *Snow White* is the tenth top-grossing film of all time. If Todd isn't whistling "Heigh-Ho," he should be.

After all, he is by no means introducing Disney into the region. Mickey's menagerie has squawked and squealed through movie houses in Egypt and Lebanon and Syria since the thirties. Indeed, everyone cheers for the Disney cartoon before the feature. This is how many Arabs have grown up. There is also a weekly publication, first on newsstands in 1959, called *Mickey Magazine*—a translated comic book printed by a state-run publishing company that crosses a broad spectrum of Egypt's literate society. Seventy thousand copies are sold a week, each copy passed among any number of young inhabitants of Caireen neighborhoods. The magazines are meant as another of those bulwarks against creeping Islamism: Nasser-era Egypt has proven that American cultural product can be used as a weapon in the war against extremism. (Uncle Walt himself knew this all too well: Loathing pinkos as much as any man alive, he personally oversaw a tacitly anti-communist *Mickey*-style publication called *Zé Carioca* in Brazil in the sixties, and made sure it was distributed free throughout that country.)

This is, in part, why Snow White and her feisty little pals have taken the long trip from their forest to Arabia. Also, it does not escape the notice of Disney executives that there are Arabs with disposable incomes that make Scrooge McDuck look like a broke-ass Cairo street urchin. This market needs to be tapped, especially as the Disney brand starts to fall off at home during the seventies.

Flush with *esprit de mission*, Todd waltzes into the Cairo Opera House, the very institution for which Giuseppe Verdi's *Aida* was commissioned way back in 1871. He hires the Egyptian soprano Retiba al-Hefni to play the titular Ms. White. Immediately there-after, it all goes to hell. The script quickly becomes an unwieldy pastiche of Egyptian colloquial Arabic and classical—or literary— Arabic. There are cultural concerns that Todd hasn't considered, such as seven little men and one unveiled women bunking together in the woods. Todd learns very quickly that Western and Arabic music work on entirely different modal systems. He's never heard of half- and quarter-tones before. There are few one-syllable words in classical Arabic, so it's a bitch setting the words to music. Does he hire more opera singers who can't sing pop, or turn to pop singers with wretched voices? While Cairo musicians are perfectly capable of playing Bizet or Mozart, no one has ever tried to Arabize "With a Smile and a Song" before.

Against these odds, the film miraculously turns out superbly. But boy-oh-boy is it ever a pricy undertaking. After crunching the numbers, Disney holds off on translating the rest of its filmography. As the House of Mouse becomes an increasingly international brand, men like Todd realize that they require a management system to monitor and produce content the world over. The idea is to set up something of an oversight body, called Disney Character Voices International, or DCVI. If a licensee screws with Goofy's persona, the lawyers shall descend. DCVI is a consummate example of cultural globalization, a means of maintaining consistent Disney characters and storylines across dozens of cultural transmutations.

The eighties are not good to Disney. It's not until 1989, with *The Little Mermaid*, that the company gets another *Snow White*–like smash. Three years later, though, and all the hard work that Todd has invested in the Middle East goes down the crapper. Robin Williams's barrel-chested Genie leaps from the bottle in the Disney blockbuster *Aladdin*, spewing improvised dialogue like "*Oy!* Ten thousand years will give you such a crick in the neck." The film kicks off the post-modern animated era, presaging star-laden, pop culture–referencing Disney/Pixar computer-animated hits, along with DreamWorks titles like *Shrek* and the raft of similar product that flows like sludge from busted studio sewage pipes. To conservative critics the world over, *Aladdin* represents a decline, exorcising the "class" from classical animation. Arabs have a special grievance: Disney has plundered the *Thousand Nights and One Night* for inspiration, only to come up with lyrics like "Where they cut off your ear if they don't like your face. It's barbaric, but hey, it's home."

It is the equivalent, as one Disney executive puts it, "of drinking from the well, then doing a number one in it." The American-Arab Anti-Discrimination Committee (ADC) is unhappy, made unhappier still by successive Disney releases. *G.I Jane*, released by Disney's Hollywood Pictures, culminates in an orgiastic firefight in which hundreds of "Libyans" spew blood onto the sands of Arizona-as-Benghazi. There is the character of Habib in *Father of the Bride Part II*—played by Canadian comic Eugene Levy—as the venal Arab trying to screw the lily-white Banks family out of their property. And those can be counted as the high points.

In 1996, Mickey Mouse's standing in the Arab world is so miserably low that the Arab League intervenes at the behest of the ADC. The committee organizes protests outside Disney facilities, and a year later the studio is forced to institute the Department of Arabic Standards and Practices. This is not only a means of appeasing local Arab-American resentment but, more importantly, a way to build the Disney brand in the very land in which they cut off your ear if they don't like your face.

Some would call this chutzpah. Others call it cleaning up the well in which you did a number one.

The man who donned the biohazard gear and waded through Disney's Middle Eastern effluent is called Ahmed Zahzah. He is a tall, tailored Lebanese gentleman in his mid-fifties, an experienced television executive who helped start the music video channel Rotana, owned by Saudi mogul Prince al-Walid bin Talal. The Disney licence recently passed to bin Talal from another wealthy Saudi named Ahmed Jarwa. Disney Middle East was, like MBC, now a Saudi entertainment business.

Zahzah's job, as head of the Department of Arabic Standards and Practices, was, as he puts it, "to precisely tailor Disney's satellite channel content to local cultural values, and thus steer the brand in the Middle East. Learning how sensitive the Arab audiences are, Disney felt there was a need to put a filter on what should go on the air. They did not want to rub cultural sensitivities any more than they had."

It was a job Zahzah took seriously. He would meticulously review an episode of a TV show six months ahead of airdate, and strip it of anything that didn't fit the rigid mandate he'd established. With the high school sitcom *Boy Meets World*, he approved the early episodes, but when the characters graduated to university, he'd start slashing episodes with any sexual innuendo (along with any reference to Judaism, an unfortunate quirk of the series). Zahzah wanted to ensure that an Arab parent would feel secure in leaving a child unattended in front of the channel. He crawled inside Walt Disney's cryogenically frozen brain and further sanitized his vision of childhood. In this, he wasn't so far off from Disney Channel's programmers in the States: Three episodes of *Boy Meets World* were axed from syndication for frank(ish) portrayals of iniquitous underage behaviour. Conservative American cultural critics frequently grumble that liberal Hollywood is out of step with mainstream American values. Zahzah didn't want even a hint of this debate to start around Disney in the Middle East.

Zahzah fully articulated the process of Arabization, distinguishing it from mere dubbing. His department's first real challenge was another Aladdin-sized cultural fumble: the dubbing of *The Lion King*. The script, an early DCVI misstep, was adapted by a bawdy septuagenarian poet named Abdul Rahman Shouki. It was the equivalent of turning *Teletubbies* into *Scarface*. ("It was really, really shocking—shockingly vulgar," one Disney Middle East insider told me. "It's one of the famous stories of the company. Jeff Miller, a DCVI vice-president, had to make sure that all copies were destroyed, every last one of them.") Little things: The direct Arabic translation of "shut up" is *ikhras*—"be mute"—which happens to be as vicious a word as exists in the Arabic lexicon. When it came time for a do-over, Zahzah used *uskut*—silence. Non-threatening, non-confrontational—it has less verbal violence in it. "After *The Lion King* debacle, we dub once—*once*—because you are creating Arabic masterpieces which should be as challenging and creative as the originals," said Zahzah. "Disney supported me—because this was very, very costly. No expense was spared. No more mistakes."

Zahzah was at first working along with DCVI, but that institution was becoming unsustainable. (The shop in Germany was so large it had a staff of ten.) Before its demise in 2006, DCVI was already starting to define how characters should be *interpreted*, rather than unthinkingly replicated. Disney was now at the vanguard of a new type of globalization, transforming what was once a completely standardized product into a culturally sensitive one. In DCVI's wake, people like Zahzah became the custodians of a parallel Disney universe they helped invent—and one of the world's most notoriously guarded cultural producers became the engineer of a very strange cultural mélange.

Indeed, the second edition of *The Lion King*, released in 2002, mostly quelled local criticism. It was an entirely Arabic film—a thorough appropriation—and through this experience Disney executives learned that if they could keep audiences suitably entertained while refraining from slights to their religion, race and country of origin, audiences would similarly refrain from firebombing their offices.

This amounted to a minor cultural revolution. And on one thing Zahzah was perfectly clear: All must hinge on language. One of his key shifts in policy was to start Arabizing into *classical* Arabic rather than colloquial Egyptian. To most Arab Muslims, classical Arabic— the language of the Qur'an—is sacrosanct; grammar and structure mistakes are not tolerated in the same way they would be in English. The source of the Qur'an's holiness is rooted in the power of the language. But classical Arabic is incredibly difficult to penetrate—as dense and illusory as Mandarin, its conjugations as tricky as Latin: For many, including the Middle East's barely educated masses, every sentence is a wall of linguistic impenetrability. Zahzah didn't care. "If you watch the Disney Channel Middle East for a year, you would never find one simple grammar mistake. It sounds theoretical—but people here detest the mistakes of dubbing. It's an insult. We absolutely eliminated that."

For over fifty years, most Arabs had been perfectly comfortable watching entertainment dubbed into the Egyptian dialect. To many uneducated Arabs, icons like John Wayne *were* Egyptian. Zahzah's movement was not a small shift—it was a fundamental realignment of a cultural focal point. And it came at the behest of the Saudis.

Zahzah calls his work "positive censorship." But it's interesting to note just how tightly he was prepared to fasten the cultural blinkers. Disney wanted to dub *Hercules* (in which the eponymous hero must save the city of Thebes along with his love interest named, with Greco aplomb, Meg), but the Zeus and Hades characters "would be very offensive to a monotheistic religion such as Islam." *The Hunchback of Notre Dame* he opted not to show, because most of the action takes place in a church.

Disney's Middle Eastern satrap was clear on what he felt would offend Muslim audiences, and in this he raised one of global popular culture's more disturbing questions (and one by no means restricted to Disney): Would cultural producers start amending original story-lines in order to cater to the absolute broadest possible international audience, including Wahhabist Gulfies? Would Americans be asked to share sensibilities with the most conservative culture on earth, where the very mention of eating pig flesh (eliminated from the Arabization of *Mulan*) or, say, Judaism, is verboten?

The Department of Arabic Standards and Practices—founded to deflect criticism from Disney's woeful betrayal of Arab characters—developed into a cultural refinery, where product was scoured of anything not only racially offensive, but also offensive to an elitist notion of local sensibilities. "I have never found burping funny," Zahzah says, "but Americans love it. So—I eliminated burping. We're not Americans, we will never be. Never. What is created for them won't work for us. I know that Disney wants all their content standardized so that it will fit every single region. I know they want this. But it will not happen."

Ahmed Zahzah wrote the handbook on Arabization. The ideas and trigger-finger sensibilities that he pioneered would be passed along to later, unrelated productions. His demand for the highest standards had only one small hitch. He had to hire writers who knew both the Arab and the American idiom, and could effectively bridge the two: poets, prose stylists, the best of the best. Such people are almost impossible to find. They need to be whip-smart, possess that rarest of gifts—cultural empathy—and take paychecks that, while almost acceptable by white-collar Egyptian standards, were paltry by American ones. These people tend to be of an independent mind. They tend to be fiery. They tend to be a problem.

The mess of papers on Amro Hosny's heavy oak dining room table suggested a psyche slowly separating from its moorings. It was a movie-set interpretation of a writer losing his shit: an outtake from *Barton Fink* maybe, or a Bukowski biopic. Set against the pleasant, if spartan, cherrywood apartment, it was a testament to the agonies of the craft. Pages and pages of a movie screenplay, Arabic letters tumbling from the margins, were scattered across every available flat surface.

Hosny lived alone in this quiet suburb of Cairo. Despite his divorce, he was still heavily involved in his two teenage kids' lives and had just taken a week off to help his son cram for matriculation finals. The holiday was, resolutely, over. Setting another can of beer before me, he cracked his third and pointed to the screenplay. "That, my friend, is a fucking disaster in the making. *Shrek the Third* into classical Arabic? A fat green Scottish ogre into the language of the Qur'an? My fucking brain is splitting apart. But you cannot criticize classical Arabic. Oh, no! If you are against it, you're against Islam. I am against classical Arabic as trying to force it as a language—which it will never be, even though I understand it very well."

Hosny's work is often indistinguishable from philology, which was described by one of its finest practitioners as "the science of compassion." Because he works within the engine room of American junk-culture, Hosny must yank an entire cultural mind apart, and put it together inside the rubric of his own. He can flit through sensibilities with the grace of a primo ballerino, pliéing between French, Egyptian, traditional Arabic, Shakespearean English, pop-culture American. While he makes harsh qualitative judgments ("Shit is shit is shit," he says; the critic requires no other mantra), he is not a classist: For him, there is no high or low art.

"Egyptians are very similar to Americans," Hosny said between gulps of beer, "and that's because we are a mixture of different cultures. We are an older culture, but a mixture of many. And you can feel it on the level of the language. Egyptian colloquial is very rich—it's a big pot. It's very simple and very expressive, like American English. I am one of the people that discovered the similarities between Egyptian and American. Classical Arabic is pure and very rigid—it doesn't accept images from different cultures. It is not a water, a liquid—it takes time and effort for you to phrase something to make it fit with some other culture. And that's why we lose ninety percent of the humor. Gone! This *Shrek* will be a fucking mess."

When Hosny started out as an Arabizer, he was doing most of his work in Egyptian colloquial. But then, over the past decade, and particularly since the latter third of 2001, classical became the pop-cultural lingua franca. Quietly, and through the medium of American sitcoms and animated film, a pure and archaic form of Arabic is being revived.

There is a precedent for attaching a cultural defibrillator to a language and jolting it out of ecclesiastical rigor mortis: Hebrew was a long-dead language in the late nineteenth century. Although the written Yiddish of the European Diaspora used the Hebrew alphabet—and a few small communities spoke versions of the tongue—the language existed only in its medieval form in synagogues and Jewish places of study. Its revival as a modern national language was the brainchild of a one-time Yeshiva student and Zionist called Eliezer Ben-Yehuda, who moved to Palestine in the 1880s and founded a Hebrew newspaper called *Z'vi*. Reviving the language was a large part of the *Z'vi* raison d'être, and over time the paper became stridently political and anti-rabbinate. Hebrew thus became a secular project, a national project. It was the adhesive agent for the growing idea of a Jewish state, which made Ben-Yehuda as responsible as Theodor Herzl for the idea of Israel.

Whether or not those behind classical Arabic's make-over as a pan-Arabic idiom have modern Hebrew in mind, no one can say. And while the example is instructive, it is not strictly analogous. There are dozens of vibrant Arabic dialects all over the Middle East. Arabic is the official language in twenty-five nations. It predates the Qur'an, by a long shot. It is by no means only a Muslim language—millions of Arabs are Christian. There are versions, written in a combination of the Roman alphabet and numbers, posted by Generation *Al Shamshoon* on Facebook and other social network websites. Yet there are those who want to standardize Arabic popular culture, tying it to conservative Islam *through* American popular culture, burying colloquial Egyptian in the process.

"But the language is too heavy," said Hosny. "It doesn't make the kids laugh. And the kids of the higher classes, and the educated kids—they will look to another language, and that language will be English. We will push them away."

Hosny has been asked by the powers-that-be to transform works of American popular culture that are manifestly postmodern—heavily self-referential, filled with in-jokes and cues to other, previous pieces of similarly postmodern pop—and transform them using a language that cannot adapt to postmodernism because its structure doesn't allow for it. American English, a stew of a language, is ineffably adaptable—the perfect vector for, among other things, animated comedies about fat, green Scottish ogres. Egyptian colloquial has many of the same attributes. Because it is so absorbent—because it includes a huge variety of modern sayings, aphorisms, axioms—it can happily accommodate the Pixar canon.

"Somehow, there is some schizophrenia here," said Hosny. "It becomes very obvious when they force you to use classical Arabic in a piece of art, or a drama, or when they hire you to write something for the TV—it's a catastrophe." Tied to a language that can't be fouled, Disney Middle East places restrictions that the product can't necessarily bear. It stops the postmodern dead in its tracks.

"There is no one who can tell you that classical Arabic is a mother tongue. Does anyone think or dream in classical Arabic?" asked Hosny.

"When I read classical Arabic, no matter the great poetry—and the images are unbelievably great—I'm still dealing with part of my mind, not my heart. Some of the characters—the villains—I find easy to put in classical Arabic. Like with the stuffy British accent of Scar in *The Lion King*. But Shrek? Impossible."

I took a battered Fiat cab from downtown into Dokki, with great billowing clots of pollution rolling over the surface of the river. The cab—iconic Cairo: black, with white side panels and luggage rack atop—almost hit a donkey and managed to clip a pedestrian with a rear door that betimes swung open on its own recourse. We stalled repeatedly, a problem the driver referred to God by muttering a *sura* every time he restarted the unfortunate car.

I undertook this minor adventure in order to see first-hand the process that Blake Todd had started, Ahmed Zahzah had perfected, and Amro Hosny had turned into a compromised art form. I found the studio eventually, sequestered in a residential block of flats half gnawed away by ivy. I entered through a security gate and was ushered by a production assistant into a small room separated from a rudimentary sound booth by a plate of glass. The walls were carpeted, a hulking engineer sat before a soundboard that resembled the blinking bridge of a low-rent *Starship Enterprise*; the couch—upon which was seated a script supervisor and a producer—coughed up a *whoomph* of stale smoke when I sat down.

A dub was in session for Sony's animated feature *Surf's Up*, another instance of a pop-cultural movement that had brought us anthropomorphized penguins in everything from tap dancing musicals to docu-weepies to this—a computer-generated surfing picture. The engineer flicked an array of buttons on the board, cueing up a scene on corresponding monitors. In the booth, playing a corpulent ice-pigeon named Big Z (voiced in the original by *The Big Lebowski*'s Jeff Bridges), sat Ahmed Khalil, a well-known Egyptian television actor who resembles less a penguin than a walrus and who possesses a rich voice, deepened by a passion for unfiltered cigarettes.

The challenges posed by translating surfer speak into classical Arabic were clearly frustrating the team. There is, for example, no equivalent term for "gnarly" in the Qur'an. The process seemed absurd, but no more absurd, I supposed, than are surfing penguins in the first place. What this little studio did prove is that there is an industry, hidden in the warrens of Cairo, where Hollywood product is run through the Arabization process. Without top-notch talent like Hosny, it isn't easy work.

According to Aisha Selim, who was producing the Arabic version of *Surf's Up* and ran DCVI when Ahmed Zahzah was in charge of the Department of Arabic Standards and Practices, major Hollywood studios *liked* dubbing into classical Arabic. "Disney did it for sales," Selim told me. "Colloquial Egyptian is the pop-cultural voice, but it's hard to sell to other regions. Disney had a problem selling to the North African market—which is a big market—who wouldn't buy Egyptian. The usual old national feuds can be papered over by pretending that this stuff isn't made in Egypt. Money became the most important thing, but the reason I started accepting classical is that Disney has a mainly entertainment/educational mandate, so it's not a bad idea that kids learn classical Arabic."

According to Selim, it was the 1998 Disney/Pixar feature *A Bug's Life* that saw Arabization come into its own. Hosny did a spectacular job on the script, effortlessly bridging Arabic classical with Egyptian colloquial before the rules had hardened. Even words like "ladybug," which few Arabs even knew existed in Arabic, were searched out and added to the lexicon. "We introduced the proper word—*da'suqa*—to a whole generation," said Selim. The *mot juste* duly inserted, Francis the Ladybug and his entomological pals could soar.

"Remember," Selim told me, "once remade, those films are *ours*. Arabic. The language, the idioms, the references, the jokes, the characters. Only the situations and the animation are Disney's. The messages, of course, are universal."

The notion of originality doesn't have the heft in some Muslim cultures that it does in the West. A film or a pop song or a literary idea becomes a husk to be rearticulated in any way another artist sees fit. Western critics typically lament the constant slew of remakes or sequels or ideas lifted from other cultures. (Remember that stretch in the eighties when French comedies like *Three Men and a Cradle* were routinely Americanized? Not exactly a Hollywood high point.) In Arab countries, a pop song or a film idea can have a constant life— remade and released in countless iterations over the years. Part of the reason is the idea of *bid'ah*—innovation—that The Poet spoke about in Libya in relation to Lionel Richie. Also, originality is not rewarded— in most Arab countries there are few intellectual property or copyright laws protecting new ideas from sticky fingers. Arab cultures also see *performance*, or interpretation, rather than *idea*, as the primary artistic force. As Westerners, we praise the New, but we should remember that this is not a universal model for artistic excellence. It would be wrong to suggest that some Arab audiences aren't often frustrated by the lack of local originality, but it would be similarly incorrect to say that ingenuity cannot exist outside of the New.

"You know, we're dubbing *Ugly Betty* right now," said Selim refer- ring to the camp soapie about bed-hopping in a New York fashion house. With *Ugly Betty*, we didn't Arabize at all. The challenge is finding actors who can act in classical Arabic, and who can say 'Buddy' like an American. We're dubbing, but we're not localizing. Yes, they drink. Yes, they have sex outside marriage. And what is the number two–rated show after Arabic movies on TV? *Ugly Betty*. It beat out the Mexican dubbed version, which surprised me, because I thought the Mexican version is closer in sensibility to us Arabs. People were worried—'Guys, we're gonna talk about sex quite openly.' But it worked.

"But let's not remove all this from politics," said Selim. "When Mohammed al-Dura got killed, the shit hit the fan." Al-Dura was a twelve-year-old Palestinian boy who was famously shot dead— according to the French camera crew who captured the footage—by

Israeli soldiers during the second intifada. The footage has subsequently come under great scrutiny, but it remains—pre–Abu Ghraib—some of the most pervasive imagery in the Muslim world of the past bloody decade. "We lost our Minnie Mouse voice talent, we lost our old script supervisor, a couple of translators. There was a dubber who sent a circular email, and said I'm not going to work with you because you support Israel, and it was translated. People were pissed off. Disney said to me, 'Close the office for three days and get a bodyguard!' It blew over, but some pop is always attached to politics. This is the way with Disney. It stinks of America the Brave."

Ugly Betty gets a free pass, while hidden messages in *The Lion King* bring Disney to its knees. On the surface this is confounding, but because soaps have long been considered meaningless televised frippery, they've escaped condemnation, and thus been allowed a lot of cultural rope. While anything that children watch must be considered holy.

I mentioned this to Hosny, to which he said, "All bullshit. Whatever they believe their justification to be, it's all bullshit. And let me tell you why it's bullshit. It's bullshit because of the way they think. You must understand that Disney is only part of the equation."

To illustrate this point, he wanted to talk about *Al Shamshoon*.

We had met for coffee in the heat of late afternoon, and Hosny had a hunted look, a condition he attributed to "that motherfucker Shrek."

"When the production house told me that we were going to dub *The Simpsons* in colloquial Egyptian, I said 'Hoorah!' I understood that this was a very American piece of pop culture, and I had to make some idea that would be the objective correlative for the Arabic people. I got the idea to make a little fictitious place called Little Arab Town—and it would give us a good reason why these people are American but Arab. The sheikhs at the channel refused that. They told the production house that they accept the writer would write in Egyptian colloquial, but they would not accept this. They felt maybe that there was some conspiracy, some plot. They don't trust the writer. So—it was Springfield, in America. There were other problems: This guy Homer drinks beer all the time, but this is a sin to the Arabs. So I told them that he will drink *she'er*—a malt drink close to 'beer' in sound, and easy for translation. But they refused this. They told me to make it 'juice.' They are motherfuckers. You think even an average Saudi is a complete fucking idiot? The guy drinks juice from a beer can? Stupid."

Hosny leaned in across the table toward me, folding his arms over the tabletop. "Unlike a lot of the Disney stuff, *The Simpsons* is a work of brilliance," he said. "It's very human. You can never feel they are fictitious characters—they are Americans, they live in a society that the writers have built that relates very much to the real world. I loved the character of Homer—he is very close to the Egyptian point of view. From some point of view you feel that he's stupid, and from some point of view you feel he is wise."

But how exactly does Homer relate to an Egyptian, or, put another way, how does an Egyptian relate to Homer?

"Please," said Hosny, waving an arm crusted with crumbs, "there are many points of relation. We have in our culture a similar demographic who belongs to the 1960s. It's not quite my generation: I'm forty-eight years old, so Homer is someone like my big brother, who was in college in '67 or '68. It was a revolutionary generation with the same hopes and feelings—against war, for peace. It was everywhere in the world the same feeling. So it was very easy for me to put phrases and thoughts into his tongue. We know this era very well: the VW Beetle, world peace, drugs, The Beatles. Homer represents a very famous phenomenon all over the world—and it was the same here."

"Even under Nasser?" I asked.

"*Especially* under Nasser. He was a socialist while the rest of the Arab world was still playing in the sand. So when I talk about this time, it's very Egyptian to me. I feel if my hands weren't tied, I could have done something good. I could have done something important."

I was starting to see where Hosny was coming from. *The Simpsons* didn't have the baggage that Disney product did. It would play on MBC—a free channel—as opposed to the subscriber-only Disney Middle East. He could reach an even broader viewership on YouTube, where Arabic TV shows frequently find an audience. Despite the fact that it was Arabized into colloquial Egyptian—or perhaps because of it—his masters had kept a particularly sharp eye on him. But what I wanted to know was whether it was even possible to keep the essence of so rarefied a piece of American pop culture as *The Simpsons*.

"I feel that these characters could be taken from a Third World society," said Hosny. "When we hear about the States, you think of everything as straightforward and above board. But the satire here is showing what is going on underneath. *The Simpsons* tells us that it's the same bullshit everywhere. Many of us here think that only we have this corrupt relationship with politicians and administrations, but *The Simpsons* shows that it happens everywhere."

Was Hosny saying that his interpretation of *The Simpsons* was, in effect, using a piece of American culture to inform the denizens of the Arabic-speaking developing world that America was not the answer?

"*Exactly*. The American Dream means very much to the people from this Third World. When we see that this Dream is not perfect— that it is full of flaws—it can give us some hope. It says that if you want to dream, dream *here!* And that over there—they live in the same world of mistakes and flaws. It was important to me to give people this impression. I'm sick, of course, at how Third World people believe that going to the States means going to heaven. It is important—vital—for them to see the cracks in the façade. Homer is a simple man—he's part of the machine, but sometimes he is pulled out of the machine—a faulty cog. And he sees, and we *all* see, the big picture."

Hosny leaned back in his chair and gazed out at the darkening Cairo street outside the bay windows of the coffee shop. The city took on a melancholy quiet at dusk.

"The Gulf and America," said Hosny with great weariness, "there is not so much difference. I'm not a big fan of the conspiracy theory—but you have to stop and think about it. It's a part of the bigger plan of selling the American way of living. With *Al Shamshoon*, as with Disney, they try to target the kids and teenagers, because they are the jeans wearers and the hamburger eaters. They must turn the teenagers into Americans, but Islamic Americans. Eat hamburgers, but don't drink Duff beer. Shop, shop, shop, but never think of eating a pig. And they want every Arab to think the Saudi way—to do as the Saudis do. This is their aim."

This was a theory, and I wasn't sure I bought it wholesale. But *Al Shamshoon*, along with the Arabized Disney canon, represents a strange case of cultural imperialism *within* cultural imperialism. Saudis owned the license for both brands, and they were trying to squeeze the idiom of colloquial Egyptian out of Arabic entertainment, replaced by the far more rigid religious—which in this case also means cultural—link to both Islam and the desert Arabic out of which it was born. The most American of pop-cultural icons—Walt Disney himself—has become a means of instituting this program of weaning the Arab world off Egyptian Arabic, thus bringing to American pop the authority of the language of the Qur'an, and therefore a *moral* authority. Egypt is a teeming Islamic African developing agrarian nation in every way differ-ent from the Gulf. But the new Pan-Arabism—Nasser's sad legacy—is an attempt to enforce values and ethos and eliminate idiosyncrasies: a new reign of Saudi ideology, via American culture.

"Such is the price we pay to be entertained," said Amro Hosny. "How much do we lose?"

I told him I'd been asking that question for half my life.

He smiled and returned his gaze to the street outside, ghostly at twilight. "I know I am complicit. But out there—in this place, Egypt—to get food, you have to do some terrible things." He sipped his coffee to the dregs, and said, with great feeling, "Fuck you, Shrek, you big green motherfucker."

Part III

'ASR

5

Turn Up the Noise, Turn Down the Suck

EGYPT 2.0

Muslim: 90%

Coptic: 9%

7% GDP

1. Wasted Land:
   Into Chaos I Lost

2. Odious:
   Poems Hidden on
   Black Walls

3. Mastodon:
   The Wolf Is Loose

Pop.: 81,713,520

Avg. age: 24.5

Capital: Cairo

Independence: Feb 28, 1922

It hurt because I wasn't expecting it—a sensation like toilet plungers placed at my ears, toggled furiously. The meat spilled from my kebab, splatting like horror movie gore onto my sneakers. Kids rushed the stage, hands raised, mouths open. Everyone was just as startled as I: No one believed the show would go ahead; no one believed it would last. Noise poured from the stage, only to loop indignantly back into the amps as wails of agonizing feedback. It was if the spirits of pharaohs, buried only a few miles from here in big brick triangles, were protesting this sonic indignity.

I was swept to the front of the crowd, limp remainders of kebab in my hand. Above me, Wasted Land, late of Jeddah, Saudi Arabia, threw their heads forward in unison. The screams came from Emad Mujalled's diaphragm, heaving upward in the clutch of his black T-shirt. Thick rolls of belly fat now had a function—to propel rage from the pit of his gut into the world. His beard dripped spit and sweat.

We came to conquer, he yelled.

The other four members of Wasted Land emitted a low growl and the innocuously named Egypt Music Gates gig was—against every odd imaginable—suddenly underway. And I wondered whether Wasted Land and their ilk—like the ancient Israelites who destroyed the ramparts of Jericho with blasts of their ram's horns—could bring down the walls that contained them with nothing more than their instruments. Outside, in the sinking light, men in suits stood smoking, watching. It was their job to kill the noise.

The air off the Nile was warm and soft, and the boats—a motley flotilla of fellucas, river ferries and retrofitted cruise ships—bobbed and blazed with colored lights. This made the sight of seven metal heads lumbering down the boardwalk, laden with the appurtenances of their subculture—long greasy hair, studded work boots, dangling chains, T-shirts depicting death in all its grisly manifestations—seem all the more incongruous. I had doubted their existence at first, but not any longer. They were Saudis, members of the bands Wasted Land and Deathless Anguish, visiting the city for the euphemistically named Egypt Music Gates Fest. This may have explained their presence among all the jeans-and-T-shirt-wearing young men and stroller-pushing families, but didn't really *explain* their presence. For that, I had to rely on the voice at the other end of my Nokia.

"I'm running late," said the man who called himself Karim, voice husky from a decade's worth of yelling along to Mayhem and Dio. "I'll be at the Dokki Sheraton in thirty minutes." I bought a cob of brazier-roasted corn, dodged offers of "special massages" from men with no teeth, and walked along the Tahrir Bridge toward the concrete hunk of the Sheraton Hotel.

Half an hour later, Karim struggled out of a toy-like Fiat cab. Six and a half feet tall, furious blotches of acne on his cheeks, Karim heaved himself forward onto the Cairo street. He stared down at me, his small eyes poking from a donut of pasty flesh, hair buzzed down to the scalp. His black T-shirt was marbled with sweat stains. Egyptian metal heads call themselves Metaliens: I half expected him to demand that I take him to my leader.

Instead he said, "I welcome you. I welcome you to real metal."

Implicit in this gentle salutation was the fact that metal is far from an anomaly in the Muslim world. There's the Dubai Desert Rock Festival, headlined in 2008 by Korn and Machine Head. There's Morocco's four-day Boulevard des Jeunes Musiciens, featuring Puppetmastaz and Band of Gnawa. There are, on the occasionally active Egypt Metal portal, thousands of kids claiming to be in metal bands. Egypt alone boasts the sonic mayhem of Hate Suffocation, Wyvern, Promised Dawn, Nemesis and Ignoramas among others. I'd seen metal T-shirts in Abu Dhabi, Doha, Dubai, Damascus, Tripoli. Even Pakistan has a brilliant hard rock outfit called Junoon. Despite the genre's seeming prevalence, Karim was jittery: As the principal organizer of the modest Egypt Music Gates concert, he was responsible for the presence of those Saudi metal heads along the Nile boardwalk. He was taking an enormous risk, and he knew, more than anyone, what the stakes were. After all, when he was only eleven years old, Karim was charged with the rather serious twin offence of "humiliating religion and Satanism."

Which means that Karim was arrested and thrown in jail for rocking out.

★   ★   ★

January 22, 1997. Dawn breaks: Imams call the faithful for *fajr*. This is the cue. Across Heliopolis, Mohandessin and other middle-class Cairo neighborhoods, men with truncheons, wearing the white uniform of the Egyptian police, gather in the doorways of apartment buildings and homes. Plainclothes Mukhabarat—the fist of the regime—keep watch. As figures walk toward the mosque, these men kick their black boots against the doors of respectable homes.

Boys lie in beds. On their walls hang posters for Megadeth, Metallica, Iron Maiden. Electric guitars stand in cases layered with stickers, alongside portable amps with band names written in whiteout. They wake startled, and listen as their parents rush to the door in alarm. Flashlights blind them. Harsh hands take fistfuls of their hair. And to the soundtrack of their mothers' wails, they are taken from their homes to nearby jail cells where they are locked up along with men who whisper the words of the Qur'an, promising to rip them limb from limb as soon as God sees fit to turn Egypt into the mother of all battlegrounds.

The raids become known as the Satanic Panic. Egyptian police swept through the lairs of young Metaliens, amassing contraband ranging from Black Sabbath to Beethoven's 5th (the cops no doubt knowing the combination had influenced heavy metal guitarist/ Zionist provocateur Yngwie Malmsteen). They ripped posters from walls, destroyed instruments and even made off with a black Bugs Bunny T-shirt—the tchotchkes of middle-class youth the world over.

Almost one hundred young suspects—between the ages of Karim's eleven and twenty-five—were interrogated about their extracurricular pursuits. Questions ranged from the theological ("Do you participate in pagan rituals?") to the morbid ("Do you spit on graves?") to the veterinary ("Do you skin cats?"). It was two weeks before the public prosecutor, citing lack of evidence, ordered their release.

Fourteen days in a Cairo jail is a lifetime. (One kid, now an engineer in Alexandria, was held for forty-five days.) The press hysteria accompanying the arrests sent ripples through Egyptian middle-class society, stifling a number of then-burgeoning music scenes and establishing in the popular imagination a link between hard rock and Satanism. The accused were reportedly strip-searched and afforded the same hospitality extended to Egypt's criminal class; the raid was reminiscent of, and organized in the same manner as, the routine dragnets that rounded up Islamist elements. This is neatly summed up by the (possibly apocryphal) story of a mother of two sons—one a metal head, the other a militant Islamist. When the cops knocked on the door that fateful January morning, the mother did what she could to clear up the misunderstanding: "No, no—Ahmed doesn't wear a beard and he doesn't go to the mosque! He has long hair, he wears black T-shirts with monsters on them and plays in a band called Scar Tissue. My God, you have the wrong son!" This is less a story of one family than it is a story of Egypt.

The storm passed, as one poetic reporter put it, "like the coming and going of the *khamsim*"; the murder of twelve Coptic Christians by Islamic terrorists grabbed the national headlines directly thereafter. Nonetheless, the Satanic Panic was a warning. Only recently have young Egyptians dared to pull on their black T-shirts once again.

The Egyptian arrests were by no means the only such incident in the region. In Morocco, for example, on March 14, 2003, there was another assault on black-clad longhairs. Fourteen young men in the capital of Rabat, all members of the country's well-established metal scene, were arrested for a range of offences including "possession of objects contrary to good morals." Again, it was black T-shirts that seemed to cause the most offense. ("Normal people," pronounced the judge in the case, "go to a concert in a suit and tie.") The Rabat arrests were met with a storm of protest—hundreds, maybe thousands of supporters rallied outside Rabat's parliament building for the metal heads' release. In an appeals trial, eleven of the fourteen were acquitted. Running the math, three Moroccan metal heads were successfully prosecuted for devil worship.

These arrests remind us of an interesting period in rock 'n' roll's inadvertent war against tyranny. In 1968, after the collapse of the Prague Spring, when massive crackdowns and the implementation of the "normalization process" retuned Czechoslovakia to the icy bosom of Communist rule, a band called Plastic People of the Universe emerged from the wreckage. Plastic People claimed that they weren't political, but they knew that merely by existing—by playing the music inspired by the avant-rock of Velvet Underground and Frank Zappa—they couldn't avoid the tag. Their very existence was an affront to the powers-that-be. Partly inspired by their arrest in 1976, Vaclav Havel and other Czech intelligentsia issued Charter 77, one of the most heartfelt and articulate pleas for the tenets of basic human rights during the dark years of communism.

There was no Charter 77 after the Satanic Panic. Rather, the scene dissipated, scuttling so far underground that it would take almost a decade to re-emerge. Support from the Egyptian intellectual class was scant. Terrified youth were cowed, sent to live with relatives here, there and everywhere. A small pop-cultural fissure that could have inspired an outcry was quickly plastered over.

The reason for this lies at the heart of why the arrests took place, going as they did beyond a mere distaste for thrash metal or a loathing for the capitalist dogs that play it. Partly, they were meant, as one Egyptian economist put it, "as a sop to keep radical Islamists harmlessly diverted while showing that the regime could be just as tough on more secularist threats." But perhaps the following offers a more plausible explanation: "Egypt was going through a particularly tough passage in its continuous struggle to come to terms with influences from the West, what the late longshoreman-philosopher Eric Hoffer might call the 'ordeal of change.' It's not really the devil, or even the West with which Egypt is wrestling," wrote reporter James T. Napoli. "It is wrestling with change." In this, it is no surprise that the authorities claimed that the Metalien's Satanist HQ was a newly opened McDonald's in Cairo's swanky Heliopolis neighbourhood.

"I was arrested for what?" asked Karim, who walked with the bowlegged shuffle of a big man in a gorilla suit. "I was arrested for *music!*" I followed him from the Sheraton, Dokki's foremost landmark, toward the Pyramisa Hotel—scene of the 2001 Pyramisa Incident. Local heavy metal lore is full of remembered tragedies, and the incident in question was supposed to be the first gig since the Satanic Panic. The authorities crashed the party, sending hundreds of kids home. It's difficult for a Westerner to understand how devastating this was for the participants. They were robbed of the one evening of communal music worship they had been craving for four long years. It did nothing short of break their hearts.

Karim pointed to a police officer in a white, too-big uniform stationed at the Pyramisa entrance. "The main guys—the guys at the top of the force—well, they understand that you can't arrest a child. But these guys barely have high school. They have no problem with it. Believe me. I know. Meantime, the Pyramisa is filled with generals and cops and spooks from all over the world, signing documents for people to get murdered. Full of scum." He spat onto the sidewalk.

Contributing massively to the low-rent John le Carré vibe was Gina, an eighteen-year-old Ukrainian diplo-brat who spoke fluent Arabic. She was as mysterious as a movie spy with the cleavage to match. Gina was Karim's right-hand woman; if she could kill someone with her shoe, I would have been unsurprised. "Gina, for the love of the Prophet, goes for weird people," explained Karim as we gathered ourselves on couches in the lobby. "But she does love this music. She does. She is heavy metal all the way." Gina looked past me and exhaled a thin stream of cigarette smoke.

"We *do* love this music," continued Karim. It was a refrain of his—a verbal tic interchanged with several others like "We *do* love our country" and "We *do* love our religion." He was constantly defending himself to some omniscient accuser, neatly summing up the contradictions of being a metal head in a country like Egypt: religion vs. music; local culture vs. imported culture; a secular social outlet vs. the mosque. These were not easy elements to reconcile, especially when the government has a massive stake in how teenagers, who make up more than half of the population, behave.

"Kids, you see, are very influenced," said Karim, after we had settled in the hotel's lobby, painted a hue reminiscent of final-stage gangrene. He spoke about the scene back in 1996 with a mixture of nostalgia and distaste. "They were dressing like Satanists, wearing inverted crosses without really knowing the meaning. Many of the children were having long hair. Many adults were thinking this was a cult; they would listen to *Master of Puppets*, which talks about devil worshippers, and think that this is what we were about—even though they knew we were not. That's just the way kids are."

"Is that the way you were?" I asked.

"Yes—I used to love my Metallica T-shirts. Look—even though I love Iron Maiden, I'm a proud Muslim. I'm proud of my culture— I have no problem regarding that. It was a stage in my life."

"It looks like you're still in it," I said. After all, we were here two days before a metal show that he was organizing. He played bass for a death metal band called, unambiguously, Eternal Damnation.

"Perhaps I am still in it. But the times have changed. They have changed. But we *do* love our country."

The times have indeed changed. During Egypt's metal heyday, kids used to hang around in downtown Cairo's Midan Tahrir and near the City Star Mall and that accursed McDonald's in Heliopolis, much the way metal heads and punkers do in most Western cities. They were identifiable, they were noisy, they were messy. According to Saif, drummer for Egypt-metal stalwarts Wyvern, the nineties scene was "Monsters of Rock big. You could have shows of twenty thousand. But after the arrests, everything collapsed."

Karim hauled his bulk forward. "It really starts with a bunch of dumb-ass journalists who say we are having group sex and killing cats—a lot of dumb-ass shit—we are doing drugs, devil worship. And the process goes on. And they do arrest us."

He was referring to a fairly standard Egyptian ploy: involve the state-run media in a social campaign, soften up the populace, follow up with a burst of stringent police activity. After the arrest, Karim was sent by his shaken parents to boarding school in Massachusetts, where he would be under the watchful eye of relatives. His T-shirts were shredded and his CDs trashed. As a bewildered preteen he had wandered from jail straight into a foreign country that didn't blink at exactly the sort of behavior for which he had been incarcerated. But he was far too young and unsure of himself to understand and fully appreciate his circumstances. He was quiet in America. It was only on his return to Egypt that a rebellious streak bubbled up in him, an impulse to raise the devil horns once again and damn the bastards to hell. Within reason, of course.

"Did you want to come back?" I asked.

"Frankly, no. Don't get me wrong—I *do* love Egypt. But sometimes we feel like an outcast here in Egypt. That's why I started this organization—Egypt Music Gates."

Gina lit another cigarette and stared at us through the smoke—it was going on two in the morning, and the hotel air was chilled beyond comfort.

"The name doesn't sound very metal," I said.

"Not at all. It's not just for metal. It's for metal *and* rock. And we don't want to look for problems.

"We do love our country," continued Karim. "Some of the lyrics that I do write is about the political situation—about the government. But not attacking the government—but about our dreams. And Palestine. The Israelis. Killing our children, trashing our cities, raping our women. We are very pissed from that. And we never insult our religion. Even at this concert—we read over the lyrics of the songs very careful—no insult to religion. No hate." Israel is, of course, exempted from these restrictions. Camp David Accords notwithstanding, that country is Egypt's perennial bugaboo.

"If any band member is caught in a drunk-type situation—they are banned. The message we're trying to send: We do respect religion, we do respect our country, we do respect authority. There can be no racism by any means. Peace! We are for that. We are against saying anything bad. We're trying to make the scene safer, better. We are very well educated people, very considerate, very kind, very classy. We study each and every message we send. They consider headbanging how we pray—how we talk to the devil. They think Pink Floyd is devil music. They are ignorant. They are dumb. And we do laugh our asses off at them."

"So this is a passion more than a political movement?" I asked.

"A political movement? No, no. We are very careful. For instance, a journalist called me up and said she wanted to cover the gig. She said she is doing a report on unfamiliar stuff, weird stuff, the abnormal stuff. I said, 'What? This is not weird, not abnormal.' Heavy metal is some of the bestselling music of all time—why it is weird, abnormal?

I said no to the interview. I said she cannot come to the show. She is banned."

"And your parents? Your family? How do they feel about this stuff now?"

Karim brought a large hand down over his face in a gesture of great weariness. There were beads of sweat on his temple despite the Pyramisa's iciness. "My parents will often ask me: 'Why do this? Why all the work, and you don't get paid? And the danger!' And I tell them this: 'Because I *love* it.'"

For a moment, Karim seemed like he was going to lose control, to hurl his girth around the veneer of this hotel—where terrible people are said to make horrible deals late into the night—screaming his rage into every corrupt, contemptuous ear. Slowly, Cairo's kids were doing a version of the same: picking up guitars, assembling drum kits. Slowly, renascent metal heads were heading back into the light, which is to say the darkness. Slowly, a spirit of gentle rebellion festered among the city's young middle class. They organized online. They blogged. They tried to make a place for themselves, virtual or otherwise.

Gina leaned in and said something to Karim in soft, Russian-inflected Arabic. He nodded.

"Gina reminds me, we are dying to make a festival at the pyramids site," said Karim. I raised an eyebrow. This was about as likely as a gay marriage benefit concert co-hosted by The Dick Cheney Rainbow Tolerance Foundation and the Muslim Brotherhood.

"It's a dream," said Karim. "But Gina would like to say that we do dream. And our dreams must come true," a notion that Gina punctuated by exhaling into the Pyramisa's frigid atrium. Karim gazed up—looking at least thirty years older than his twenty-one—and watched Gina's cloud dissipate. The visual metaphor did not seem lost on him.

There must have been something in the pop-cultural water. While I was engaged in my own quest, there was a surge of similar heavy metal punditry. In 2008, a book—*Heavy Metal Islam* by professor and metal musician Mark LeVine—and two fine documentaries were released, all covering aspects of heavy metal in the Muslim world. The first film, *Global Metal,* was a sequel of sorts to anthropologist/metal head Sam Dunn and director Scot McFadyen's *Metal: A Headbanger's Journey.*

"7 Countries. 3 Continents. 1 Tribe," screams the film's tagline, and it is Dunn and McFadyen's contention that this most-maligned form of Western music has been adopted, transformed and absorbed into the cultures of embattled societies the world over. The film was an attempt to understand the cultural nuances of globalization rather than the mechanics of globalization itself. The resulting message was as warm as a hug: "We are all one, united through subcultures like metal."

The second film was something of a revelation. *Heavy Metal in Baghdad* is the tragic story of an (or rather, the only) Iraqi heavy metal group, name of Acrassicauda. The film looks at the Iraq war and its bloody aftermath through the eyes of four young metal heads, articulating just how high the stakes are for teenagers in countries like Iraq and Egypt, especially when they decide to hitch their identity to a pop-cultural black sheep like metal.

To many, heavy metal is a nail-studded baseball bat to the temple, administered by a sweaty ingrate in leather pants. I've always sat uneasily on the fence. I'm never sure how a band like Cannibal Corpse (their lead singer's voice is in a key the residents of *South Park* call the "brown note"—a register low enough to loosen bowels) manages to get ten people into a venue, let alone ten thousand. And I'm not sure what to think about a musical genre in which something called a "death grunt" (don't ask) is a legitimate stylistic technique. Still, Guns N' Roses remains a—if not *the*—significant milestone on my lifelong musical journey, and my pocket money contributed to the smack budget of hair metal bands Whitesnake, Def Leppard and Mötley Crüe. Where these bands stand in the taxonomy of true metal is endlessly debatable, but there it is.

Despite my vacillations, I've always understood the *impulse* behind metal: the rage, the noise, the power chords, the pointless umlauts. And I've understood, since my late teens, that the more dense and unlistenable the music, the more entirely it is owned by a particular sub-culture. Hardcore music is not meant to adhere to any established sense of aesthetics—your Great-aunt Ethna, cool though she may be, is not supposed to get off on Wretched Animal's "Scrotum Death Machine." This sort of music is designed to be exclusionary. And in many countries in the Muslim world, that exclusion doesn't merely result in arguments with one's parents. It results in a fundamental argument with one's culture.

For Acrassicauda in Iraq, as it was for Karim in Egypt, metal is the only outlet that makes sense, and it becomes the only thing worth fighting for. The bands and their fans take serious personal risks in trying to put on shows, in growing their hair, in identifying with anything "American." In Western cultures, and especially in America, where the idea of the individualist is inviolable, we cultivate a sense of being outside the mainstream that buys into the very mainstream idea of portraying ourselves as outsiders. In other words, we've tamed the notion of being an "outsider," because *all of us* are outsiders. This is how we've managed to subvert, own and make cash-money from rebellion.

Heavy Metal in Baghdad reminds us of what it means to be a real outsider. The documentary depicts, among other things, Acrassicauda's last Iraqi show in Baghdad's Al Fanar Hotel—played to intermittent blackouts and the background accompaniment of gunfire—and how much the success of the show means to the participants. "If we cannot find some fun here," asks one audience member, almost begging the camera, "then where?" It is the same question that could be asked wherever there is a metal scene in the Muslim world. It was the same question asked by Karim.

On a very basic level, *Heavy Metal in Baghdad* warns us not to dismiss the appeal of junk-culture and shows us how important a bridge it can be between so-called opposing civilizations. "There is a kind of universality with youth culture—a lexicon of common cultural references that can act as a dialogue," director Eddy Moretti has said. "This stuff touches young people at a time when their lives are open, and it can be kind of revolutionary in that respect."

But that isn't really the point of the film. Moretti has depicted the plight of ordinary Iraqis through the lens of a pop-cultural idiom. I recognized the adult weariness, the sheer exhaustion in the eyes of Acrassicauda's members: I had seen it in Karim, his life knocked off course by his preteen brush with the Egyptian legal system. I remember him saying to me, looking at his feet, partly chastened and partly defiant: "We *do* love this music. We *do* love it. But we know the music is weak. It doesn't have the answers that the great religions do. But we do love this music. And we will not give up."

Misguided courage? A quixotic tilt at a windmill with a V-neck guitar? Why risk pulling on that black T-shirt, I wondered, when it can lead so easily to more metal, this time administered to the ribcage by one of those young men of the Mukhabarat?

I lay on my bed in Cairo's Berlin Hotel and held aloft the flyer Karim had given me. *Metal Fest!* it promised. *Keep it Metal!* it implored. The band names were inscribed with the standard metal iconographic ornament: spiders' webs (Dark Philosophy, from Egypt), inverted crosses (Tyrant Throne, from Jordan), bats' wings (Wyvern, from Egypt) and a combination of all three (Deathless Anguish and Wasted Land, from the Kingdom of Saudi Arabia).

That was, I thought, one mother of a lineup.

My iPod was blaring the music of Odious, a Euro-based Egyptian band that effectively married heavy metal to Eastern music in a rather ass-kicking synthesis of two disparate cultures—all in the service of making ears bleed. "*Apophenia formed another living lie,*" screamed vocalist Bassem Fakhri on "Invitation to Chaotic Revelation." Huge drums, the wail of an *oud*, bass so low only insects can hear it, guitar as meaty as pumped pectoral muscle.

But the mourning cannot hear
Debilitating the unsightly pyramids of horror and fear
And when the mutilated tongue creates new letters
We will fight for writing the brave words and believing them
When the hand can rise and hold we will fight to be inside
But a mirage was the idea of sin 'cause we were born so blind
Born killed hope of salvation

I did not interpret this as happy music. Metal's lyrics—at least since the genre shed the sex-drenched blues influence of Led Zeppelin—have been famously inchoate. What, one asks, does all this *mean*? A better question would be: What does it evoke? The genre, wrote Jeffrey Arnett in *Metalheads*, "is the sensory equivalent of war." If so, Odious put me square in the middle of Fallujah, *circa* 2004, frags exploding around my bewildered head. Jacked as I was on week three of Cairo's mayhem, it was like having my soul exfoliated.

Metal lyrics in the Muslim world are almost always allusions to the standard geek-noir imagery of Tolkien and *Dungeons & Dragons*. One must dig deep to find even a hint of Islam. There is an odd, loopy, overblown poetry to them: Anne Rice meets Edgar Allan Poe by way of Elvira, garnished with a Christian-Goth sensibility: I pictured knights, swords, horses with burning eyes, demure babes with ruby-red lips. Where were the Saracen warriors, the veiled chicks, the flapping green banners? Middle Eastern metal was a fantasy space, borrowed from scenes in Norway, Britain and the United States. It was an effective way to conjure life here, this moonless, agonized lyricism.

But they do occasionally share vocabulary, imagery and outlook with crazed fundamentalist mullahs. Your average terrorist spokesperson, for instance, could pen a pretty cool metal song. Metal "hyper-aggressively [embraces] the death instinct, regimented chaos, deliriously fetishiz[ing] morbidity," writes cultural commentator Howard Hampton. So do most of the folks on the Pentagon's Most Wanted list. They speak a version of the Metalien's unsubtle adolescent-ese. That's not to say that said Metaliens were terrorists-in-waiting.

Metal has another dark secret: It is as Karim noted, some of the bestselling music of all time. Until flannel-wearing grungers decimated unsuspecting hair bands, metal moved records like no other genre except pop. Even after metal was in supposed death throes at the hands of Kurt Cobain, Metallica's self-titled album has sold twenty-two million copies. Indeed, Metallica has moved one hundred million records over the course of its career; Iron Maiden has sold over seventy million; and, by way of random example, Skid Row sold two million copies of its ineffably shitty 1991 record *Slave to the Grind.* But then MTV cancelled *Headbangers Ball* in 1994, and in the wake of the highly publicized murder of a Norwegian black metal vocalist/Satanist Euronymous in 1993, metal was pushed underground, and two very interesting things happened.

Outside of the officially sanctioned mainstream, metal sprouted myriad branches, categories and subsections. Black metal, death metal, doom metal, glam metal, thrash metal, grindcore. Each was more cloistered than the next, and metal garnered so many stalwart acolytes precisely because of these divisions. "Death to fake metal," as the maxim goes. In this, metal, more than any other musical genre, is like a major religion.

That's not a metaphorical observation for its own sake, but rather shows why metal—and the attendant inter-genre antipathy—is so prevalent in two of the Middle East's most restrictive societies: Egypt and Iran. There is a familiarity to the genre's social formula. It easily becomes a proxy religion and follows a familiar pattern of behavior for those who can no longer stomach the irrationality of theological squabbling. After all, it becomes preposterous for local metal heads to debate whether there is a hidden twelfth Iman (a major point of ecumenical contention between Shiite and Sunni) when they could be arguing whether Mastodon's *Blood Mountain* is great speed metal or crappy death metal. Metal allows the fan to stake an extreme position, to become a believer. And to constantly and consistently argue the validity of one's position, without irony, and without brooking disagreement. At a certain point, metal is no longer a hobby. It becomes life, a vital part of identity. To strip a metal head of that black T-shirt would be like tearing the prayer raiments from a *hajj*.

It was Friday the thirteenth, shortly before noon, and throughout the tony neighborhood of Zamalek, mullahs' sermons blasted from speakers out onto the streets. I took a slug from a surreptitious can of beer, trying to get into a metal frame of mind. The sidewalks were lined with strips of Astroturf, and men knelt, listening—overflow from the sidewalk mosques. As they bent in unison to pray, it looked as if they were prostrating themselves before Zamalek's Nike boutique, bowing before Phil Knight's swoosh, praying to sweat-wicking tank tops and heel-supporting sneakers.

In Cairo on Friday, Islam infiltrates all public space. Mullahs' words own the street, public address systems crackle with the exhortations of skinny, often very young, men, who fulminate in high voices, while rows and rows of the devout stare forward at a spot in space and time where there is only pure faith. On one hand, it is a show of facelessness that was extraordinary in its scope. On the other, it is a beautiful expression of communal faith and brotherhood, played out on a huge human canvas.

Today, Karim and his fellow black-clad head bangers would perform a similar ritual, on a smaller scale. Within metal, the outsider is an insider: It is a ring of safety, a community. If the establishment Muslims praying on Zamalek's sidewalks were to behold a room of slobbering metal fans, they would probably be revolted, but to watch people carried away by anything that captures their soul, be it Mohammed or Motörhead, is a disquieting experience.

At that moment in Egypt's history, choices were being defined. The Muslim Brotherhood—Egypt's longtime Islamist agitators—is fragmenting, breaking up into factions, some of whom wear the suits and spew the rhetoric of young politicians from the Western world. They do not preach suicide bombing, but rather the processes of liberal democracy in the context of an Islamist state. Was there space for Karim in their vision of a future Egypt? Was there room for these cultural and generational differences that young people everywhere will always insist upon, to their eternal credit?

Prayers over, men streamed into the streets, holding hands, stunned into silence from the heat. Against their tide, I saw Karim struggle his way toward me.

The pyramids loomed through the smog like the barely remembered lyrics of an ancient ballad—hunks of geometry shimmering in the fierce lunchtime heat. The cab, its shock absorbers long since dead, crunched along the highway.

Sweat poured down Karim's face as if he'd just stepped from a rainstorm. Apropos of nothing he said, "We are *not* terrorists."

Our cab turned off onto a rutted street lined with jerry-rigged resorts that would not have been out of place as set design for *Revenge of the Double-D Pharaoh Queens*. They stood alongside flimsy "official" government papyrus museums—elaborate set-ups for tourists guileless enough to take the term "official" in Egypt as anything but the opening movement of a con job.

The cab turned down a long drive and dropped us off at El Bodega Village, a faux-Spanish villa that was fronted by a concrete patio hung with Chinese lanterns. The hall was a wide room decorated with bright-red tiles. Men in tank tops shifted equipment around, building a wall of speakers beside a makeshift stage. This was Karim's backup venue. The municipal authorities had forced him to use it.

"It so sucks," said Karim, "but we moved it here. Don't worry, we're about to make a new history." Gina appeared beside him, smoking, staring at me.

"You know," she said, vowels crawling under the weight of her accent, "there are men watching us. They want to stop this. It may not happen, still." I looked outside and saw two men in suits that hung like flesh from sun-dried carcasses. They smoked with the same urgency Gina did.

As incongruous as those Mukhbarat hacks looked, what on earth seems more bedraggled, more hopelessly out of place than a metal head in daylight? These are nocturnal creatures, best suited to the cover of darkness. There's something especially poignant about a Saudi Arabian metal head in daylight. This is a person born to another world, a Metalien who will likely never find a home here on our planet. Emad Mujalled of Wasted Land was a big lad, his long hair tied back in a ponytail matted with sweat, his long beard somehow metal rather than Islamic. Like Karim, he was gently geeky rather than intimidating. Did the men in suits know what they were up against here? If they were expecting to take a Jack Daniel's bottle to the head, they were bound for disappointment.

"In Saudi," Emad told me, "we have started the scene about three or four years ago—we're still improving, and we are trying to get the government to allow us to make gigs. You need to get a license if there is to be a gig, and it's not easy to get a license. So we usually just do it in private places—and we just jam. But the last show we had in Jeddah—we had about three hundred to five hundred people—all local Saudis. So hopefully we get the chance to improve the scene."

There have been four semi-public metal shows in Saudi Arabian history—the last called S.A. Metal Gig III, which was, as the title suggests, the third such show, and apparently the best. All have been heavily monitored by the *matawa*, a semi-formal religious police force that keeps Saudi behaviour in line with official notions of propriety.

"We got into this music because we want something different," said Emad, "not just the hip-hop all the time. So we find ourselves looking at rock, and we go even further backward, and find ourselves looking toward metal. Then, of course, we find Metallica. And everything changes. But for me, it was the guitar that counts. It is all about the guitar. I think metal becomes big because it is something new—it is strange in our country—and we want to get people used to it, to make them see that metal is not a problem."

"And is this happening?"

"It's hard to reach people, but it is also very hard because many in the country are very religious, and this music is very upsetting to them. These people don't like the Western stuff. Hip-hop and rap is fine—everyone is listen to that—but rock is maybe too heavy. People in Saudi is very concerned at how they look, and rock is very noisy, while hip-hop is always on the TV and the media."

That mainstream American hip-hop is tacitly accepted by the *matawa* in Saudi Arabia while rock and metal are verboten may at first seem utterly confounding. But hip-hop, as we'll learn later, conforms to at least a notion of traditional Arabic percussion. Jay-Z's fleet of Maybachs and Ferraris would not be out of place in Riyadh, nor would the genre's surface sense of rapacious consumption. Meanwhile, the very sound of the electric guitar is the wail of decadence, remembered by ultra-conservative Saudis as the rot that made the hated Petro-Boomers supplicants to the sixties.

"Despite all, we are hopefully looking to expand the music," said Emad, "by explaining that it is not something to be afraid of. The Internet is very helpful—we send demos, upload it to MySpace—and it is doing well. Someday, we hope we will play in our country without any problems."

"There a chance Slayer will ever play Saudi?" I asked.

"Yes—maybe after one thousand years," said Emad, deadpan. "They will die and come back to life first."

There was an awful tension in the hall, as if we were blood cells in a constricted artery. Outside, the men in bad suits looked in, black circles around their eyes. Gina smoked as though she was trying to raise the global price of tobacco. Band members chewed fingernails. I sucked at a bottle of water, wishing it were a Stella.

Egypt Music Gates had become a gathering of young people—a broad cross-section of Egypt's middle-class youth, along with a smattering of young foreigners like Gina. Hosni Mubarak's regime did not look kindly on gatherings of this sort. They used as an excuse the hardline Islamic prejudice against music—attributed to the so-called *lawh al-hadith*—which is considered a ban on instruments, vocal performances or anything else that could possibly lead to rocking out. The roots of the *hadith* are traced back to Sayyidana Abdullah bin Masood, a boon companion of the Prophet, who said, "I swear by Him besides whom there is no other God, that [the *lawh al-hadith*] refers to *ghina'a* (singing)." This plays into the usual religious rhetoric decrying the corrupting influence of music, as common with strait-laced pastors as it is with imams.

But Karim and his black-clad crew—along with many Muslims similar in outlook—could find no specific reference in the Qur'an that forbids music. They remind their opponents that the Qur'an is a recitation of God's word as it was told to Mohammed, and therefore even the Prophet's *hadiths*, or sayings, can never supersede it. If God didn't think to outlaw music, then it clearly wasn't worth outlawing, at least according to those who consider the *hadiths*—most of which were written hundreds of years after the Prophet died—a corruption of a simple religion that should by rights have but one ecumenical source. Whether God was anticipating Axl Rose in all this, no one can say. But it does serve to show that a Muslim music devotee can offer as many Qur'anic zingers as his anti-music counterpart. The matter remains inconclusive, and is—as with the Taliban—usually settled by the party with the bigger gun.

Suddenly, from the stage, a hammering of war drums. Those of us in the hall looked up sharply. Karim nodded and walked over to the members of Wasted Land, had a quick confab, nodded again. The sun was setting; the world outside was the purple of a three-day-old shiner. Emad Mujalled hauled his bulk onto the stage, stared at the microphone. Ahmed Khoja picked up his guitar. I sipped water. The men in suits watched. Fear moved through the crowd like a ghost. Karim nodded.

Then came the noise.

★ ★ ★

We came to conquer!

They rushed the stage: scions of Egypt's middle class—their metal T-shirts freshly washed and pressed—a handful of expatriates, and even a few girls. Two mothers, thick wads of cotton wool jammed into their ears, followed the kids toward the stage; a squeal of feedback sent them reeling toward the exit.

The bass nestled in my gut like a fat slug, writhing, looking for an exit of its own. Each chord felt like two fists driven hard at my sternum. I looked over at Karim. There were tears in his eyes.

I marched into the field of living memories
Looking for forgotten dreams.
My freedom been locked within the key of resisting gates
Hold up my men!

The road to triumph paved by warrior's agony
This is the sign of rambling thunders
Unleashing my innermost brutality
The bells of death falls in the tottering towers.

The tiles along the walls looked like dried blood in the low light of dusk. Thumps of bass from the amps pushed heat from the stage in thick waves.

It occurred to me, from my place inside this crush of young people, from my vantage point within the eye of their obsession, that heavy metal made an important claim to local legitimacy. It filled a most surprising vacuum. This music cradled the ancient Arabic notion of *tarab*—the ability for music or poetry to transport the listener into a state of transcendental ecstasy. It's a discipline that has almost entirely disappeared from contemporary mass-produced Arabic music, what with the preponderance of garbage pop and fourth-rate trance that blasts from the vehicles of the Caireen *shebab*. But there was *tarab* here in the El Bodega—as pure and untrammelled as it exists in the music of the great singers that Karim's parents would have worshipped. *Tarab is* a beautiful, natural escape hatch—a way to find a space apart from the horrors of this world. It is a way to commune with the exceptional. It is a prayer rug woven from sound.

Later, on the patio, I sat across from Sameh Sabry. He called himself Slacker, and he is the scene's unofficial archivist. We were worn out, wrung dry, stupid with dehydration. Still, Slacker arranged himself with élan on the plastic patio chair. He spoke like a philosopher steeped in both Socrates and Scorpions.

"Basically," said he, "any society is made on human power. And for me, I consider this as emotional music—with emotional words, painful words. It touches my soul. Why don't I like rap? It only mentions the girls he slept with or the car he drives. The music I listen to has so many meanings. It changes my life.

"My question to you is: Would you stop listening to the music you loved if someone was going to throw you in jail for it? If the answer is yes, then you don't love the music enough. I have been charged for Satanism; I have been called a devil worshipper. Many times. My name has been in print—with my age, my school—I was waiting for them to come for me. I did not change. I did not hide. You want a piece of me—come get it. Others are into it for fashion—but I really believe. For me, I think the music we do is preaching community. There's this community—and it's powerful."

Slacker leaned back in his chair and moaned at the sky. "I love the

American spirit—because it encourages you to be a hero. They make you feel big even when you are doing something small. And the reason why I love America is that I see the differences and I like the differences."

This from a man who has in no small part sacrificed his health for metal, or at least staked his well-being far beyond the bounds of acceptable risk. He told me that he had a heart condition, that he collapsed regularly from the stress. "It is crazy to live in this Middle East. The humiliation from Israel. The humiliation from America, even though I love the spirit. The humiliation from crazy governments. The crazy people. The crazy traffic, the noise, the pollution. We are the *damned*, man. Sometimes I don't know how long I can last. I fight for my life, buddy. I should give this up. But I can't."

We sat in silence, listening to the El Bodega shake from the rage of the music within, fluorescent lights flickering under a dirty Cairo night sky.

"It is the same here in Egypt as it is everywhere, is it not," asked Slacker. "A gathering of friends who love a small piece of culture beyond anything else. Here are young Egyptians and Saudis trying to find their identity. Through this, we assert some kind of difference from the crowd. This is the way of the Western childhood since the fifties, no? It *can't* be a bad thing. After all, where would all this aggression otherwise go?"

Karim lumbered up to us, soaked in his own sweat and that of his ecstatic patrons. He clamped a hand on my shoulder.

"Tell your friends back home," he said. "We dream here. We *do* dream. And look what can happen."

I returned downtown in a rusted cab. It was early morning. Thumping along the pitted on-ramp, I looked toward Giza and saw the pyramids lit up, beacons of an enormously distant past. The weight of that image overwhelmed my exhausted brain, shutting it down like a nuclear reactor after some great emergency: There was nothing but the low buzz of my damaged ears.

Forty-five minutes later, as I lay in my bed looking up at the Berlin's cracked ceiling, the power plant clicked back online: I wondered how we are supposed to reconcile the past and the manic present—how we are meant to make sense of the two—without bowing to some profound lunacy. How were Egyptians—or Saudi Arabians or Iraqis for that matter—supposed to square their forbidden passions like metal with decrepit regimes, religious or otherwise, that fill the crannies of everyday life? What I had seen that night was on some small level a revolution—or at least a concentrated act of defiance—played out to the fuzz and wail of heavy metal music. I had seen kids assert their right to rock.

There is this expectation, a shared if unarticulated belief that these bands—like the legendary Plastic People of the Universe, who carried the ethos of revolution inside the psych-swirl of their avant-rock—herald some hope for future freedoms. Regardless of lyrical content, simply by existing, merely by banging head, Wyvern, Deathless Anguish and company are harbingers of change. What sort of change? None of these young men and (very occasional) women seem to know. But at base, they seek change that represents the freedom to turn it up to eleven, to grow their hair, to scream at the devil, to find an outlet that isn't mandated by the government or their religion.

Outside on the patio during the concert, I had met a young woman in a hijab who was a reporter for the magazine *Al-Shabab—The Youth*. She had come with her brother, and they had stood out painfully at the show, wincing at every guitar lick. "This is so strange to me," the brother said. "Music should be pleasant. It must be about the refinedness of the melody. It must connect to your heart. It must connect to your soul. Please, Mr. Richard—I wish for you to think of the old Egyptian singers."

The reporter was looking away into the middle distance, and said something sharply in Arabic.

"I didn't catch that," I said to her brother.

"She says," he told me, "that this is not Egypt."

This is not Egypt.

I recalled standing on the top floor of a skyscraper in Cairo's Mohandessin district some weeks earlier. The view from the twenty-fifth floor of the Nahdet Misr building confirmed Cairo was more than a city; it was an entity, carpeting the earth to the horizon, fading into a soft-focus strip of pollution along the edge of the world, spilling off into the south, into Africa. "Cairo," a voice behind me had said, "is Egypt."

But what exactly was Egypt? Bent, poverty-stricken workers farming patches along the Nile? Aggressive touts peddling camel rides at the pyramids? Loving families strolling along the boardwalk? Disney Arabizers? Men on their knees on Astroturf listening to the wail of the mullah? Sharp-suited ex-military politicos doing deals in the Pyramisa? Or Karim and his love for a form of music that has few friends outside its network of passionate devotees?

The answer is, of course, all of the above. Between the authoritarianism of the government and their Islamist enemies, Karim and company were just trying to define some small space for themselves. Would Wyvern and Wasted Land be denied even the small concessions they were battling for? Certainly, they would have to fight for each death grunt and drum roll. In this, their mission was both tacitly political and explicitly, beautifully human.

They came to conquer. And in some small way, they had.

6

Ain't Nobody's Bitch

INDONESIA

Muslim: 86.1%

Protestant: 5.7%

Roman Catholic: 3%

Hindu: 1.8%

23% GDP

1. Silver Jews:
   Punks in the Beerlight
2. Wire:
   Reuters
3. The Brandals:
   Ain't Nobody Bitch
4. Teenage Death Star:
   Johnny in My Head

Pop.: 237,512,300

Avg. age: 27.2

Capital: Jakarta

Independence: Aug 17, 1945

The stage was a riser with a drum kit, two amps, four emaciated Indonesian kids. Everything in the room was carpeted: the floor, the walls, the ceiling, the doorknob. We had removed our shoes; the room stank of feet and vomit. I felt like I was in a deep-sea cave into which some vile leviathan had crawled in order to scream itself to death.

"You know Tumor Ganas—you know what this mean?" asked the kid next to me. His mohawk listed drunkenly in the heat of the cramped studio.

"It's the name of the band on stage, no?"

"Not just a band. You know what this means, Tumor Ganas?" he asked again. The kid had a vicious scar on his right bicep, a knot of damaged skin pocked with the remains of a tattoo he had burned off with a clothing iron.

"No idea," I said.

"You are lucky. Tumor Ganas is disease of the cock," he said, grabbing his crotch and making an "ouch" face.

The four members of Disease of the Cock assembled onstage; discordant fuzz screeched through the broken amps. The name was appropriate. I had met the lead singer earlier, outside, while drinking from a plastic bag of arak with the members of the punk outfit Hello War. He hopped off a Yamaha scooter with two Tumor Ganas band mates, their hair somehow maintaining architectural integrity under the weight of their helmets, and greeted me with the Nazi salute. He was all lean muscle; he had "Fuck Work" tattooed on his neck.

"Sieg, sieg *heil*," said Fuck Work, his face a magniloquent tangle of piercings.

I sipped from my baggie and looked at the tarmac.

"He does not like foreigners," said Hello War's bassist.

"Seems that way."

I scrunched up my baggie, tossing it on a pile of garbage growing steadily at the entrance of Stupa Studios, nestled against the train tracks that marked the city's southernmost limits. The air was heavy with the smoke of braziers and the *ojecks* that tore along the main road, their headlights cutting into the thick night. Shadows flitted along the red-tiled roofs; Jakarta seethed to the north of us like a coiled boa.

Inside the studio, feedback morphed into a roar. Fuck Work crouched over the microphone:

Fuuuuuuuuuuuuuuuuuuuuuuuuuuuuuuuuuuuuuuuuuuuuuuuuuuuuuuuuck!

The room heaved forward in a single movement, like a gag reflex before puking. I felt the kick drum in my sternum, the bass somewhere inside me. The crowd met the aggression head-on:

Raaaaaaaaaaaaaaaaaaaaaaaaaaaaaaaaaaaaaaarrrrrrrrrrrrrrrrrr!

Inside this pocket of fury, body slammed against body, sending ripples of flailing arms down to where I stood by the door. Each song was a ninety-second thrash punk ditty, yelled in a mulch of Bahasa and English. Fuck Work swiped at the crowd with his microphone, kicked at a kid who was on his knees. He looked up and over at me, and screeched *boulay, boulay, boulay*. White boy. Motherfucker.

In this room, anything was possible. Time slowed; droplets of blood and perspiration hung in the air, bodies froze in mid-combat.

"*This is fucking puuuuuuuuunk!*" screamed the kid next to me, his scar seeping pus.

This was punk indeed. All the pressure of Indonesian life—the crash of the markets, the crush of Jakarta, the rich getting richer, the poor getting poorer, the looming shadow of Islamism—all of it was set loose in this small studio. Whatever I believed punk was, I had never come close to its very *spirit* until I arrived here, the faraway jungle island of Java.

"*Fuck you* boulay," screamed Fuck Work.

"*And fuck you too*," screamed I. He grinned a gap-toothed grin, and lunged at me from the stage.

I made for the exit, and in my haste suffered a carpet burn from the door.

"Breakdance," Ari was saying.

He wielded the Vespa with impressive physicality, hauling it around corners, hopping it over sluices, bringing us side to side with a Camry and staring into the passenger window to intimidate the driver. We would come to a traffic light, line up in a huddle with dozens of other scooters belching fumes, and then tear off down a sluiced alley that in olden times flowed with cholera, chlamydia and oleander petals. This was once the poison jewel in the Dutch colonial crown: the great, pestilential city of Batavia. It is now called Jakarta.

"Breakdance," Ari was saying. "In the late eighties, all our parents say: 'Don't do it!' But we love it. Then skating. Then Metallica. Then punk. When Nirvana comes, we suddenly have a new consciousness. We are born again." He had a habit of turning to make eye contact. His helmet—more of a hard-shell yarmulke—dipped dangerously low on his brow.

I clung to his Black Flag T-shirt as we rounded into Jalan Masjid. Mosque Street. It forms the main artery of Jakarta's notorious Blok A neighborhood, where the homes are hutches, built on top of and inside one another: If Mordor had conquered Middle Earth, this is what hobbit houses would have looked like. Tweaked *preman*—street hustlers—guided us down a cobbled road barely fit for a mule cart, demanding coins like bridge trolls. Their pupils were dilated; they wore studded belts and Doc Martens. Fuck Work's spiritual brethren all.

Ari made for a scrawl of graffiti sprayed on an outside wall: *Food*, it read, *Not Bombs*. We drove under a line of laundry and straight into the living room of a house. Ari killed the engine, hopped off and disappeared.

I sat for a moment, trying to settle my thumping heart. In the gloom, I made out punk posters on the walls, revolutionary texts in both Bahasa and English arranged on a bookshelf dominated by a fetid toy Kenny from *South Park*. Cassettes lay pell-mell; a tin of Harrods malted biscuits sat on a shelf, as out of place as a tiara would have been on the large punk sitting cross-legged on the floor leafing through a back issue of *Rolling Stone*. She did not greet me, but burped loudly by way of salutation.

"I'm making you coffee," said a voice from deep inside the gloom. I swung myself off the scooter, found the kitchen and watched a hunched young woman scoop Nescafé with a higher quotient of mouse shit than coffee granules into a mug. "I hope you don't take milk."

"Black's fine." The milk here I could do without.

"What you think of this place?" she asked, handing me the coffee.

It reminded me of all I'd read about the MC5 house in Ann Arbor where Iggy Pop and The Stooges came of age, or Arturo Vega's New York City loft where the Ramones were based in their heyday. In other words, nowhere I'd want to spend more than ten minutes without refreshing my hepatitis booster.

"I love it," I said.

"I'm glad. This place here is important. It is one of Indonesian punk's homes. I wanted to show you how I contribute." She waved her own mug, splooshing coffee on the floor, pointing out a shelf lined with stapled zines, all warped by the humidity. "I document, I inform of history, what is going on, what will happen."

This was Ika V., local punk's doyenne, keeper of the records, muse. She's thirty-two years old, with a lip piercing, a cheek piercing and an advanced punk fashion sense—flowing skirt, hoodie pulled low, spiked bangs, combat boots. There's a softness to her features, a matronly roundness. I'm not sure what they make of her at her day job: Ika is a senior creative director at Young & Rubicam Indonesia. Despite shilling Procter & Gamble product to Indonesia's two hundred and thirty-seven million souls, Ika is punk through and through. She was determined to show me that the local scene is not an idiosyncrasy to be hastily tossed in the "South East Asia: Weird" file. Punk is *big*, Ika tells me. Go to any small village in West Java, she says, and you'll find a scene. Kids will sell their motorcycles to finance the gigs; they'll gut you with switchblades if they doubt your punkness.

"For me, it starts in high school, when I bought cassettes of the Sex Pistols and the Ramones," said Ika. "But then, in the moment, I started to read about punk as well as listen to it—we passed around old books, because this stuff was hard to come by. And I'm surrounded by these people, these punkers, and it becomes my life."

Which brings us to the trick question about Indonesia: How has such a musical mecca developed in the most populous Islamic country in the world? How had it been able to flourish here, alongside a growing and increasingly militant Islam? In what way did the conditions differ from Egypt, or from the Gulf? And did Indonesia suggest something fundamental about how Islam could interact with popular culture?

"I know, this may all seem weird to you," said Ika. "It is weird for me, with my background. My father is a typical Javanese Muslim, in the way he values life and sees things in both Javanese and Muslim way. But my mother is a Muslim mother. Get married this, and go to the mosque that. As such, maybe she can drive me a little crazy. They look at my life as if to say 'What the fuck?'"

One could look at Indonesia and ask the same. The country's Muslims "constitute a majority with a minority mentality," according to *Jakarta Post* columnist Thomas Barker. Ninety percent of

Indonesians consider themselves Muslim, yet Islamic political representation—at least the kind that doesn't involve plastic explosives—has traditionally been restricted by successive authoritarian regimes. And the Islam practiced across the archipelago is by no means homogeneous: There is the syncretic Islam of Java, the hardened Islamism of the extremist urban fringes, the Wahhabi-influenced Islam of the rural *pesantrens*—Indonesia's Saudi-backed *madrassas*.

"So yes, we have Islam here," said Ika. "But Islam is Islam. And punk is punk. You know that [San Francisco–based punk zine] *Maximumrocknroll* say Indonesia has the second biggest per capita punk scene in the world, after Brazil? We have very few places to play—because the government doesn't want us to—but the biggest punk show of 2006 was German punk band Cluster Bomb Unit. Seven thousand people came to see them. But it's not easy here.

"Slayer was banned from Malaysia because according to the authorities they spread dangerous messages. Anthrax was not allowed to play on Java because their name refers to a disease of the cow." (Disease of the cock is apparently a more benign pathology.) "Punk zines are 'tools of ideology' in Singapore. Black T-shirts are banned in Malaysia. But for the most part Indonesia is far more open than the rest of the region. For the most part."

Ika says that most of the Westerners who come to Indonesia are hilarious: They'll leave with only a CD sampler of gamelan music, the two-thousand-year-old classical percussive "gong"-style instrument that dates back to those long-ago days when Indonesia was mostly Hindu-Buddhist. Islam arrived in Indonesia in the thirteenth century, taking three languid centuries to establish itself as the dominant religion (excluding Buddhist holdouts like Bali). In the seventeenth century, the Dutch colonized the region. And while a centuries-long cultural stew like this one is by no means unique, the way Indonesia spiced it might well be.

"Come—pass me that." Ika was pointing to my guidebook, which I had managed to hold on to throughout the Vespa ordeal.

We sat beside each other on a patch of relatively unfilthy floor and

I opened the book at a map of Indonesia. Ika passed a fingernail with chipped black nail polish over the strewn mess of the archipelago: the geographical remnants of tectonic plates angrily separating Sydney from Shanghai. Seventeen thousand islands, six thousand of them inhabited, however sparsely.

"Each island musically is different," said Ika. "Well, not *each* one, but the bigger ones. You see here: Sumatra and Java in the west are the largest. Bali everyone knows from the bombings, and look, up here in the north is Kalimantan. And far, far here in the east, Timor. Also Irian Jaya."

There are several skewers running through this variegated island satay, one of which happens to be North American music. "You see here?" said Ika, her fingernail on the far end of Java. "This is Surabaya, a big, very conservative East Java city. In the late nineties, all of a sudden there comes a big pop revival from there. Here we are in Jakarta: indie rock, commercial rock, punk. Bali is the rockabilly scene." Her finger jumped back to Java. "The city of Jogja. Pop again. A Jogja band called Sheila On 7 sells more than a million copies of their latest album. And then we come to Bandung." The fingernail landed a half-inch or so below Jakarta, and tapped twice for emphasis. "This is the student city. It is where all the scenes start."

We were interrupted by a cheerful "hello, hello." Ari was back. He ruffled Ika's hair, pulled a Dead Kennedys shirt over his mottled belly. He's a founding member of three established Jakarta punk bands— the Idiots, Grave Dancers and Peace or Annihilation—and a pioneer of the scene. He swung a heavy bag of records over his back, and walked back to the battered Vespa.

"Isn't he cute?" asked Ika over the chug-chug of the engine.

"Sid to your Nancy," I said. Ika smiled.

We rose, and I strolled around the house, flipping through zines, stepping over the slumbering body of a teenage punker. I half expected a member of Bad Brains to leap from the shadows and jab a needle of uncut speed into my neck.

You go anywhere in the world, thought I, but where will you find one so bitter as a punker from the West? Who is so misanthropic, so bleak in outlook as an American punk fan who came of age between 1975 and 1979, who knows that *anything* can be co-opted, any ideal tamed, and that capitalism, to paraphrase the old truism, will buy your revolution and sell it back to your tattooed ass for ten times what you got for it? I knew this better than most: In the dying days of my previous career, I produced music videos for Canadian sugar-punk bands, scions of California sun-punk outfits like Green Day. These scrubbed, apple-cheeked youth infused me with a depression I'm not entirely sure I'm over. They "wore anarchy as a badge of conformity rather than an alternative way of living," as Stephen Colegrave and Chris Sullivan put it in *Punk: The Definitive Record of a Revolution*. Punk was dead, and I'd helped drive a stake in its heart. This I did not tell Ika, in case she told the female punk by the door, who made Fuck Work look like a choirboy.

"But in Indonesia," said Ika, "punk is punk. It *lives*. When the best punk band here, called Marjinal, appeared on TV earlier this year, the outcry within the scene was such that no other punk band would do the same. Now Marjinal speaks to no one. They hide."

Ika clanged her coffee mug into a heap of discarded crockery. "This is not always a happy political country, so I do what I can. I run this house, which is a free creative space for neighbors and friends—people crash if they need a place—whether it's kids kicked out of home or touring bands. I really enjoy the spirit of the DIY punk. Of course, it can be cruel and harsh and mean. But also very open. Just like Indonesia."

The studios of Aksara Records—located in a warren of streets behind the Blok M complex, a gargantuan shopping mall that forms the gateway between north and south Jakarta—were state of the art, as was the attitude of the four members of The Brandals who were draped on a large couch, fiddling with their mobiles. Two other members were in the recording booth cutting the guitar track that was currently sandpapering my eardrums. The group resembled a harder version of a New York lo-fi revival band—note-perfect reinterpretations of eighties no-wave meets garage rock meets The Stooges. The signature song in their repertoire is a track called "Ain't Nobody's Bitch." It opens with a lissome jangle-riff, a staccato hammer on the kick drum, feedback buzz humming at the corners of everything. Then, in a voice ground down to the adenoids by unfiltered cigarettes:

> You ain't nothing. Nothing but another knock on my door
> You ain't nothing. Nothing but another break on my floor
> Gotta keep it, gotta keep it, gotta keep it awa-ay
> I'm not begging, I'm telling you I'm not here to stay
> Gotta keep up, gotta keep up, gotta keep up with me-e
> When you got what you want, then you gotta gotta gotta go-o-ooo

The Brandals's hair and outfits were precision cool, so spot-on an approximation of East Village ennui that it was if I were sitting in the CBGB's greenroom, *circa* 1983. I told David Tarigan so. He smiled patiently; the expression he wore when talking, listening or thinking about music reminded me of thirteenth-century paintings of saints done by Italians.

David gestured me out of the racket of the studio. Implicit in his manner, and in his intellectual and aesthetic approach to the music in his country, was the following: Beware the assumption that Indonesian rock and its dizzying subgenres are an exotic cargo cult.

The quintessential indie music geek, David was to be my Virgil. He was rangy with a slight belly, skinny jeans, his long, greasy hair arranged in a modish sweep. His music vault was a repository of Indonesia's forgotten 7-inch singles, recorded by bands whose output would long ago have dissipated into the humid mists of the archipelago's jungles if it weren't for his diligence. His erudition reached far beyond the shores of the Indonesian archipelago: His collection included Madchester post-punk, California hardcore, Chicago indie and all manner of arcana and obscurity. He was still, except for a jittery right knee that hopped up and down when he sat.

It would not be a stretch to call David a music historian; it would be entirely accurate to call him a prime mover in the current Indonesian independent music scene. He runs the Artist and Representation Department for Aksara Records, a Jakarta-based label that releases an astounding roster of local talent and culls the finest international independent music for local distribution.

The majors are, for the most part, alive and well in Indonesia. In the EMI offices, seven Indonesian artists have found a place on the "million sold" wall, and only one international act has done the same: Coldplay. Eighty percent of the market here is local, with seventy percent of all music sold on cassette, which is both cheaper to produce and harder to pirate. Much of it is solid, commercial rock and adult contemporary—nothing that would be out of place in North America. "We ship three hundred thousand records of a local rock band," an EMI executive told me, "and lose no sleep." All this in a region where piracy is rampant.

Aksara's top seller is the twee pop outfit White Shoes & The Couples Company, with twenty-five thousand copies sold. Sister label FFWD Records have moved over seventy-five thousand copies of power pop band Mocca's shimmering *Friends*. These are decent numbers for indie labels anywhere. There are radio stations, TV stations, a local *Rolling Stone* and other publications all supporting the industry. The Indonesian indie scene even has its own version of *Singles*, the Seattle-set grunge movie that moved the genre into mainstream popular consciousness. The film is called *Garasi*, or *Garage*. David thinks it's a piece of shit. The previous year, he provided music for a soundtrack to a film called *Janji Joni*, a far more accurate portrait of Indonesia's hipsters, and curated a 2004 compilation called *Jkt:Skrg*, featuring a host of Jakarta bands who regularly played the city's scant venues.

According to the album's distributor, "the shows were more often remembered for what was destroyed than what was performed." But what was performed, if *Jkt:Skrg* is anything to go by, was ludicrously awesome. There's The Brandals's "Ain't Nobody's Bitch," the Frank Zappa-ish snooze-a-delia of Sore's "Cermin," the Pavement-meets-Weezer mash-up "Mosque of Love" by The Adams, the unhinged *chugalug* power punk of the superbly named Teenage Death Star. Piece of shit or no, the *Garasi* folks were onto something: This was as vibrant and coherent a scene as nineties-era Seattle.

David held a theory: The popular music scene in Indonesia evoked the same spirit as the '77 punk explosion in America. Ever the historian, he saw music with an epic Edward Gibbon–like bird's-eye view: If vital, life-changing music had a core facilitator, it was rebellion. Genre mattered not at all. What counted was the *driving force*. Extreme rock or punk or indie rock or twee pop, so long as the music was propelled by a spirit of rebellion, it was worthy of his consideration.

"To understand all this, you must meet some people," said David. "Through them, you will understand much." David had started to sound like Yoda crossed with Mr. Miyagi.

"Meaning?"

"You must go places, and meet people. Don't worry, I will help you."

Before he asked me to levitate an X-wing, I followed him downstairs, toward the car parked in the covered garage.

Islam for Life, read a banner draped on a wall outside a tottering village, *Life for Islam*. We traveled into a town, bouncing along the main drag trying to avoid a small herd of goats. Banana trees and mangroves necked with thick jungle foliage to form an arced avenue. Light from errant sunbeams twinkled off the water in the sluices. The road was lined with people and *warungs*. A rhesus monkey tethered to a post cawed busily as we turned into a fenced compound. Palm trunks shorn of their fronds lined a short driveway at the end of which, in an open bamboo shed, a man named Yon Koes was playing pool with two of his sons.

If I wanted to understand the career of the diminutive, bowlegged man waving at us with the pool cue, insisted David, I had to understand the sweep of Indonesian rock history. In this, the long drive from Jakarta had been something of an education. David popped a CD into the player, and an alternative universe of rock 'n' roll flooded the speakers.

First track: Muffled, sepia-tinted 1950s island music, courtesy of the label Irama—an Indonesian game-changer.

Next track: more Irama, this time with a distinctly Latin beat—influenced by the records coming from Cuba. And then we start tasting the West, with vocalist Oslan Husein and his smash rendition of an Indonesian standard called "Bengawan Solo," the most covered Indonesian song ever. Between the island lilts, there are shades of The Platters, Elvis Presley, with Jerry Lee Lewis hiccups: an aborning rock sensibility.

David then twirled a new CD in his hand and flipped it into the player in one neat movement.

The unmistakable sound of rock 'n' roll. Prompted by the Everly Brothers records that drifted through the dense, jungly airwaves from a bleeping Voice of Australia radio tower in the northernmost town of Darwin, brothers Yon and Yok Koes would come to redefine Indonesian music. Track after track, they summed up the journey rock 'n' roll took, from early Elvis Presley and Paul Anka to the exuberance of The Beatles and beyond. "But it doesn't stop here," said David. Outside, the fringes of Jakarta: shanty slums pouring into filthy gullies, a tangle of found material clustered in the shadow of vast factories.

Next up: The Brims, who cut a track called "Anti Ganja," which sounded—no doubt accidentally—rather like a celebration of the good weed: "*Ahhh, ahhh, ganja. GANJA-aaaaAAAAA!*" wailed The Brims, accompanied by swirling Pink Floyd synths, leading toward a full-blown stoner crescendo.

David clicked forward to the hard-rock guitar heroics of one Rhoma Irama, "the undisputed *dangdut* superstar of the 1970s."

While President-at-the-time Suharto's New Order policies allowed for a certain amount of openness after the despot-minded Sukarno was ousted, it had tacitly encouraged local popular culture movements in opposition to Western influences. Thus, the *dangdut* genre reigned in Indonesia, an everyman's South East Asian–influenced pop style that was the equivalent of country and western to an Arkansan. *Dangdut* would come to expose a cultural rift between urban and rural, between the burgeoning middle class and the more traditional working poor. It became redneck music.

"Basically," said David, "because of a number of reasons—*dangdut* one of them—we missed the whole punk scene here in the seventies. There was disco, eighties pop—songs for sissies—slow ballads about love. But Indonesia missed the 1977 punk rock explosion. The fashion caught on, but the music didn't. There was just no punk consciousness. Until . . ."

The unmistakable torrent of Nirvana's "Smells Like Teen Spirit." The last time I heard this song I was bowling in Balkash, Kazakhstan.

"Suddenly," said David, "we have this option: three chords, four chords. It changed things for many, because suddenly we know the four-chord wonders, and the new rebellious genres rained upon us. And underground rock from America in the eighties flooded in— Dinosaur Jr., Sonic Youth, Pavement—all of a sudden we had access to their music. Anything can happen."

And anything did happen. With the sluice gates open and music flooding in, Indonesian kids were looking both backward and forward. Any middle-class kid who came of age in those heady days was drowning in music. With the jungle thickening outside the car, I heard the vicious noise of independent pioneers PAS Band—the first to release under their own power—Puppen, Full of Hate, the chirp pop of White Shoes & The Couples Company, the jangle rock of The Brandals. "It didn't matter the type of DIY music," said David. "It mattered that it was DIY. Rebellion was the main ingredient.

"So, this new form of expression became available for us to choose from. It's so eclectic—you can choose every kind of genre. Basically, we now have an outlet for this angst. And it grows from there. There is bands and fanzines and private labels and everything in the same spirit."

Which brought us, by and large, to the gates of the Koes compound, and the small man with the pool cue who was now leaning into the car window shaking David's hand.

Yon Koes spoke rapidly in Bahasa, the linguistic equivalent of a spirited pinball game. He brushed back his dark, shoulder-length hair, showing off a nose that would have looked more at home on a Miro.

"Come, come," said Yon Koes. He exchanged the pool cue for a guitar, and waved us through the jungle of his garden.

"How old you think I am?" asked Yon, through David. Despite the dark hair, there was a mess of crow's feet around his eyes, a milky quality to his gaze.

"Twenty-five years old, maybe thirty," I lied.

He laughed. "I'm sixty-two. I have seen many things, played much music." Behind us, a rumpus room covered with Koes Brothers memorabilia: ancient posters of the boys in Beatles-style suits and in seventies regalia. Yon now spent his days painting, and his oils transformed the room into a salon. A fat child in a *SpongeBob SquarePants* outfit hovered close by.

Yon lifted up his battered guitar in a swift movement and rested it on his knee. "Now we sing." He strummed some Cadence-era Everly Brothers, and then segued into the Beatles "Michelle"—his voice was cracked, an old man's voice, but still a good voice, a strong voice. His second wife, a plump women at least thirty years his junior, joined us. As Yon played, a sweat stain bloomed on his chest.

"Sing!" implored Yon.

"Mr. Koes, you do not want to hear me sing," I said.

David joined in with a sweet, timorous voice. When the performance ended, I applauded.

"Very good, very good. Do you remember when you first heard the song?" I asked.

Koes's eyes went distant. "Oh, yes. Back then, we were so young and what was cool in the Western world was cool to us. We were young and in search of identity. We paid a lot of respect to all the acts—Everly Brothers, Elvis, Paul Anka. But after The Beatles everything changed—they offer us freedom of expression: shouts and wailings. Energy."

Yon raised the guitar like a weapon, slamming the guitar strings with his small, worn fingers: "Love Me Do" played by Johnny Rotten. I'd never heard The Beatles laced with such ferocity. It was like hearing them for the first time, unspoiled by their ubiquity. It was a revelation.

In 1960, the Koes brothers first signed to Irama for two albums. Shortly after the release of their debut album, a little track called "Can't Buy Me Love" was pinged out from the Darwin radio tower. See ya later, Everly Brothers; the band hurriedly became a quartet (including brother Tony, who became the de facto band leader) and started doing Beatles covers. That's where the trouble started.

"There were warnings," said Yon. "They told us not to play The Beatles. Nothing Western. Remember the Dutch, they say. Others say: We are Muslim; this is not our music. But we don't care. We played."

After a particularly spirited show in July 1965—the birthday party of a local colonel—the Koes Brothers' take on the Lennon/McCartney songbook drifted over the walls and was heard by the wrong ears. Stones started flying, thrown by enraged neighbors. The band went home, and the following morning men from President Sukarno's secret police came to put an end to all this rock 'n' roll nonsense, which they did by locking the Koes Brothers in prison.

"They caught us because of subversion. They said we were doing this against the government." For three months, Yon Koes and his brothers did time, "in a cage, like in one of those cowboy movies."

"Were you angry?" I asked.

Yon's eyes darkened; the kid in the *SpongeBob* outfit noticed this change in his father's mood and moved closer, grabbing his leg. "Rather I was sad, and confused. I only wanted to sing good songs. Why I had to go to jail?"

And then one day the warden came and with no explanation set the band free. They were released on September 30, 1965, and the next morning Sukarno's regime fell.

Their post-arrest album, a dark conceptual affair titled *To the So-Called "The Guilties,"* must stand as one of the rock 'n' roll triumphs—in any country—of the era. The band hammers at their guitars with a viciousness that seems pathological; the album veers perilously close to punk. "Tony Koes was the composer—and Tony Koes was *mara*—angry," Yon told me. "Those songs were for Sukarno. Tony was never the singer before this, but after jail Tony wanted to sing." Tony passed away in 1987—cancer—and was angry until his dying day.

In later years, the band branched out as Koes Plus, releasing a Christmas album (their wives are Christians, so it was something of a gift) and even a children's album. And Koes Plus are still going, more of a novelty band now.

"I would play every day if I could. I still play gigs with young musicians. And I still play Koes Plus songs."

Yon grabbed his guitar again, and implored me to sing. "Come on, friend. Sing!"

"I can't, Yon," I protested. "I only sing hip-hop."

"No, no!" protested Yon, laughing. "Then you must go!"

And so we did, with David wearing the look of a man who has just met a legend, or a god.

"You see," he said to me, "you cannot have punk, real punk or DIY, without musical history. It can't just arrive, like in a vacuum. I wanted to show you this."

David was talking about *lineage*. He was reminding me that punk was not sui generis, something dreamed up by Lou Reed during a Bowery heroin binge. It was a reaction to the bloat of seventies progressive rock and hippie jam-band excess, both a return to the essence of rock and a rejection of the status quo. It changed in character when Malcolm McLaren schlepped it to Soho and injected it into the anarchic spirit of Johnny Rotten and company, but to truly understand punk outside of its own particular mythology—and to enjoy it as one of the most remarkable passages in the development of Western musical culture—I have always liked to remind myself of its links to simple, three-chord blues rock. This is why the scene felt so real in Indonesia. It was situated, part of a legacy.

"And of course, you cannot take punk outside of proper history," said David. "It needs a match to light the fire of the spirit."

"And what lit the fire in Indonesia?" I asked.

We stood under the shade of the tapang tree; David summoned his driver with a wave. "Nirvana. The end of Suharto's New Order regime. But more than anything," said David, "the Crisis."

It was the evening of August 25, 1997. A young stockbroker named Mohammed Kasagia walked to the *bajaj* stand in Jakarta's central business district, his suit drenched in sweat that had nothing to do with the pestilential heat. He would never, he swore to himself, forget this day. He was in a daze, pale as a *boulay*. He slumped into a *bajaj*, breathing shallowly, running through the events that had just unfolded on the trading floor: Asian stock markets had not just crashed but imploded. The JSX lost 4.5 percent of its value that morning, representing hundreds of billions of dollars of evaporated wealth. The same thing had happened across the region. Trillions of dollars had disappeared into the sticky air. It was one of the greatest financial disasters of the twentieth century.

Kasagia went home, put Nirvana on the stereo, listened to it loud. He didn't know what to tell his mother, his father. He even opened the small Qur'an the family kept in the house. He felt Asia's looming misery close around him like a fist.

"We're fucked," he thought. In this, Kasagia was a far more adept speculator than he'd ever been on the stock market. In the four months following the crash, Indonesia's rupiah would lose eighty percent of its value, while the stock market plunged a further thirty-five percent. The fallout would be the most socially transformative event to hit the country since Suharto overthrew Sukarno. The Asian Tiger was defanged. In one year, Suharto himself would be gone.

Kasagia, who was twenty-three at the time of the crash, remembers arguing with his father during the dark days that followed. You are soft, his father would say. You never knew war. You never knew deprivation.

This *is* my fucking war, said Kasagia.

But it wasn't a war. For a middle-class twentysomething like Kasagia, his life was now defined by a measure of deprivation, at least compared to his high-flying pre-crash ways. Mostly, it was defined by boredom. He had closed his Qur'an the day after the crash. Others had kept theirs open, finding succor in their faith. Many, many more—Indonesia's tens of millions of indigent—saw no change at all in their circumstances. But for Indonesia's equivalent of Generation *Al Shamshoon*, the future had been erased. It created the very nihilism that defined punks in Britain in the late seventies and hardcore music fans in America during the Reagan era.

Kasagia, like so many young Indonesians, referred to the collapse of the economy, followed by the fall of Suharto's regime, as the Crisis. And it forced young Indonesians to become some of the more self-reliant, entrepreneurial people on earth. They either innovated or fell by the wayside. The Crisis was simultaneously energizing and enervating. It was a time of renascence. It was an age of ennui.

Growing distant from his parents, Kasagia didn't know how they could have sat by while Suharto raped the country. He grew distant from his own past—his time on the trading floor—where he was a trained monkey for the bastards who lived in Jakarta's Menteng, where the thug peasants who stole more money than they knew what to do with hid inside Greco-Roman compounds dusting coke from their noses.

Mohammed Kasagia did not know who he was or where he belonged. The only person who spoke to him was Kurt Cobain, but Kurt Cobain had blown his own brains out, and that didn't seem like much of a plan. His friends were the same way—lost—until they found themselves in a rundown bar called Park listening to—no, *experiencing*—a band called Teenage Death Star.

Sir Dandy, or Dandi Achmad Ramdhani, the lead vocalist, has left very few pieces of stage equipment undamaged. He's gloriously grizzled, so much so that he was recently asked to audition for the part of a drunken master in a TV commercial. Sir Dandy is a perfect post-Crisis Indonesian—an industrial designer, a gifted painter, a sometime actor, a clothing entrepreneur and a musician. He's harnessed his creativity and his energy to make a series of cottage industries work, because there were no other options, no government support. But the band is special. "It's all an experiment for me," he has said. "I just do what I do. I like the Libertines, Black Flag—crazy shit—where the vocalist and the other members, they always get drunk and naked on the stage. I always like the band with the most exciting performance. It's not just about the music—it has to be about spirit."

Kasagia embraced the spirit. He inserted his thumb in a number of indie pies, working alongside his friends, all of whom were doing the same thing. Mohammed Kasagia was remaking himself.

He got wasted the day of the Bali bombing—when members of the Jema'ah Islamiyah blew up Paddy's Pub and the Sari Club in the Kuta District, killing hundreds in 2002. He got wasted during the cartoons-of-the-Prophet crisis, when Jakarta's Danish embassy burned. He got wasted to forget this shit, to keep it at bay.

But Indonesia, like Kasagia, is still trying to make sense of itself and define itself as a *modern* entity. I recalled something Ika had said of punkers: "These are very lost kids. Very lost. They know the music but they don't know what punk *is*." This is true of kids in suburban or small-town North America—they've chosen punk, but couldn't quite say why, beyond the fact that "punk rules!"

"But this is the same as Islamism," added Ika. "They have just happened to choose punk. For now."

I do as David Tarigan orders: I go to Bandung, one hundred miles southeast of Jakarta, along a highway lined with terraced rice paddies, through clouds so low they begin at the tarmac. When I arrive, I hop on the back of Helfi's motorcycle. Helfi (one name only, like a soccer star) is a punk pioneer, used to manage Puppen, wears a Teenage Death Star T-shirt. He runs the record label FFWD Records and a clothing label called Airplane Systm.

"Bandung was in the Dutch era famous for food, fashion, music, architecture, design," says Helfi, who shares the Indonesian predilection for talking while madly piloting a two-wheeled vehicle. "I want to base business on Bandung model—to synergize."

This was once, during colonial times, an open city, and its richness derives from centuries of interacting with other cultures, while its citizenry—the better-off ones—are beneficiaries of that legacy. And so, in turn, are many of Indonesia's two hundred and forty million citizens, especially those who work in the creative industry, because Bandung is a feeder town, sending forth musicians and graphic designers and architects and filmmakers into the archipelago, dispensing the fruits of Bandung to all and sundry.

I cling to the Teenage Death Star T-shirt as Bandung whips by: stately Dutch residences with their dirty red sloped roofs; Frank Lloyd Wright–inspired modernist structures; outlet stores with papier mâché Supermen flying from the walls; stores called Jeans World and Spiderman Party Store; hyper-designed glass and steel boutiques that would not be out of place in Zurich or Montreal. Which is not to say that Bandung feels like anywhere other than Indonesia: there's something distinct in the architecture, the febrile jitter of the calamitous weather, the jungle foliage, the intensity of the traffic.

Later, Helfi gives me directions to the hamlet of Indramayu, site of a punk show that Ika told me about, where one thousand or so punkers descended on a small town that foolishly rented out a space. It is about a hundred miles outside of Bandung, surrounded by rice paddies descending toward the ocean in a giant mossy staircase. There is little here other than a traditional market covered in places by blue tarpaulin, a motley line of bamboo-rigged *warungs* and a single road leading to a rusted syrup factory that reeks of rotting sugar. A Cronenbergian menagerie slithers through the underbrush; bird calls sound like babies dying in agony.

I ask around, wondering what the locals thought of the show, which took place in November 2006, and no one has forgotten. It was a bad thing, a father of two barefoot children tells me. What do these kids want? he asks. No work. Just noise. They fouled our town.

No, says an older woman. When we were young, we danced to all the songs from the West. Kids need something to do. This is good. It's just that they were messy. We were upset. There was vomit on the ground.

This conversation is as old as rock 'n' roll itself.

Then I do what most visitors to Indonesia do: I make for the island of Bali. This is what one hundred and sixty-four tourists did in 2002 when they met their fate in the Kuta district. On October 12, a series of bombs blew up, murdering them along with thirty-eight Indonesians. I stand in front of the memorial on the site of Paddy's Pub, on Legian Street. The memorial is made of large pieces of precisely carved stone, fronted by a swirling Balinese motif presiding over a chunk of dark granite inscribed with the names of the dead. The sky promises meteorological mayhem. This monument marks the spot of one of a series of awful events that kicked off the millennium, devastating attacks on the soft underbelly of Westernized commerce, culture, pleasure.

I lie in a bunk bed in a hostel, listening to raindrops pummel the thin glass of the windows, and wonder what music was playing in Paddy's Pub when a man walked in with a case full of explosives. How was David Tarigan and Mohammed Kasagia's spirit supposed to defend against that? Was it ever meant to?

That night, I drift off and dream of a distraught Johnny Rotten tearing down Legian Street, the whole place in flames, body parts littering the ground, his hair melting. I wake up in a sweat, and swear off the street food.

I pack my bag and book a flight for Jakarta. I have booked a meeting with the man who stands at the meeting point between the id of punk, and the ego of terror.

"This," said Mr. Iwan—the corpulent and mysterious Man Friday—of a canvas depicting the Virgin Mary in what looked to be Gotham City reimagined by da Vinci, "is Maria in a gothic style." He pointed to another set of paintings. "These, I do not know what they are"—they were replica Caravaggios, or at least I hoped they were replicas—"and this is the great spiritual leader, Shaikh Mohammed Nazim Adil al-Haqqani," he said, indicating two heroic portraits of a holy man in the aspect of the devout Sufi. Opposite these, in glass display cases, collector's-edition guitars: a Hendrix Fender, a McCartney Les Paul, Van Halen's pink V-neck. Above them, a row of fifty or so pairs of Adidas sneakers, collectible editions all.

The salon nicely represented the Jakarta neighborhood I found myself in: an amalgam of upper-class suburban, inner-city urban and down-home rural. Outside, goats grazed in abandoned lots, men walked with bundles of cane balanced on their heads, late-model SUVs lined the sidewalks, abandoned lots were adorned with swaths of accomplished graffiti. The neighborhood revealed a strange architectural proclivity among the city's parvenu: neo-classicism. Ruffled, gilded mansions, columns rising forty feet into the air, loomed over the street like the fever dreams of snuff addicts in the court of Louis XIV.

However odd the houses here may be, none is stranger than the structure in which I was standing: a baroque-cum-Greco-cum-Ming Dynasty monstrosity. The house and the studio/office beside it—enormous black and red structures, the comic book palace of a villain we'll call Fu Ming von Baronstein—so perfectly explicated the mentality of their owner that there is not much left to say about the guy.

His actual name is Ahmad Dhani. He's the biggest star in the South East Asia rock 'n' roll firmament, the Yon Koes of his day. His band Dewa has sold over six million records. He was once a callow rock star, but since he got sucked into a war, he's become much more than that. Ahmad Dhani is Indonesia's Bono. And as anyone who has heard U2's last several records and *doesn't* own a minivan knows, this can be both a good and a bad thing.

Dhani's retainer, Mr. Iwan, ushered me upstairs and sat me on a couch facing a library of DVDs. It was a long moment before I noticed Dhani, who wore his thinning hair shoulder length, a long wispy goatee terminating on his slight paunch. Dhani did not make eye contact: He sat in a yoga pose. I found him unnerving.

"My grandfather on my mother's side was named Kohler, a Dutch-German," said Dhani, by way of greeting. "The path of my father was to be a member of the [hardline] Dewan Dakwah Islamiyah Indonesia [Islamic Propagation Council of Indonesia]. His father? He was of Dar ul-Islam, who were outlaws fighting for an Islamic state in Indonesia. This explains much. Do you understand?"

I said that I didn't.

He shook his head disappointedly. I was failing some sort of test. "My mother was obsessed with Western music, pop of the fifties to seventies: Henry Mancini, George Gershwin, Elvis. Voice of Australia was the soundtrack of the home. She played in an all-female group and taught me the guitar. Forced me to play piano. When I am eight years old, I watch *Flash Gordon*. This is where I am introduced to the music of Queen. To this day, I love Queen. This movie changed me. Seven years later, I started Dewa. I will not," said Dhani dryly, "be fighting for Islamic state of Indonesia. I have chosen."

As his discography reveals, Dhani chose to hoover up a great sweep of rock 'n' roll genres, keeping an eye all the while on the underground that bubbled beneath his platform boots. He represents the mainstream Indonesian rock industry, but he has been buffeted by the wave of indie music that has so excited the local music press. He asked me what I thought of his music. I told him I liked it. He nodded.

"It's very idealistic—very new for the time. I make real music, sophisticated music. Sometimes I have to adjust to people's taste. If I go too high, people will leave me. I have to wait for them to catch up."

That's one way of looking at it. But Dhani was the one playing catch-up; Dewa, at their best, sound like a Beck and Kurt Cobain jam session, assuming they sang in Bahasa and were taking the day off from being geniuses. I found Dhani interesting for two reasons: for how he was mining the rich veins of the underground, just as so many mainstream artists in the West do, and for how his work had invited opprobrium that no artist in the West has had to suffer.

In 2005, Dhani and radical Islam met head-on. It was perhaps inevitable that the highest-profile group in Indonesia's music scene would at some time clash with the extreme end of Indonesian society, but it took a confluence of apparently random circumstances to provoke the Islamic Front Pembala Islam's—or FPI—jihadi ire.

The catalyst was the seemingly incongruous cover art for Dewa's seventh album, adorned as it was with an eight-pronged star, which some Muslims consider an inviolable image. It didn't cause much of a stir until Dewa made a TV appearance promoting the album, where the CDs were laid out on the floor and Dhani—who happened to be wearing an emblem on a chain that looked suspiciously like a Star of David to the members of the FPI—sang the song "*Satu*," or "Oneness," which is a ditty that has significant Sufi sensibilities *not* shared by Dhani's newfound enemies.

The FPI could no longer take this proliferation of offenses sitting down and stormed the offices of Dewa's then-label, Aquarius Musikindo, armed with brickbats, knives, two-by-fours, gas for dousing others and themselves. If FPI has a modus operandi, it's vandalism and extortion, and this particular initiative kicked off a busy season for the jihadis. One hundred acolytes ran the booms in Dhani's neighbourhood and raged toward his studio in a display of menace that was followed by weeks of death threats. Several days later, they turned their attention to Jakarta's Kemang neighborhood, where they bashed in windows and tore down the signs of nightclubs along the strip.

It was not a pleasant experience, and because of it Dhani has become something of an Indonesian mouthpiece for tolerance. It is his role in the LibForAll Foundation that has won him accolades from abroad and turned him to an activist rock star in the Geldof/Bono mold, although Dhani seems laconic about the whole thing.

"I do it when I have the time. It takes much time," he told me. That said, he neatly packaged his views into his hit song "Warriors of Love"—*If hatred has already poisoned you against those who worship differently, then evil has already gripped your soul, then evil's got you in its damning embrace*—and this was what brought Karen Hughes, long-time Bush crony and then undersecretary of state for public diplomacy, to Dhani's studio.

"She told me that she was very appreciative of what I've done. I don't know why my song is so important for the Americans; I don't know why it brought Karen Hughes. Even my government doesn't do that for me."

LibForAll must send shivers of joyous hope down the spines of those engaged in the War Against Terror, many of whom occasionally make their way through Indonesia. (This is, after all, Obama's home turf. He famously spent the better part of his childhood here.) The organization's philosophy is summed up on its website, where it claims that "it shall promote the popular culture of liberty and tolerance in the Muslim World, so as to influence the general public, and not just an intellectual elite. Dhani deftly employ[s] [his] knowledge of human psychology to discredit religious extremism in the eyes of the public in a form of ideological justification."

Dhani was subsequently invited by the Department of Homeland Defense to come to Washington and address a special committee, and has spoken to NORAD in Colorado. Dhani, in the words of those who invited him, is a "weapon against terrorism," a sort of Stinger missile with an electric guitar as payload.

"They wanted me to speak about Muslims in Indonesia. I tell them that we have the potential to be a radical Muslim country or a moderate Muslim country. We have potential for both. It depends on how the American government support the moderates, because the radicals already have support from foreign country—they have money and resources."

Strolling from Dhani's home to the studio, with Mr. Iwan a few steps behind us, I asked whether those hardened Terror Warriors bought his "music can help us out of this mess" message.

He nodded sagely. "If people love music very much, they don't have time to think about fighting other people or to think about vandalism. If the young generation in Indonesia love music, universal music, Western music, then they don't have the time to think about different religions or race. The government have an important role to play to make Indonesia more musical—not me."

"How would they do this?"

"Through education. And more television."

"More television?"

"Yes. Like more MTV."

"More *MTV*?"

"Not just MTV. More music channel. More Western film. Hollywood film. I think a lot of Hollywood is good."

"Okay. In what way is Hollywood good?" I didn't think that Sufis went in for superhero sequels.

"It persuades tolerance. A lot of Hollywood movies have deep-meaning stories that can make people think, even if they don't know they are thinking."

"But what do you say to those people who say that the influence of American culture is destructive, that it ruins local cultures, that it is rotten?"

"Not cool. No—I don't believe that. Some movies are garbage, but most are really good. Hollywood is like mankind—some good, some bad. But even the bad—are they really so bad? How many people die when it is a bad movie? I am different. I see a lot of Hollywood films.

Sometimes just for fun. Sometimes for entertainment. But sometimes they are very educational. But I still keep my Sufi way. It doesn't change me. It is still my religion. In Sufi, this is not an issue. In other Islam, maybe this is an issue. For some. But not all." Dhani stopped walking and stared at me, making eye contact for the first time.

"And let me say this—what you call pop culture, this will save us. It's very easy to make this place more Western. We need more good Hollywood movies. Otherwise we are *finished*. We are lucky here. We have malls, movies, music. It is a start. It will be hard to topple that. I often thank God for these things."

Post-meeting, Mr. Iwan and I broke my Bali no-street-food resolution and bought lunch from a vendor who had retrofitted a bicycle with a Plexiglas and wood crate—a roving restaurant complete with burner. We sat in the foyer of the studio and ate noisily while Mr. Iwan showed me posters of shows past. One in particular caught my eye: Dhani in an armed personnel carrier, he and his Dewa band mates wearing flak jackets, the densely packed streets bristling with armed men.

"We were the last band to play Aceh before tsunami, and the first to play afterward," said Mr. Iwan. Banda Aceh was once Indonesia's Gaza, a heavily militarized zone rife with Islamic extremism. Then, on December 26, 2005, the tsunami hit.

The next set of photos showed Dhani with his head in his hands: Aceh had been swatted from the earth by the back of God's hand. There was nothing left; the devastation was utter. "This," said Mr. Iwan, "is what happens when Allah is angry."

And also man, I thought, recalling the aftermath of the Bali bombings. It occurred to me then that the notion of Islamizing a country like Indonesia, with so vibrant a popular culture, would require a period of sustained and crushing brutality to reshape it into a full South East Asian theocracy. A tsunami of war. It is, of course, possible, but pop here, and the arts scene, and those massive malls—while they may attract the ire of the radical faction and provide Islamization with ideological impetus—make its implementation less of a practical possibility. That's why Dhani wanted more MTV, more music channels, more Western movies. They pushed his enemies further to the fringes. They built a wall.

From an upstairs studio, I heard the roar of guitars.

"There," said David Tarigan, pointing to a huddle of a hundred or so punkers, gathered next to a clinically bright Kwik Stop. We made our way toward them and were promptly stalled in a fetid stairwell that stank of piss, all the while serenaded by a preteen punk with miniature guitar, wearing a too-big Buzzcocks shirt that slipped off his bony shoulders.

I was the only *boulay*, which drew a considerable amount of attention, especially from a tall fellow in a bowler hat and suspenders, name of Pancia.

"You, my friend, are with me. My guest." He wobbled dangerously and guided us upstairs to get our thumbnails daubed with purple nail polish. "Come, my friend. Let's get fucking punked!"

The hall was empty but for the punkers who were slowly making their way in. The ceiling dribbled mucous-like condensation; the bathroom, leaking water into the hall, was an environmental emergency. Suddenly, a wall of sound, prompting a rush of people up from the jammed stairwell.

Within minutes, kids were smashing into each other, diving the stage—there would be blood. Pancia draped his arm over me, guiding me forward into the fray. I looked back plaintively at David, who could only shrug.

A guitar squeal cut through the shouts of the mob, physically pushing us back. Then a kick drum pulled us forward. We rippled like this for the length of the set, owned by the music. Boots cartwheeled by; a comatose kid was dragged out—the night's first casualty.

"Man, let's get some beer," said Pancia. We made our way down the stairs to the Kwik Stop, Pancia insisting that the other kids eyeing us "Go fuck! Go fuck right now."

"Okay mister," said one, "this is not your country."

Down at the Kwik Stop, drinking Bintang from oversized bottles, Pancia told me that he is a teller for HSBC Bank. The bassist in his garage band is a school teacher. "But punk is life, man." He wobbled on his feet, took a slug of my beer, and said. "You are my friend. Tonight, I will show you what punk means."

And Pancia did. Back upstairs, he took the stage with his band. They played ska-tinged doo-wop, a constant wail of feedback tranforming it into pure noise. Pancia batted stage-divers away, shakily hammering away at his bass, keeping time to who knows what—a song, perhaps, that he'd heard once, in a place far away.

In the throes of this manic crowd, I thought that the Indonesian punk mystery must come down to openness. An official policy of cultural acceptance like that of Suharto's New Order had a huge role to play, but also the openness of the people, a willingness to absorb, to suck in, but also to *enjoy* other forms of culture from abroad. In the same way that the archipelago, excluding Bali and sundry other isles, chose Islam—picking what made sense and discarding what didn't—Western pop has similarly been ransacked for what worked (where is hip-hop and R & B?), and was either accepted wholesale or rolled into Indonesian forms. It's tempting to call the Indonesian way imitative, but that wouldn't be quite right, because it's absorbative—Indonesian punk *is* punk. It's unmitigated, it exists in a pure form, it plays a vital social, cultural and political role in the lives of hundreds of thousands of young Indonesians. Thus, punk is as Indonesian an art form as it is an American or British one. It's the real deal.

But while David Tarigan's vaunted Indonesian DIY spirit was alive in this rancid hall, it was cut, of course, by typical punk aggressiveness and nihilism. Many of these kids did not believe in the future, could not conceive of it. Ideologically, they were adrift, subject to the pull of other forces. Which is why David worked so hard to archive Indonesia's musical history. He could say to both punks and their opponents: Look how *old* this stuff is. It is tradition. It belongs to us. And if it belonged to Indonesia—no matter how political or apolitical Pancia and his like may be—it formed a part of Ahmad Dhani's wall of pop culture, keeping the real bad guys at bay.

Pancia ended his show with a roar of feedback so raucous that I feared for my eardrums. That was it for me. I made a run for it, and stood outside sucking in humid air, watching the blinking lights of a nearby mall.

7

You're the Terrorist

PALESTINE / ISRAEL

Muslim (Israel): 23.6%

Muslim (Gaza): 100%

Muslim (West Bank): 98%

NEG GDP

1. Dead Prez:
   Police State

2. Ramallah Underground:
   Min Il Khaleof

3. Dam:
   Min Irhabi

Pop.: 7,112,359

Avg. age: 29.3

Capital: Jerusalem

Independence: May 14, 1948

The tricked-up Honda rolls by in hip-hop video slo-mo. Spinning rims kick up shards of sunlight; the car rattles with thumps of bass, like waves off a bomb blast. A tinted window lowers. Behind the cigarette smoke, four Arab *shebabs* wear black shades, chains, attitude. Their faces are scarred, their hair spiked with gel. It is 11 A.M. in the birthplace of Saint George, patron saint of Palestine, not thirty-five miles from Bethlehem. But you will never see this place featured in "Follow the Footsteps of Christ" travel brochures.

Under the shadow of hulking factories, the mixed Israeli city of Lod—home to 67,000 at last count—looks like an empty set for a Run DMC video, a desert reimagining of an old-skool 'hood. Busted tenements swoon against broken community centers, spilling into the embrace of barbed-wire barricades. It's a place that evokes the Bronx, mid-1970s, from which rap was born—the cataclysmic low point of American inner-city blight. The first hip-hop generation was raised on streets like these. Their music crossed the borders between boroughs: into Brooklyn, into Queens, into Manhattan, beyond.

And rap has found a home in the Middle East's most violent, crime-riddled burg, gutted as it was in 1948 during the Israeli War of Independence (or the *naqba*—the Disaster—depending on your affiliation), when the bulk of Lod's Arab citizens were expelled from the city in a ragtag huddle. This broken city is a metaphor for the local condition: Severed by concrete, it speaks to the divide. Lod is ground zero of the Israeli-Arab hip-hop scene, home to Palestinian rap's biggest deal: Tamer Nafar and his DAM crew.

Which is why I stood on a cracked slab of asphalt, eyeing the Honda Accord warily, and waved at a cab that seemed to have been there since the Pharisees ran the show. I gave an address that turned out to be a minute's drive away. A decaying four-story tenement: Cocks crowed; the jacarandas bloomed as if in irony. On the second floor, metal slats clacked open.

"Come round the other side," I heard someone say in glottal English. "I come fetch you." At the foot of a concrete staircase scarred with graffiti stood Palestine's foremost MC, wearing denim hip-hop shorts and a Fela Kuti T-shirt. Despite the fact that he didn't look physically healthy or powerful—pale, patches of stubble, raccoon eyes—there was a strength and tension in Tamer Nafar's shoulders. He carried himself with the hunched swagger of a heavyweight boxer before the first bell of a title fight. He said nothing, started walking up the stairs. Where was the welcome flute of Cristal? Jay-Z's crib, I mused, this wasn't.

Gunshots: The staccato hack of an AK-47, a hip-hop leitmotif since Public Enemy at least.

But on September 14, 2005, in the dust and heat of the Gaza Strip, these particular gunshots were live to air. And as good as an AK-47 sounds over a hip-hop breakbeat, a group called P.R. The Palestinian Rapperz and the fans who had gathered for their show were not at that moment able to enjoy it. A gaggle of hardline Hamas youth were furiously spraying bullets into the air. The show was, resolutely, over.

"They were singing disco," screamed a seventeen-year-old Hamas member, Mohammed, at a reporter. "This goes against the Holy Book."

Palestinian Rapperz do not in fact sing disco. What's more, Mohammed would probably agree with much of what they do sing about. After all, the offending concert was held in celebration of the Israeli withdrawal from the Gaza Strip. But in a burgeoning theocracy, rules are rules: In Hamas-controlled territory, loud music in public is frowned upon. "The Hamas guys were mostly upset because a lot of girls were excited about us and they were waving their hands as we sang," said another Mohammed, this one a member of Palestinian Rapperz.

While hip-hop in Palestine seemed, at least on the surface, like a freakish pop-cultural glitch, my iPod was no stranger to rap made by Muslim artists. The subgenre took shape in France's riot-ridden *banlieues*, where young immigrants found corollaries between their situation and that of blacks in urban North America. From there it spread to Lebanon, where by 1995 the hip-hop, graffiti and B-boy scene was so significant that, "you had wars, man, between kids who believed they was East Coast and kids who was West Coast," Lebanon's premier MC and turntablist, Lethal Skillz, told me. Hip-hop had also made it to North Africa, where Moroccan rappers like Salah Edin (who raps furiously in the Moroccan dialect of Darija) built a hardcore local fan base.

Borne on the back of speedy Internet connections, mainstream American rap is all but ubiquitous in the Muslim world. It's prevalent in Saudi Arabia, as we learned from our Metalien friends in El Bodega near Giza, Egypt. Indeed, when I asked the marketing director of Universal Saudi Arabia what the bestselling album in the Kingdom was, he didn't hesitate: "Akon, *Konvicted*."

That record was the soundtrack to my life: Wherever I went, Akon was there to greet me. I heard him pumping from vehicles on the Muscat corniche in Oman during the Shiite festival of Ashura. I heard him pimping from sound systems in Qatar, Syria, Abu Dhabi. (I didn't hear him in Afghanistan or Pakistan; he had not caught on in Indonesia.) In Yemen, a young man painstakingly explained how the rhythm of the Arabic *dubke*—a percussive dance—was stolen by

Akon for his record. Doubtful, but it wouldn't be the oddest thing a rap producer has borrowed.

Mohammed of Hamas, who shot up the Palestinian Rapperz show, would not like Akon, because Akon raps about, mostly, fucking strippers. (His smash hit "Smack Dat" is a Keatsian ode to girls who work the golden pole.) But while hip-hop had a history, however brief, as an Arabic art form, I wanted to know how—and why—it had made its way into the madness of the Gaza Strip and beyond.

In this, the Israeli town of Lod was about the best place one could start. The only moving thing I'd seen on the baked, deserted streets was the Honda Accord. Lod was ghetto fabulous; it felt like rap's last stand. "For those within the culture, hip-hop is much more than just music," wrote Rodrigo Bascunan and Christian Pearce in *Enter the Babylon System: Unpacking Gun Culture from Samuel Colt to 50 Cent*. "It is a way of life, the practice of being yourself." But what happens to the self when the practice thereof is steeped in such enmity, and mired in constant conflict?

Tamer Nafar trailed a hand along the stairwell, the concrete walls of which were liberally scarred with one of hip-hop's four essential elements: graffiti. "Fuck world," read one scribble, reminding me of my old pal Fuck Work a million miles away in Jakarta. I followed Tamer through the murk, past a wrought-iron security gate into a family apartment. His mother, washing dishes, didn't acknowledge us as we filed by. The home was clean, the walls whitewashed, but it was hard to breathe: There were bars on the windows, partially opened metal slats, a heavy security gate—a prison dressed as an apartment. In a corner, the Nafar patriarch sat in a wheelchair, reading. Four streaks of Lod sunlight cut across his withered legs.

"This is how we live," said Tamer. "The whole of us are always in this place. Nowhere to go outside of here. There is nothing in this town."

We entered the cramped room Tamer shared with his brother and fellow DAM-ite Suhell, who sat on the bed alongside the third member, Mahmoud Jreri. A television mounted above the door played video-clips, a computer hard drive was humming, PDAs bleeped text messages. I noticed a considerable DAM shrine—CD releases, a tangle of lanyards from shows around the world: Montreal, Paris, Berlin, Istanbul. On one wall, a Tupac and a Che flag. On the other, "Suhell" was helpfully tagged above Suhell's bed.

Tamer waved his hand at hidden speakers, which were, in the endlessly self-promotional way of the hip-hop artist, playing DAM. "This from the new album, *I Don't Have Freedom*," he said. We listened in silence.

I heard plaintive, aching *oud* strings, the high keen of a *doumbek* drum in a 2/5 beat. Then a chorus of male voices singing a traditional, lachrymose Arabic *qasidah: Everywhere I go I see borders, imprisoning humanity. Why can't I be free like other children in this world?*

Then, a 4/4 hip-hop breakbeat lands like an elbow to the temple, followed hard by Tamer's honed, guttural flow. We have leapt generations, oceans, genres, sensibilities, yet nothing is out of place. Tamer hurls the words from his mouth, spits them in a rat-a-tat rhythm. Mahmoud kicks in with a throaty flow tinged with the *huzn*—melancholy—of those voices in the chorus. Then follows Suhell's Stygian rap, shaded by the plaintiveness of the *oud* refrain: *All the biggest armies in the world are weak against the hope of the children.* Finally, the track strips down to the *doumbek*, leaving a girl to read a poem:

> We want a new generation
> That does not forgive mistakes
> That does not bend
> We want a generation of giants

A new, unforgiving, unbending generation of giants. DAM's hip-hop dream is Israel's worst nightmare. Trickles of sweat ran from my underarms.

"It's hot," I commented.

"It's always hot," said Tamer. He was looking at the ceiling. "If it's not hot, it's cold. It's the desert, no?"

I waved toward the slatted windows. "Seems like a rough town."

DAM gave a collective dry chuckle. "A rough town," repeated Tamer. His eyes narrowed. "A *rough town*? Before the second intifada, this apartment is worth a hundred and twenty grand. Now it's worth thirty. A rough town? Drugs is what this town is. Kids getting the shit kicked from them by the cops, for what? For nothing. For being Arab. Art? Nah, man. Culture? Nah, man. When we shoot our first video here, it is the first time anyone ever puts a camera on this place that isn't a news crew. A rough town?" Tamer clucked, and returned his gaze to the ceiling.

There ensued several moments of hummus-thick silence.

He waved at the window, mimicking my earlier gesticulation. "You've seen this place, bro," said Tamer. "You know what it's about. So if you're me, and you're watching *New Jack City*, or Tupac in *Thug Angel*, or a Biggie video-clip and outside is the 'hood, what you gonna think? You gonna think it's the same damn place.

"We listen to Public Enemy, Gang Starr, KRS-One and, of course, this guy"—Tamer pointed to the flag on his wall—"Tupac Shakur. He is the one who got it started for me. Everything he said, especially in the earlier songs, well—he spoke of my life perfectly. We listen to his 'White Man's World.' We think—ah, this is what it's about!"

The Tupac connection made sense, and not only because the rapper was a famously recalcitrant interview. "White Man's World" is both hard-edged and sentimental, the lament of a jailed gangsta. There are gunshots and tears, dead homies and crying mammas—an urban-style *qasidah*. And Tupac's legend runs deep: His mother was one of the twenty-one Black Panthers arrested in 1969 under suspicion of planning terrorist activities. She had links to the Nation of Islam, her adopted last name is a derivative of the Arabic *shukran*, meaning "thank you," or in this case, "thanks to God." In prison, she wrote a rather uncompromising epistle to her captors, promising "a war—a true revolutionary war—a bloody war. And we will win."

She would later undertake a career as a committed crackhead, affording 'Pac a wide-angle master shot of American indigence. Harlem, Baltimore, Oakland, Compton: Wherever he landed, it was the same old story. His "Thug Life" manifesto, an incensed call for those under the boot of poverty and violence to stand up and be noticed, along with his signature double-barreled bird-flip, made him a powerful Fuck-the-Man figure from Brooklyn to Bahrain. Tupac embodied the genre, combining social commentary, a vivid depiction of urban violence and battle rap into one slick package. He came to a definitive end in 1996 on a Las Vegas boulevard, courtesy of assailants unknown. His posse, the badass Fruit of Islam, was in this case of no assistance.

"DAM is part Tupac, but not all Tupac," said Tamer. "Consider our name. DAM means Da Arabic MCs, but the word also means 'eternal' in Arabic, and 'blood' in Arabic and also in *Iv'rit*, Hebrew. If you combine this, you have 'eternal blood,' meaning that we are *way*—way! above politics.

"Us, we don't sing of bling," Tamer continued, staring at the ceiling. "What bling, my friend? Bitches? We don't sing of that. Nah, we're trying to change all of that. We rap about the problems women have here: *Prisoner, choked, cut off from your dreams and ambitions. Keep your head up sister, just keep your head up. Lost in our customs, primitive and stupid customs.* DAM is about change. And it starts here in this town of Lod."

Da Arabic MCs. Eternal Blood. Converging, combating identities. Tamer Nafar has rapped in English and Hebrew—a language most Israeli-Arabs are taught in school—since his early teens. He cut his first demo when he was fourteen, but it was near impossible to make the leap in consciousness to rapping in his mother tongue. ("It's really difficult to rap in Arabic, but you have to start somewhere," Lethal Skillz told me. "I'm sure French hip-hop sounded like crap at first.

There needs to be a starting point—you need pioneers to measure your flow against, to get things right.") It took years, but Tamer kept at it, and as his proficiency grew, so did his profile. He rapped about the social issues he saw around him—no money, no job, drugs—and then he turned to the political situation. *Too many songs*, rapped Tamer, *and not enough messages.*

He recorded constantly and in October 1999 cut the first official DAM track, called "Innocent Criminals," about "the crimes Arabs do because we have no choice." It was embroiled in minor controversy when radical Israeli musician Aviv Geffen shot a video-clip in which Tamer, dressed as an Israeli soldier, kicked away at the prostrate singer. Subtle it wasn't, and however well intended, the video hinted at the fact that Israeli-Arab protest music could only exist if co-opted by the Israeli left. Nonetheless, during this period—pre–second intifada—Israel had a minor appetite for the small amount of Arab rap trickling into the country, much the same way that white suburban America has long fueled sales for gangsta rap. (Tamer's music was recorded and engineered in Tel Aviv by Israeli Jews supportive of his work.)

"Tamer Nafar is a household name in Israel," *Time Out* music editor Dror Sher told me, "but no one knows why. No one knows what the guy wants to say, except that he's controversial. He's not seen as a rapper, a musician. And this happens when your message isn't a simple one, when you're a complicated artist." Indeed, Tamer's rhymes come off as rage-filled but plaintive: *To all the people of love and peace,* he raps, *how can we have co-existence when we don't even exist?* Palestinian agitators aren't supposed to be this agonized.

"The thing about Tamer," Sher continued, "is that he is confused, and always was confused. He has too many identities. He wants Tel Aviv to listen, he wants the Palestinian Territories to listen, he wants Arabs in the rest of the world to listen. And unfortunately for him, *he* listens."

In 2001, DAM cut a single that dropped like a daisy cutter. "Min Irhabi." *Who's the Terrorist?* It was an underground Internet smash hit, downloaded over a million times from now-defunct ArabRap.net and included on a complimentary CD in the French edition of *Rolling Stone*. The band was mentioned on every news service from CNN to Al Jazeera in breathless, bemused tones. DAM gained an international fan base just as MySpace was breaking as an online venue—establishing Palestinian hip-hop as an Internet phenomenon. (And without the Net, Palestinian hip-hop doesn't exist. There are, simply, no other channels of distribution.) But this wasn't a music story, it was a *news* story:

> You're a Democracy?
> Actually it's more like the Nazis!
> Your countless raping of the Arabs' soul
> Finally impregnated it
> Gave birth to your child
> His name: Suicide Bomber
> And then you call him a terrorist?
>
> YOU'RE the terrorist

This, at least, is DAM's official, oft-repeated founding myth: Hip-hop stars, like politicians and superheroes, require one. But there was one particular character that has been excised from the tale and the story makes no sense without him.

A parking lot outside a club in Haifa, 2003. It's late. Streetlamps bathe everything in sallow light. Tamer leans against a car alongside a man who looks unfortunately like Sacha Baron Cohen's Ali G. This is Subliminal, a.k.a. Ya'akov "Kobi" Shimoni, Israel's mega-selling über-Zionist hip-hop sensation. Their accompanying posses—ball caps backward, basketball jerseys, tattoos—are tense, pacing. This is not a cordial meeting.

"Listen to me, you son of a bitch," the hulking Israeli rapper The Shadow says to DAM's Mahmoud Jreri in Hebrew, "talk to me like that one more time and I'll fuck your ass."

"Kobi, talk decent, have a word with your homie," says Tamer. "Threats and violence don't work with us."

"Did you see a blade?" asks another. "If we were here to fight, no one would stay alive."

This is a final gathering of one-time collaborators. Subliminal—The Light from Zion—owns a label, a roster of recording artists and a burgeoning hip-hop shmatte business. According to his own mythology, he's sold over a million records in a country of six million people. As the hip-hop avatar of Israeli nationalism, he voices the fears, nightmares and anger of his generation: *Blood is spilled and it spills more blood . . . I am dying to live but living to die.* So, to the great beefs of Tupac and Biggie, Nas and Jay-Z, 50 Cent and The Game, we can add Tamer Nafar and Subliminal. Their relationship is documented in a film called *Channels of Rage.* The filmmaker, Anat Halachmi, calls it "a hip-hop tragedy."

Four years before the incident in the parking lot, Halachmi films those same posses on a packed tour bus. "Everyone together," says one kid. Subliminal orders Halachmi to "film the coexistence." He has an arm around Tamer, who has the wide-eyed glee of a kid who can't quite believe where he is. "Why can't we all just get along?" asks The Shadow, ironically. It's a self-conscious challenge to the powers-that-be, a spit in the eye of the status quo. Of course we can all get along. *Everyone together.*

A hip-hop nation.

This is before the Oslo peace accords are properly dead; it is five years after Israel suffered the trauma of president Yitzchak Rabin's assassination at the hands of right-wing Orthodox Jewish extremist Yigal Amir. It is a period of tentative renascence, of weary hope. But there are portents: At a concert in a tightly packed club in Haifa, when Subliminal raps, "*The country is still dangling like a cigarette from Arafat's lips,*" Tamer, alongside him, looks nauseated with discomfort.

"*People*," he says into the mic, "*only hip-hop will bring us peace.*" He does not rap it like he means it.

Then 2000, and the second intifada: Israel is under lockdown. Subliminal tacks hard right, urging concert-goers to proudly wear the Star of David. (They come free with his CDs.) Meanwhile, Tamer loses focus, struggles in the studio, starts moving toward a powerful Arabic rapping voice. "Min Irhabi" is in his sights. *You're the terrorist.*

What, I wondered, had drawn Subliminal and Tamer to each other? Did Tamer need Subliminal to get a leg up, to learn? (He could have done worse; Subliminal is a remarkably gifted rapper, with an effortless flow that lands somewhere between Dr. Dre and silk bedsheets.) Did Subliminal need Tamer to add Arab cred to his crew of Russian, Ethiopian, Iranian and Tunisian Israelis? Or did they both desperately need to believe that through the music they loved—music that was a fundamental part of their selves—they could bridge their differences? But if mainstream hip-hop is about street cred—who is harder, who has been shot more times, whose Bentley Continental has a louder stereo—then Palestinian and Israeli hip-hop is about who has *suffered* more. About who has the *right* to suffer.

"The problem isn't between Tamer and Kobi," says Tamer in the garish light of the Haifa parking lot. "If it were, just a few rap beats and everything would work out, right?" Tamer's face is already carved from the same emotional marble that I'd seen in the apartment in Lod. He is barely twenty-one, but there is no inkling of a kid in him. His youth has evaporated.

"Wanna hear something funny?" asks Subliminal. "The problem *is* between Kobi and Tamer." Subliminal hangs on to the dream he has helped destroy. No one dies that night, except for the hip-hop nation.

It comes down to a word, a beautiful Arabic word and one of my favorite in any language: *Biladi*. My land. Subliminal had appropriated it in his own rhymes. Like the *bap bap bap* of an AK-47, it peppers DAM's lyrics. *Biladi.* Hip-hop has arrived at a regional cul-de-sac. Where to go from here?

In that cramped Lod bedroom, I asked Tamer if there was a way this could move forward, a way to bridge the divide.

"We're a cancer in this society," Tamer told me. "The Israelis want to cut us like a tumor. And we are enemies to the Arabs. Traitors. Subliminal isn't my problem, bro. Being a bridge isn't a problem, bro. I got *real* problems."

Tamer is, after all, an Israeli-Arab. Which means he is a Palestinian. Of a kind. Palestinians in the West Bank and Gaza wouldn't call him Palestinian. Nor would many Arabs elsewhere in the Middle East. To the Israelis, he's a ticking demographic time bomb. Tamer Nafar does not belong. Nazareth-based hip-hop producer Anan Keseem put it to me best: "Who are we then? The '48 Arabs. The Israeli-Arabs? The Inside Arabs? Leaderless, featureless, identity-less. All the time we are confused." (Naming anything in Israel, including "Israel," is exhausting. Words are boomerangs: No sooner have they left your mouth than they spin back toward you, bent on taking your head off.)

"We're not looking for a bridge," said Tamer. "Not us, not as DAM. We're trying to make a bridge between other Palestinians and other Arabs. I don't look for a bridge with Zionists right now. Why would I? They are the ones with the power. It's all about power, bro. Who has the power, who doesn't." And if there is an essence to DAM's music, it must be this paradoxically powerful sense of powerlessness. The enraged bark of the underdog.

Tamer escorted me to the door. As we walked out, I saw the Nafar patriarch at the kitchen sink, slowly, meticulously drying each piece of crockery. I assumed that DAM made a decent living from touring, and I asked Tamer why he and Suhell didn't spring for their own pad.

"Partly choice, combined with tradition," he said. "We don't have an American lifestyle because we are not American." He shut the security gate behind me, the bolt clicking home like a gunshot. "We are Palestinians."

★ ★ ★

"It's hard to defend this shit."

So said Chris Rock of hip-hop, something I've loved since I was sixteen, and I've tried mightily never to question that love. I don't adore hip-hop because it's street poetry or an insight into frayed inner-city consciousness or even for the clever rhymes, but for the same reason all suburban white kids love it—the elemental rage, the bravado, the braggadocio, the nihilism, the misogyny, the portrayal of illicit goings-on in a galaxy far, far away. I've apologized for hip-hop's sins a zillion times using the lingua franca of the doctoral dissertation, but at this point, fuck it. To each their own. That's what iPod earbuds were made for.

As hard as it is to defend hip-hop, it has, arguably, become harder to defend Israel. Growing up in South Africa, I never discussed Zionism with any of my fellow Jews. That's because an allegiance to Israel was assumed. But as I stood in modern-day Lod at high noon, a wave of weariness washed over me. In the eye of the storm, nothing made sense. It was hard to line up the players, follow any one argument, figure out the heroes and the villains and the dudes in between. Same thing happened every time I touched down at Tel Aviv's Ben Gurion Airport. Sheer confusion. It was like I'd swallowed seventy Paxil, a shot of laudanum, and a half of Canadian Club. One took a moral position, only to have it undermined by that morning's headlines. But it wasn't my job to take sides. It was my job to take notes. Standing on that empty boulevard, I wrote one word in large print: *OY!*

I strolled through Lod—along deserted boulevards lined with dusty palm trees, the air thick with heat and rage. The Honda Accord I'd seen when I first arrived, full of *shebabs*, slowly rolled by, rims flashing like shivs. I looked at my feet, brought out my iPod, cued up DAM:

We've been like this more than fifty years
Living as prisoners behind the bars of paragraphs

Of agreements that change nothing
We haven't seen any light, and if we peek between the bars
We see a blue sky and white clouds
In the center a star reminds me that I'm limited . . .

He is Sameh Zakout, and he walks with the swagger of a gangsta: golf shirt, New England Patriots cap, heavy chain. He raps as Saz, is part of the DAM clan, a cousin to Tamer. He lives in Ramla, next door to Lod, although Israel is so divided that nothing is next door anymore. Ramla cred in Israel is *real* street cred—it's a hard town, defined by poverty, ethnic tension, drug-related gang war, and falafels so tasty they can only be the work of a munificent God.

"The Internet," Saz said, as we rounded a corner into a Ramla market, "saved our fucking lives. Oh no, my friend, *believe* it. From the other Arabs, from Palestinians who think those of us stuck inside this Zion place are traitors, who think that we want to live here, to live in this fucking place. Through the Internet, with hip-hop, we can tell people our story. Nowadays you can see people like me. And I am true hip-hop. It belongs to me. The difference is that the black minority in the States called it hip-hop. We could have named it a hundred years ago. Ramla is the fuckin' sixth borough, bro."

Everyone owns hip-hop; any culture that adopts it claims proprietary rights. In Israel and Palestine, because it is tied to the identity—to the self—of so many young people, it is a battle that speaks of the larger war. Hip-hop came to Israel during the early 1980s, when the cultural battlements were remarkably porous. The sabra—native-born Israeli—had plenty in common with his Arab counterparts. His slang and his culture were peppered with Arabic: He watched Egyptian movies on TV, he listened to revered Egyptian chanteuse Um Kalthoum. When the demographics of the new country changed with the influx of Eastern-European Jews—followed by a surge of PLO terrorist activity that led up to the five-year-long first intifada in

1987—a stark cultural alienation developed. This endangered a small but vital empathy that is all but gone; without it, peace becomes less possible by the minute. Forty years ago, Israeli and local Arabs ate from the same cultural platter. Now—especially after the second intifada—they would rather starve.

Israeli hip-hop has definitive links to the Orthodox Jews in the country, who have always been partial to Rasta music. (Matisyahu, the Orthodox reggae indie-phenom is just one in a long line of such musicians.) A gentleman named Nigel Admor was Israel's proto reggae/dancehall/hip-hop religious fundamentalist, releasing a slew of novelty songs in the early nineties, when music stars with long beards and *peyot* were still fresh. He has now retired to concentrate on teaching a special brand of martial arts he claims to have rediscovered from his ancestors—each move based on a letter of the Hebrew alphabet. (Go ahead and try this without a good warm-up: א)

Admor was produced by a session bassist and studio whiz named Yossi Fine, who played with David Bowie and Lou Reed among others, and was turned on to rap when he came across the Sugarhill Gang's "Rapper's Delight" in 1979. (Hip-hop historians agree on but one thing: "Rapper's Delight" is mainstream rap's foundational hit.) Fine's radio program, *The Funk Corner with Yossi Fine*, played on the Israeli station Galgalatz from 1981 on. *The Funk Corner* didn't care if you were Arab or Israeli. Yossi Fine just wanted you to shake your ass.

The music scene in the country (notwithstanding the awful pop) is extraordinarily vibrant. There are a number of producers who can crank out professional demos on the cheap. There is also a diversity of nationalities within Israel, all claiming to be marginalized, all angry. Then, of course, there are the Israeli-Arabs and/or the Palestinians. In this tiny sliver of planet Earth, there is enough animosity to fuel a massive hip-hop scene, never mind an endless ethnic/religious factional war. All these hip-hoppers feel a sense of ownership; they find hip-hop in the roots of their culture.

"When Public Enemy rapped about a 'fear of a black planet,' they probably had no idea they would one day be a source of inspiration to Arab kids living in Israel and the West Bank," wrote a blogger of the phenomenon. Perhaps not. But Afrika Bambaataa, the South Bronx–based hip-hop pioneer, never saw it as anything *but* a global movement. With remarkable cultural sensitivity, he understood the deep links as clearly as he saw the fault lines. To Afrika Bambaataa, "hip-hop was not merely all-city. It was global—a Planet Rock," writes hip-hop historian Jeff Chang.

It gets complicated, this Planet Rock. "You think I don't hear hip-hop every day when I'm a kid?" asked Saz. "I hear it coming from the muezzin, man, calling for the prayers."

He had a point: Hip-hop traces back definitively to the rhythm of Qur'anic recitation. Its poetic cadences, when properly rendered, are both sharp-edged and liquid, the literary equivalent of an exquisite martial art. There is no baroque in the Qur'an. It *flows*.

Battle poetry—another hip-hop fundamental—also has local roots. The early followers of Mohammed had to smack down not only the other major faiths but regional start-ups as well. Consider the words of Hind bint Utbah, the wife of the Prophet's foster brother, who incites her husband "to write verses against the Prophet and against the religion of Islam"—an early form of Battle MC-ing. Hind, herself a poet of some renown, was more than the Lil' Kim to her era's Biggie—she followed her husband onto the battlefield, as was the custom in those days. When the Quraysh armies of Mecca defeated the nascent Muslims at the Battle of Uhud, she mutilated the corpse of the man who had the previous year killed her father and brother in battle, cutting out his liver and consuming it raw.

To its enemies, the Qur'an states, "Let them render a chapter like it. But if you cannot—and indeed you cannot—then guard yourself against the fire." The Qur'an means, literally, "recitation": It is meant to be performed, called from ramparts. As religion scholar Reza Aslan points out in *No god but God*, "In Mohammed's time, the medium through which miracle was primarily experienced was neither magic nor medicine, but language." In this, the Qur'an becomes the opening salvo in fourteen hundred years of enmity in verse, and the fulcrum in a strong Arabic tradition of oppositional poetry. The Qur'an is not a narrative text, like the Bible or the Bhagavad Gita, but rather an act of language.

The cadences of Qur'anic recitation have been reflected in centuries of prose and poetry all over the world. In the Bronx, the flow of the Five Percenters and the Zulu Nation preachers were borrowed from Islamic imams—culled from *suras* and verses—even if these preachermen had no real knowledge of Arabic. This in turn influenced the flow of those early MCs laying rhymes over a 4/4 breakbeat, whether they were conscious of it or not.

"You see, man, hip-hop is in my bones," said Saz. We had stopped in the market to drink lemonade poured from a large samovar. "This is a prison. Don't dream. DON'T HAVE ANY DREAMS. But I dream. I represent. Hip-hop lets you dream. Hip-hop makes you free."

That's a tough notion to swallow in Ramallah, the biggest city in the West Bank.

"The traffic here is crazy. Just crazy," said Nisreena, a friend of a friend. Her Opel caught air over a bump, slammed into a pothole and roared down one of the city's vertiginous hills.

"Maybe it has something to do with the drivers," I said, gripping the holy-shit handle and clenching my butt-cheeks.

"Possibly," she said. She had offered to drive me from the bus station to a meeting. I had no idea it would be a theme park ride.

Earlier, I'd caught a bus into the West Bank from a station near Jerusalem's Damascus Gate. The land east of Jerusalem has been left to rot, ruined by garbage and rubble and tendrils of smoke that rise from the sand. A saddled horse nuzzled for feed in a rubbish-strewn clearing, creeks bubbled like warm oatmeal. In the distance, the separation wall ran like a row of concrete dominoes, waiting to be flicked down by the finger of a gleeful deity.

Ramallah's hills, once verdant, are littered with the remains of wars and a slew of poor engineering decisions. What hasn't collapsed shall shortly do so; what hasn't been bulldozed will be bombed. Like its topography, Ramallah architecture goes up and down and up again.

The Opel zoomed past sullen young men in jeans and T-shirts loitering around cars in the clogged streets. Knock-off jeans clothed armless mannequins in paltry stores. Faded martyrdom posters lined the walls of buildings. They are the tattered memories of boys sent to their doom, poorly Photoshopped in front of gold-domed al-Aqsa, an AK in each hand, bombs strapped to their stomach. There were martyrdom posters pasted to the lion monument in al-Manara Circle, as if at the centre of this city lies a willingness—inverted as a necessity—to sacrifice the young men who crowd its streets. It struck me, with hollow dread, that these posters are advertisements, meant to look like Hollywood action-flick posters. Or hip-hop album covers. What other way is there— among all these faceless, futureless young men—to be remembered?

Nisreena brought the Opel to a shrieking halt just long enough for me to stumble out. Ten years ago, Ramallah was arguably the most cosmo-politan city in Israel, and there were still hints of this in the Sangria Pub. It was a Thursday evening, the beginning of the weekend. Young Palestinians filed into the bar, the girls dressed in ersatz D&G gear. I sat drinking a beer with a twenty-one-year-old kid named Boikutt, who was as thin and gloomy as an Edward Gorey drawing. His real name was Jad Abbas, he wore a T-shirt, jeans a size too big, Chuck Taylors. Smoke rose from his Gauloise, smoke rose from *sheeshas* burbling at tables behind us, smoke rose from backfiring cars and from the garbage burning on the hills beyond. Boikutt records as one-third of Ramallah Underground, a loose arts collective and hip-hop outfit, along with Stormtrap and his brother Basil, a.k.a. Aswatt. Activist hip-hop stalwarts Dead Prez have given them props; the Kronos Quartet has played their composition "Tasheesh." They are skirting genuine international renown.

Boikutt spoke quietly with none of the stridency of Tamer or swagger of Saz. He was measured, parsed out his words carefully. And he told me a story.

It was the second intifada and Ramallah was burning. Tanks were parked at the al-Manara Circle, which just a few weeks before bustled with traffic and pedestrians. Curfew—the whole city under lockdown. When there was electricity, middle-class Ramallans flipped from CNN to Al Jazeera, trying to make sense of what was happening on their doorstep. They needn't have bothered. In Ramallah in those days, the news came to your front door.

The news came to then sixteen-year-old Boikutt, and his nineteen-year-old brother, Aswatt, by way of a squad of Israeli special force soldiers performing house-to-house searches throughout the city. The apartment block was close enough to al-Manara to be a focal point for the action, affording splendid views of the city to the north along the hills. Most of the residents knew the drill: You heard the buzzer, followed by the hammering of machine-gun butts against your door. You opened up, filed downstairs. The family had been expecting just such a visit for weeks.

But nothing prepared you for the knock. Aswatt had just finished his hourly ritual: a bump of coke in the washroom, the high of which he planned to exhaust at the controls of his PlayStation. Drugs made it easier to get through the days. The apartment was filthy: liquor bottles, wrappers, tin cans, unwashed plates. Weeks into curfew, the family was rotting in its own filth. When the knock came, it sounded like gunfire. The Abbases filed out to stand in the hallway.

The soldiers found some curiosities in the Abbas apartment: two turntables, a midi, several mixers, music posters, a keyboard, a hard drive and monitor. But they also found a U.S. Army jacket hanging in the closet and a mock advertisement tacked to the wall: "Absolut Gaza." In a parody of the Absolut Vodka ad campaign, the printout pictured a young man in the act of throwing a cocktail of the Molotov variety.

Not good.

A soldier, in thick Iraqi-accented Arabic, called for the owner of the army jacket. It was Boikutt's, a present from his uncle. He was ushered upstairs by the four heavily armed men. They wanted to chat about the "Absolut Gaza" ad.

"Who is the man in the picture?" the soldier wanted to know.

"I don't know," said a baffled Boikutt. The soldier grabbed him, slammed him against a closet, reframed the question. "Tell me who the fuck that is. Now!" When he opened his eyes, Boikutt was looking at the barrels of four M16s.

"It was in an email."

"Who sent the email?" asked the soldier.

"I dunno, man. It was a forward."

When there are no answers, things get broken—in this case Boikutt's room, with its music equipment ordered in the meticulous way of the teenage obsessive. His mother had made her way upstairs brandishing his American passport. "Look," she said. "He is an American citizen." The soldier knocked the passport from her hand and asked, "Where were you born?"

"Arizona," said Boikutt.

"What city? What street did you live on? What zip code?" Tough questions for someone who was two weeks old when they left America, born there just to claim the document the soldier had thrown to the floor.

The soldiers stormed out of the room. Boikutt waited, staring at the floor. And waited. It was an hour before he felt safe enough to move.

Story finished, Boikutt drained his beer. At that moment, Hamas and Fatah were locked in an internecine struggle for control of the Gaza Strip, and the area was under a strict lockdown.

"It's funny," he said. "Once we were demanding our country back. Now, we are demanding electricity."

Boikutt is a product of his parents, who have long been involved in both politics and music: His father was a trumpet player in the Fatah martial band and had been part of the organization since he joined in the sixties as a sixteen-year-old. His parents met in Lebanon, and Boikutt was born in the States so he could secure that semi-useless American passport, then moved to Cyprus, coming of age in Jordan. He attended music school for two years in Washington, D.C., after which he returned to Ramallah.

"This is where we live, man," said Boikutt. "This is our home. My father needs to be here. He's pretty easygoing—supports what I do, pays for most of my equipment. I think he cares too much for Palestine—he's always trying to help, always advising people. He's really tired now, though—he has problems with his heart. Still, he goes to all the Fatah/PLO meetings, trying to move things forward, to make people aware. Life was hard for him. He had to take his family always on the move." I thought of Tamer's crippled father: Imprisoned, dead or compromised patriarchs are a running theme in hip-hop. To some degree, the genre has always been about asserting—and thus distorting—manhood that was otherwise absent at home.

"Look up 'rap' in the dictionary—it means 'protest,'" said Boikutt. "It's a form of resistance—even if it does come from a different situation. I'm not comparing, y'know, black Americans to Palestinians, but they were resisting many of the same things—racism, no opportunity, brutality."

The history of American music is shot through with protest: spirituals, John Coltrane's "Alabama," James Brown's "Say It Loud (I'm Black and I'm Proud)," Woody Guthrie, Bob Dylan. But rap didn't start out as protest music, even though a disgust for the status quo existed at the heart of the original block parties run by the likes of Kool Herc and Afrika Bambaataa: "Peace, Unity, Love and Having Fun!" promised the Zulu Nation, reaching out from the South Bronx. And while "Rapper's Delight" was an ode to the sybaritic arts, when Grandmaster Flash and The Furious Five (reluctantly) recorded "The Message" in 1982, rap had its first protest song: *Don't push me, cause I'm close to the edge, I'm trying not to lose my head, it's like a jungle sometimes, it makes me wonder, how I keep from going under . . . HA HA!*

Those words kicked off a movement, branching off into either NWA's gangsta rap "Fuck Tha Police" or A Tribe Called Quest's contemplative *The Low End Theory*. Socially conscious hip-hop never defined the genre, but it once played an important role in its makeup. And it still does, at least outside the mainstream. That, as much as the definitive cultural links, is what has always drawn young secular Arab intellectuals to the form.

"I see rap as a weapon," said Boikutt, "a social weapon, a political weapon, an artistic weapon. It's the same form of resistance, using the same weapon, for a different oppressor. I don't know who created the sword, but other people use it. I don't know who created the gun, but there's plenty of them here. You know—it doesn't matter whether it's Western or Eastern—it's just another way to fight. It's non-violent, but it's a weapon."

This echoed something Saz had said: "For me, the microphone is my M16. And my words are my bullets." But were Boikutt and Saz not concerned that when something like Palestinian oppression becomes a *cause célèbre*, protest degenerates into a T-shirt slogan, a bumper sticker, a rigid set of ideologies? To slightly mangle Bertolt Brecht: Yelling and screaming via a cultural medium like hip-hop can end up deflating genuine social criticism. In other words, all the bitching leads to little more than further bitching.

"The question is, can you be a Palestinian hip-hopper and not profit from the cause?" asked Boikutt. "Well, you can if you are real about it. The frustrating thing is that most of the people who listen to you are not hip-hop lovers—they're activists. So the conversation is dead before it starts."

Palestinian hip-hop is still gestating, and it threatens to be stillborn. The genre has always contained an unwieldy duality: sometimes "Rapper's Delight," sometimes "The Message." Surely hip-hop needed to embrace all elements of Palestinian existence to be culturally vital? Life in South African townships can be hell, but kwaito—a local derivation of hip-hop—sells hundreds of thousands of records because it is both culturally relevant party music *and* protest music. Can Palestinian hip-hop be anything other than Palestinian protest music?

"I know what you're saying, man: You can feel it when you're on stage," said Boikutt. "The audience is there to wave a picket—they don't know anything about hip-hop." He drained his beer and sank into his chair. "Thing is, this is a producer's medium, and we're producers first. The goal was to make something that would fit alongside real music in a mixtape—nothing more. But we also wanted to make a Ramallah sound. I knew when I listened to hip-hop that I wanted a new Ramallah. That's my mission."

I sipped my beer and thought: mission accomplished. Ramallah Underground is what I'd describe as Eastern urban. They are the sound of an *oud* string, the wail of a muezzin, a sampled ululation snaking over a diseased breakbeat, a record scratch, a heaving synth— sonic flits kidnapped from the streets. Then there's Boikutt's throaty flow, thick with fury, the voice of a towering creature of the Territories. Arabic consonants land like brick on windshields; words explode like stun grenades. *Keep your voice loud as if an XLR cable is connected to your tongue and welded on your teeth.* This is not world music. This is the music of war.

"The question is this: What is Palestinian culture?" asked Boikutt. "Is it what happened here ten thousand years ago, fifty years ago or three years ago? People change, systems change. But don't talk to me about real Palestinian culture. How the fuck do you know what that is? Why *can't* it be hip-hop?"

According to Anan Keseem, one of Palestine's premier producers, there are currently about forty hip-hop outfits operating in Arab Israel, Gaza and the Territories, everywhere from Jenin to Gaza, Bethlehem to Nablus. "The older generation is even starting to appreciate it," said Boikutt. "If your uncle heard you listening to Run DMC, he'd be like 'Turn that shit off.' Now, he hears it in Arabic, so it becomes Arabic music, and he appreciates it. There's growing up a generation who gets introduced to hip-hop through *Arabic* hip-hop. I have a little cousin in London—he doesn't know nothing *but* Arabic hip-hop. It's Arab music—obviously it's a hybrid, because we're hybrid. We *are* Palestinians, and *this* is the reality of Palestine. I'm telling the Ramallah story."

★ ★ ★

The al-Kasaba Theatre is a short walk from central Ramallah on a street crammed with shoe shops and more convenience stores than was convenient. Sunset lasted an hour. In the darkening sky, Venus—never brighter than in the East—was swarmed by three flapping kites: comets of play. The air was thick with smoke, the sky tinged an ethereal puce. In Yemen, locals call this Solomon's Hour.

A Belgian-based NGO had organized a cross-cultural concert, featuring Boikutt and headlined by a band called Rumpelstitchkin, four Belgian rockers in their early thirties, their manner with one another suggesting a long week on the road following a career of near hits, almost breaks and summer rock fests in Brussels's parking lots. At twenty-five shekels (twelve dollars at that day's exchange rate), I wasn't sure how many of Ramallah's young rap/rock fans would be able to afford it. But there were about a hundred kids in the hall when I arrived.

The band assembled on stage with some of the Palestinian musicians: a superb young *oud* player alongside a dreadlocked rock guitarist. When I'd spoken to Boikutt before the show, he'd confessed that he was nervous. "It's the fastest I've ever rapped, especially live," he told me. He was now sitting in the front row, eyes on his Chuck Taylors. The music built slowly, the *oud* finding space between the guitars to glide up and out from the stage in ripples of melancholy. This was Boikutt's cue. He stood, almost invisible against the mass of the auditorium. He took the three steps to the stage in one leap, grabbed the mic between his hands, and then something remarkable happened.

Boikutt *grew*.

It was as if he had uncoiled, all the energy inside him revealing its purpose. The eighty or so kids in the auditorium rose, as if they understood that in order to bear the force of what was coming they'd need to be on their feet. Then, like a point-blank blast from a sawed-off shotgun:

> They're passed out
> They pulled out
> They sat down
> They shut up
> Got cut up
> Got sewn back
> Open your eyes and see
> The destruction of a liberation organization
> Open your ears and hear
> The sound of the earth move
> I have come from underground
> A raw Palestinian
> Live and direct from the frontlines

The crowd—a gathering of local middle-class kids and expats with American or British accents—expanded, filled the auditorium as if Boikutt's perfect, pointed rage was some kind of battle armor that they had all donned. His flow increased in velocity—a broadside of verbal ordnance. *Paralyze all obstacles, be convinced of your movement, get on the streets and represent!* The band behind him had receded; the auditorium was filled with young Palestinians, hands in the air, yelling.

I was, momentarily, among a generation of giants.

Some nights later, I slept on a bunk bed in the basement of the Austrian Hospice in Old Jerusalem's Arab Quarter, along the Via Dolorosa near the third station of the cross, where Christ stumbled with his burden for the first time. At four in the morning, church bells battled with the muezzin's call to *fajr*, and I blundered through a dream of a mathematical construction that I somehow knew was the formula for working through the regional conflict. To solve this equation would be to come to the bottom of things. I woke up frustrated, wisps of algorithms disappearing as consciousness dawned.

The dream felt especially elusive as I walked through a checkpoint and into the teeming mess that is Shu'afat Refugee Camp, a short ride from East Jerusalem's Palestinian bus station. This was a city of children. They moved in packs led by barking girls in hijabs, passing under fluorescents that jutted like warring light-sabers. The sky sagged with knots of cables. Like the territorial spray of a tomcat, graffiti on a wall read: *Welcome to G-Town.*

Muhammad Mughrabi met me at the foot of a broken road. He is the lead MC of the hip-hop crew advertised in the graffiti. He had shy, long-lashed eyes, wore a basketball tank top, two twinkling earrings, a heavy gold chain. I said that Shu'afat didn't seem like a place where it was advisable to wander around drenched in bling.

"We have money here," he said. "Money we don't need. But you have to be strong here. You have to survive. People know me. They know my family. They know I am strong."

It was dusk. We wound our way through streets that smelled powerfully of cooking oil. Muhammad swung open two rickety saloon doors and led us into a concrete bunker with three battered pool tables. He gently shooed some kids away and racked up.

"The first time I hear Arab hip-hop was in a car driving through the camp," he told me between shots worthy of an ESPN highlight reel. "I think—what the fuck is this? For the first time, I am struck. I know that I must do this. Be this."

Muhammad learned his English from an esteemed faculty including professors Dr. Dre, Tupac, Eminem, among others. At sixteen, he entered talent contests in East Jerusalem where this new form of "song" captivated audiences. He was soon taking home prize money.

"So in 2002 it is time to start a band. I download my samples from an Internet café, but no one will record me, because they think rap is

YOU'RE THE TERRORIST 219

50 Cent and bitches and money. But one guy does record me. And so we start."

The group was initially called G-Camp, but the name felt wrong. "I knew from American hip-hop about the 'hood, the ghetto. I look up ghetto on Wikipedia, and I find that it was the name of where the Jews lived in Poland, and now they make us do the same damn thing. In Arabic, Poland is *Poleen*. It rhymes with *Falesteen*. And Shu'afat is not really a camp. It has become a town. So, I come up with Ghetto Town. G-Town."

At twenty-one, Muhammad is already an experienced MC. He has a lazy flow, always a nanosecond behind the beat, as if his *huzn* is too much to bear: hip-hop as dirge. But this is what distinguishes Arabic hip-hop from its ubiquitous chintz-pop counterpart: Muhammad, like Tamer and Boikutt, sees his music as something more than mere lamentation.

"On stage, I can convince any of these kids to do anything you want. They are *waiting* for me to tell them what to do, for me to say something. Where are our leaders? There are no leaders. Who is the man in charge of Gaza, of West Bank? Tell me his name. We have no leaders. Just me." With that, Muhammad cranked the eight-ball into a far pocket with the force of a mortar blast.

A gaggle of urchins bustled into the bunker and crowded around Muhammad, who patiently proffered high-fives, and I thought of something Janne Anderson, a Danish activist organizing a series of hip-hop workshops in Ramallah, had said to me. "I see Palestinian hip-hop really as an upcoming youth culture. Nobody believes that this stuff is purely Western anymore. It has a purpose, a reason. Parents want anti-drug songs. It's become part of the value system. People identify with it because it's a street culture. There's only one other thing that's like this. And that's the Islamic movement."

"The Islamic movement?" Boikutt had said some days before, when I put this to him. "Nah, man, those guys don't make trouble for us. They know we are singing of serious things. Maybe five years ago they care. Now, though? Nah."

Hip-hop will certainly pop up on the local Islamist radar at some point if it hasn't yet. There is also the cautionary tale of the female rapper Sabreena Da Witch, a DAM-affiliated MC who went into voluntary exile because of resistance from her traditional extended family. It's one thing for dudes to MC, but it's a whole other thing for females to do the same. These are the kind of walls that Palestinian hip-hoppers are trying to level.

"Come," said Muhammad. "Let me show you something."

We walked the half block to Muhammad's sprawling family compound, a five-story concrete structure that didn't look like it could withstand a loud burp, never mind the massive tremblor Jerusalem's seismologists are promising. He sat in front of a PC and played me a recent G-Town track called "1 March 2008." It was a thumping lament, garnished with the sonic palette of conflict.

"If you listen close, this track is at 60 BPM, for the sixty years of the *naqba*. It is like a history book. I am telling kids what happened that day. I am telling them that Palestine is Palestine. Does any of us hip-hop guys sing about Fatah? Hamas? No. We are outside of that. Everybody is so sick of politics. Everybody is so sick of bullshit traditions. We are the new way. We are the new dawn."

My last day in Israel/Palestine/Whatever: I sat with Saz outside a Ramla falafel joint, watching traffic. The town was at boiling point. It's a wonder there weren't hourly drive-bys.

"G-Town?" said Saz. "Nah. Never heard of them."

"They're from the Shu'afat camp, outside Jerusalem."

"I know where it is. I never heard of them."

And therein lies the problem. Being a Palestinian no longer means being any one thing, if it ever did. It's broken into subsections, divisions, genres. G-Town belongs to the refugee camp genre, whereas Saz belongs to the inner-city Israeli-Arab genre, distinct from DAM's Lod genre, which is different from . . . well, you get the point.

"Being a refugee is fucking difficult," Muhammad Mughrabi had told me. "You go to Ramallah, they say you are Israeli. You go to Jerusalem, the Arabs say you are from the camp. People hate us."

A white Acura drove by; Tamer and a homie hopped out. We drank juice, talked about the new Snoop Dogg album. I asked Tamer what he thought of G-Town. He hadn't heard of them either. I asked him what he thought of Ramallah Underground.

"Those guys? I do a show with them once, here in Ramla. They know me. I see them in England for a show, and they can't say wassup. Maybe I'm not good enough for them. I'm from Lod, they from Ramallah. It's bullshit, but that's how it goes."

Saz said that hip-hop has saved the Israeli-Arabs from the rest of the Arab world, but it has yet to heal *Palestinian* divisions. They are divided: by walls, checkpoints, but also class, stigma and desperation to own the story of suffering. It's the problem encoded into hip-hop—the battle for cred. It killed Biggie and Tupac. It's what ripped Subliminal and Tamer apart. It's what keeps Palestinian hip-hop from properly contributing to Palestinian culture.

Dror Sher put it best: "Ramla and Lod may be so close, but the conditions are so horrible that they are far away. So Palestinian hip-hop is in the same place as Palestine. There's no direction. There's no five-year plan. Reality changes every five seconds, and you have to take care of your own. To grow, maybe it needs to leave Palestine. But then it becomes something else."

When Tamer called for a generation of giants, who exactly should be included in that generation? Until that question was resolved, Palestinian rap would be just a crack in the wall. And *that* would be a hip-hop tragedy.

"Come," said Tamer to his homie. He looked at me hard, nodded. "We go back into the nightmare." They climbed into the Acura, and were immediately lost in Ramla's traffic.

Part IV

MAGHRIB

8

Stop Watching the News and Get in the Game

SYRIA, FEATURING YEMEN AND PALESTINE

Sunni Muslim: 74%

Other Muslim: 16%

Christian: 10%

Jewish: trace

20% GDP

1. The Cardigans:
   My Favourite Game

2. Roy Orbison:
   I Drove All Night

3. White Shoes &
   The Couples Company:
   Runaway Song

Pop.: 19,747,586

Avg. age: 21.4

Capital: Damascus

Independence: April 17, 1946

The landscape is empty except for the scars
of war: bullet holes in walls, craters in
the asphalt. Ahead, a tank: a Star of David
flutters from the turret. It shudders, fires
a round into the distance.

The boy with the *keffiyah* is armed with a
slingshot. He aims it at the broad frame of an
Israeli soldier, drops him. The soldiers come in
steady waves, firing heavily. The boy is hit. Red
splats mark his body. He ducks into an alleyway,
leaps for a medical kit. The wounds vanish.

He runs for the tank, felling four soldiers with
his slingshot. He leaps onto the smoldering
vehicle, drops a grenade into it—*BOOF!*—snatches
the Star of David.

As he raises himself upright, bullets pepper his
back. He freezes—a martyr's pose—then falls to the
ground. This time there is no medical kit.

An Israeli soldier approaches, points his weapon
at the kid's head, pulls the trigger. Nothing: gun
jam. The soldier tosses the weapon aside, his face
locked in a scowl. He grabs a chunk of concrete
from the street, raises it high, and brings it
down with all the force he can summon.

The boy's legs twitch. Then he is still.

<end>

We left in the evening. Traffic snagged us at the outskirts of Damascus, where teetering buildings gave way to hills that fanned out into a desert ribbed with grit. Alongside us were hunchbacked trucks, buses, loaded wagons—a Soviet-style exodus to nowhere. I dozed and woke surrounded by desert plains tinted blue by the gloaming, eucalyptus trees bent under the *shamal* winds particulate with all the Middle East. This was Syria. Rogue state. Pariah.

"You were drooling," said Radwan Kasmiya. He turned down the Toby Keith, handed me a wet wipe from an array of cleaning products he kept at hand, then resumed his ten-and-two grip on the wheel. I wiped goop from my shoulder. The *ad'han* sounded from Radwan's Nokia, a portable muezzin.

"You know why I do this—program the *ad'han* into my PDA?" asked Radwan. "It is my clock—my internal clock, like a circadian rhythm. Also, when I deal with the Saudis, I must know not to bother calling them at this time."

Radwan is a Prospero, a wizard practicing his newfangled art in a land where magic is a dangerous business. He is also, undeniably, a dork: a Syrian nerd, modeled directly on the American nerd: doughy, with a pocket protector and a short-sleeved shirt tucked into Dockers. As the country's top software mogul, but more importantly the Arab world's premier video game producer and 3-D digital guru, Radwan had an email inbox groaning with twenty thousand emails, many of them death threats, most of them accusing him of making games that would turn a generation of tech-savvy Arabs into terrorists.

We were on our way to the first of two key points on the Syrian map that spoke of ancient enmities one would like to think had long been settled. One destination was the great crusader castle Krak des Chevaliers. The other was Qala'at Salah ad-Din, the mountainous compound won by the Saracen hero. The first was a Christian holdout, the other a Muslim one. Franks vs. Mohammedans, and that sort of stuff. Radwan had excused himself from the company of his wife and three-year-old daughter to drive me to these places in his silver Kia he called "Sara." He thought this brief road trip would provide a breather.

"Oh, look at that," said Radwan. "Your shoulder."

"My shoulder?" I said.

"You missed a spot."

I took another scented wet wipe, and dabbed at the drool.

In a perfect case of a brand reflecting the nature of its founder, Radwan Kasmiya's company is called Afkar Media, which is Arabic for "mindset" or "ideology." The logo is an intricate calligraphic rendering of an eye. It evokes mulishness, vision. A three-dimensional version of the logo stands outside Afkar Media HQ, a drab three-story glass building within the Damascus Free Zone compound. Inside, twenty or so programmers work on an array of new-media projects. This could be any North American suburban computer company, assuming the suburb had been recently bombed. Afkar's mandate is sweeping and poetic:

> To communicate with Moslems in a way that respects their colorful heritage and spiritual privacy as a way to get them out of the shell they were put in and enrich the civilization of the 21st century with a touch of justice, acceptance, and love.

In order to do this, they produce violent video games.

I learned of Afkar during a few days of media hand-wringing over a Thomas Friedman column in *The New York Times* titled "Giving the Hatemongers No Place to Hide." Writing during the wave of revulsion following the 7/7 London Underground terrorist bombings in July 2005, Friedman reminded his readers that the West was losing the "war of ideas within Islam," and followed that with an impassioned call to expose hate speech wherever it hid. The situation was dire, as evidenced by a police raid on the Iqra Learning Centre bookstore in Leeds (hometown of the bombing cabal), which traded in everything from ballpoint pens to Islamist hate literature. According to a *Wall Street Journal* report quoted by Friedman, the Learning Centre was the sole European distributor for U.S.-based Islamgames, which produced video games featuring "apocalyptic battles between defenders of Islam and opponents. One game, *Ummah Defense I*, has the world 'finally united under the Banner of Islam' in 2114, until a revolt by disbelievers. The player's goal is to seek out and destroy the disbelievers."

Banner of Islam! Disbelievers! Sounded scary. But I wondered if Friedman or the *Journal* correspondent had actually played *Ummah Defense I*. The "Disbelievers"? Pixilated robot-like doodads. The "defenders of Islam"? A UFO uncannily resembling a steaming cow paddy. Even as out-there allegory, *Ummah Defense I* is a bit of a stretch. If something sinister was going on, it was perhaps that someone was attempting to return gaming technology to the glory days of the Islamic caliphate. Islamgames, with its vaguely educational mandate, is as tame as it gets.

Hezbollah, however, is not. Their Central Internet Bureau, part of the organization's sophisticated media wing, developed a game called *Special Force* in 2003, which echoes the title of a U.S. military-developed game called *America's Army: Special Forces*. (Hezbollah has its own satellite station called Al Minar, among other media initiatives. The organization has a hyper-conservative Islamist *Martha Stewart Living* meets MTV meets the *700 Club* branding model.)

"The goal is to create an alternative to similar Western games where Arabs and Muslims are portrayed as terrorists," Hezbollah spokesman Bilal az-Zein told Reuters at the time. The game's website provides the following expository narrative:

> In the Name of Allah, Most Gracious, Most Merciful. One time I was walking in Beirut, the capital that 'defeated the greatest army of the world.' I stopped by one of the computer game shops dispersed widely in Beirut and most Arab cities. I saw the children playing the game of the invincible American hero, who's never out of ammunition and who continually wins. I asked one of the children, did you like the game? He replied, 'Yes, but I wish I were playing as an Arab Moslem fighting the Jews as the Islamic Resistance did in Lebanon!'

We have this fun-loving and articulate youngster to thank for Hezbollah's craptastic *Special Force*. But I did wonder at the logic. I've made it my business to game in over thirty cities in the Muslim world, and I've found that for the most part kids don't give a Nintendo Wii whether they're the American hero or the Bangladeshi hero so long as they get to blow heads off the bad guys, whatever religion, creed or species they may be.

I'd started my gaming research in Yemen—in Old Sana'a—under mudbrick skyscrapers that made one think, fondly, of the eleventh century. If one were to close one's eyes and conjure up the perfect Bill O'Reilly ideal of a backward, sullenly religious Islamocracy, Yemen would be it. Nonetheless, I gamed with many young boys and men, most of whom still wore the *futa* and shawls of their great-grandfathers. And according to the official literature, they still subscribed to ancient clan-based blood-for-blood mores. More to the point, they spent their afternoons in subterranean chambers playing video games on battered PCs while their elders chewed qat.

My guide in Yemen was a loquacious eighteen-year-old named Abdul-Hamid. He liked to play the notorious *Grand Theft Auto* franchise (sample line: "Kill the Haitian dickheads!"), in which the gamer plays a criminal who must rise through an urban underworld doing things that would get one flogged and/or beheaded in the alleys of Old Sana'a. The franchise has sold over seventy million copies. Factor in bootlegs, we're talking probably a quarter of a billion *GTA* games smeared over the planet. Abdul-Hamid owned several of them.

"I love this game, because when you fight in the streets, it is very good," he told me, after I asked him how a devout Muslim could reconcile the more insalubrious elements of *GTA* with a pious lifestyle. "We do not do these things in real," he reminded me. "But my nieces and nephews—some who are three years old—like to watch me play."

Around the planet, bootleg copies of every game imaginable are available for a pittance, and Yemen is clearly no exception. While soccer games for the PC are by far the most popular, we played *Knights of the Temple: Infernal Crusade*, in which the gamer becomes Paul, a Templar, who must battle the Devil's Bishop and kill demons from hell. ("This," Abdul-Hamid told me, "I like.") We played *Conflict: Desert Storm II: Back to Baghdad*, which is a squad-based military game in which . . . well, you get the picture. We played *SOCOM U.S. Navy SEALs: Combined Assault* and more of the same. In all cases, there was no obvious connection between the ostensible meaning of the game and the art of playing it. Language and media-literacy barriers ensured this. So far as I could tell, Abdul-Hamid and his peers weren't interested in anything but kicking virtual ass.

But that's just not how game developers and media watchers see it. "Video games matter," wrote Thomas Friedman. Hezbollah agrees: In Beirut, a media operative for the group told me that "*Special Force* was not meant to be played—we know it isn't good enough. It was meant to get media, to show the problems of American games. And to recruit."

Despite Hezbollah's best efforts, the history of Islamist gaming is short and desultory. There is the 2006 first-person shooter *Quest for Bush*, which was a free online modification of an American game called *Quest for Saddam*. Before that, there was *The Stone Throwers*, a free download developed by a Syrian medical student just after the beginning of the second intifada. There was *Legend of Zord*, developed by a now-defunct UAE company, along with *Zoya: A Warrior from Palmyra*, an awful *Tomb Raider* knock-off. There have been others, including an array of free game-like downloads available on Islamist sites. Out of 1.3 billion Muslims, less than a few thousand have availed themselves of these online opportunities.

There are, however, a plethora of successful games published by American gaming companies that have been developed by the U.S. military complex and sold as entertainment when their actual purpose is decidedly otherwise. The Marines in particular have at least a fifteen-year history of "looking at commercial off-the-shelf computer games that might teach an appreciation for the art and science of war." Those games, having been modified for the military's purpose, have in turn been marketed to the public. Authenticity is their selling point. The Kuma\War series, for instance, recreates actual events—the killing of Saddam Hussein's sons during the early days of the Iraq invasion, an assault on Iran's nuclear facilities—and spins them for fun. But Kuma\War has an agenda. It is "a series of playable recreations of real events in the War on Terror. Nearly 100 playable missions bring our soldiers' heroic stories to life, and you can get them all right now, for free. Stop watching the news and get in the game!" These games enrage most educated Muslims. Hezbollah decided not to get mad. Instead, it tried to get even.

What's the net result of this techno-ideological back and forth? No one knows. There is no solid, appreciable scientific data on whether games influence political or social behavior, even if they do possess, as celebrated game designer Ernest W. Adams puts it, "the power of rhetoric." ("The only thing that everyone agrees on is that playing videogames makes you better at playing videogames," comments another cultural critic.) What presumably terrifies commentators about gaming is that, unlike film or television, the player *takes on* the persona of the principal character. This engagement—this mind melding—*must* be dangerous: To play a terrorist is to become a terrorist. But there is significant evidence to suggest that games—even the murderous first-person shooter genre—make kids smarter and faster, increase their critical faculties and inculcate in them the rather Protestant notions of consequences, perseverance, hard work and reward, while keeping them otherwise occupied so they don't perpetrate the actual crimes at which they have become so virtually competent.

Let's assume there are a host of cognitive and scientific reasons for a teenager's predilection for *Grand Theft Auto*. This still doesn't explain *how* or *whether* a specific cultural product changes an individual's world view. (Or adds to an accumulative change.) One thing is certain: Games provide a remarkable ideological open-ground: No film, TV show or comic book could get away with such in-your-face propaganda. A game's ideological point of view is coded into its architecture. Gamers expect secrets: They look behind doors, check under rocks, peek down Lara Croft's tank top. Because video games are technologically open-ended, they are heavy with what academics call "paratext." To derive the maximum enjoyment from a game, a player must refer to the production company for online patches, updates, cheat notes, and must engage with other gamers or experts for additional intel.

While other media have paratext, none is as all-encompassing as gaming, which can work as an effective ideological conduit like no other pop-cultural medium in history. (Hezbollah's *Special Force* was heavily advertised in game shops in Southern Lebanon, which were decorated to resemble the organization's cave-like bunkers.) The net result of all this cyber-syllogism is unclear but, as Keith Halper, head of Kuma Games, has said, "It's propaganda, but it's also a form of debate. We have made a point, they have responded."

★ ★ ★

"I believe that a creator must make society a better place to live, not a worse place to live," says Radwan Kasmiya, which is not the usual video game developer's rhetoric. But he is not the usual video game developer. His international notoriety derives from two thematically linked games released in 2002 and 2005, entitled *Under Ash* and *Under Siege*, and another released in 2006, called *Quraish*. The first two are standard first-person shooters set in Jerusalem and Gaza, played from the Palestinian point of view. (Which is enough to classify them in some circles as a terrorist training tool.) The latter is the first Arabic 3-D real-time strategy game that follows the sixth-century rise of the House of Islam. "Was it 'AL JIHAD' the holy war that makes them conquer?" asks the press material. "Was it the tolerance of this spiritual religion? Or is it the wiliness of their gifted leaders? Well . . . you will have to choose it by yourself."

No one believes in the educative—which is to say the propaganda—possibilities inherent in gaming more than Radwan Kasmiya. In *Quraish*, the player must pick one of four "races": Muslim, Christian (or Byzantine), Persian (or Sassanid) and Bedouin. Battles and sieges—the mechanics of war—take up the bulk of the player's time, as they do in most strategy games. "Notice the bars of the characters' heads—one is for health, but the other one is for morale," Radwan points out. "This is not just about happiness, but it is about how the soldier *feels*. If you sack a town, you will become rich and even healthy, but your morale will go down. You see—I'm not just doing this for fun. Not at all." In this, *Quraish* depicts Radwan's historical interpretation of the ascendancy of the Islamic caliphate. "I am proud of how humane the soldiers were. There was almost no bloodshed," Radwan says. "Europeans should learn a thing or two from us." As far as he is concerned, so should every young Muslim. And this they can do by purchasing his product.

Radwan's oeuvre inverts the typical storyline: The good guys are now the bad guys. They are complicated, nuanced examples of the tit-for-tat pop-cultural battle being played out in the Muslim world. The games are portentous, heavy with the other side's version of history. *Stop watching the news*, they assert, *and get in the game.*

```
<begin>
```
The man in the *keffiyah* dodges the bullets ripping up the mosque. The corpses of worshippers litter the prayer rugs. He ducks behind a pillar, zigzags, pauses.

A thickset assailant in dungarees and a yarmulke sprays the mosque with gunfire from an Uzi. *Gakkakkakkakakak.* Men crumble before him.

Move now! someone yells. *He's reloading.*

Rounding a pillar, the man approaches at a fast run.

Careful! Goldstein has detected you.

Goldstein slaps another clip into his Uzi,metal on metal. The man with the *keffiyah* pounces, throws a right hook, a left hook, another right.

Goldstein hits the floor. There is no more gunfire.

```
                                                   <end>
```

Radwan's office was a Sam's Club of his obsessions. It sported a hundred or so bootleg DVDs, everything from *The Bourne Supremacy* to Romanian winners of the Palme d'Or, filed on a bookshelf dominated by a Shrek doll and a series of *Lord of the Rings* figurines. There were *Seinfeld* and *Curb Your Enthusiasm* and *The Simpsons* box sets. His desk was large and largely empty, his PC set off to the side. A Post-It note on the monitor read, "Please come out—We missing you," scrawled by his concerned staff after he did not leave his chair for sixteen hours straight.

"They care about me," said Radwan, firing up his PC. "Which is nice." He swung the chair toward me and turned into Professor Frink.

"Put a shovel in this land and you will dig up a history. Underneath this very floor? History. And when it comes to telling history, much of this I got from French comic books. Then," he paused dramatically, "I find the computer."

"Blessed are the meek: for they shall inherit the earth," promises Matthew 5:5. Replace "meek" with "geek" and we're getting somewhere. The rise of the nerd as an economic and social force—praise be to William Gates, Jr., and Steve Jobs—coincided with the advent of the personal computer. In Radwan's case, "it was a Sinclair and it was my first gate to computers. I was in the seventh grade, and the minute I switch it on, I was hooked." He spoke about it as if it was his first girlfriend.

"The computer was, of course, an English make," he told me, "and my first program was to make it write Arabic letters. You can call me a computer nerd, I suppose, but I have always—since the first days—used computers to help me. And to help other people. To help them live in a better way."

Radwan Kasmiya was born in Damascus—in a hill-bound neighborhood called Salihiya (or Place of the Good People, a reference to its preponderance of mosques). He spent six years of his childhood in Morocco, playing among olive trees, fig trees and Roman ruins, "where the smugglers kept their horses." Not unlike Syria, there was history in every fistful of dirt.

"I used that time to learn French," said Radwan, who is always using his time to learn something. As a boy, he pored over history books, piecing together the battles that once ravaged this land, villains sailing from the far West bearing pennants emblazoned with blood-red crosses. Radwan's father was of Palestinian stock—a teacher turned entrepreneur—his mother was from an aristocratic clan that traced its lineage back to the time of the Prophet. Radwan's home was upper middle class, with French manners, silver cutlery, bookshelves lined with the great works of the Western canon.

Halfway through an electrical engineering degree, Radwan had already started SuperSoft, which he describes as a "Syrian Microsoft," developing accounting, auditing and multimedia presentation software. (Certain Microsoft applications are ineligible for export to Syria under U.S. Government regulations, as are components such as fast processor units and large-capacity memory cards. Radwan builds most of his hardware from skimmed parts.) By the time he started his compulsory military service, he was raking it in. He would go to base for roll call, then change hurriedly into civilian gear under the bleachers, race back to his basement office, and get to work.

Radwan is something of a Syrian anomaly: an entrepreneur in a country that doesn't support entrepreneurship, where the brightest enter the cushy civil service or flee to the West. His original SuperSoft partner currently works in a high-level computing job for NASA. "He said to me, 'Okay, Radwan, I am leaving to follow my career.' I think about it a lot, but I think I have no regrets. What would be the point? To leave would be to lose."

To lose what? I wondered. And to whom?

Radwan saw video game development as a way to bring his passions for technology, history, film and comic books together in an artistic repository for all the riches geekdom had to offer. In 2000 he partnered with Dar al-Fikr, a major Arabic publishing company, so his vision could be realized. But Radwan was not content to stop there. Afkar has become a full-fledged new-media company, producing a series of computer-animated short films about a puckish lad called Kareem, each five-minute piece commissioned for Kuwaiti television. Another game, called *Swords of Heaven*, was in development. And there was the first wholly Arab-produced computer-generated feature film, called *A Wall in My Backyard*, about the Israeli-built security fence (or Apartheid wall, depending on which side of it one happens to live) destroying a Palestinian village. In this, Radwan was remarkable, but not just because he had poured his obsession with the occupation into his work.

★ ★ ★

"I'm a gamer, and I'm a reader—I read many, many books—and I can see now that games can influence a wider slice of society than any other media," Radwan told me. "And I'm a gamer who is lucky to have a very big historical background. When I play *Empire* or *Construction*"—two hugely successful real-time strategy games that influenced *Quraish*—"I could sense what is the hidden script."

"Hidden script?"

He smiled. "I don't like this mono thing—one thing pitted against the other. The problem with video games is it is putting more strains on the majority to think that the world is just black and white. In movies, not always the good guys win. In video games, the good guys *always* win—and this narrow view is affecting the teenagers. If we continue like this, we'll have a new wave of extremists, on both sides. An American teenager playing *Delta Force* or *Counter-Strike*, and in the game he is invading Iraq. What do you think he will do if he is actually in Iraq? This is dangerous. Very dangerous."

"So you've decided to counterbalance this with more of the same?"

Radwan smiled again. "You know—when I made my games, I didn't make them tit for tat—it's not like that at all. I purposefully built in levels that you can play without a weapon. At the end of *Under Siege*, most of the heroes die—what kind of game is this? No matter how well you play—you die! Most games are based on instinct. I try to focus on the heart and mind. Most games—you just kill what's on the screen—an alien or a Third World misfortunate. Me, I am using action to tell a story. You will activate both heart and mind to understand it." He beckoned me over. "Come, come. Sit."

I sat alongside Radwan at the PC. His fingers moved over the keyboard like a virtuoso pianist.

"Remember this—I am always against the guy with the guns." We scrolled through the *Under Ash* demo: There were guns aplenty. This is a simple first-person shooter with a twist. The game, set during the first intifada, was inspired by a photograph of a lone Palestinian boy hurling a rock at an Israeli tank. It is narrated by an insurgent who fought against the British (and, of course, the Jews) in the Arab Revolt between 1936 and 1939, then moved from his idyllic home in Palestine into the "big prison" that is Gaza. There, he lost his willingness to fight, until "the intifada made me reconsider."

This is the romance that has gripped Radwan's imagination. His Palestinians are underdogs—a mother taking care of her young, a teenage boy, an old man without a family, a resistance fighter affiliated with no particular group. His scenario of resistance is set during the first intifada, rather than the far messier second intifada, in a fantasy Palestine free of infighting, sectarianism and brother-on-brother bloodshed. Radwan—and many other Arab artists of his generation—have conjured a Palestine that serves as a popular-culture touchstone. It is a place of righteous struggle.

Under Ash's tagline is "It's Our Right—To Live in Dignity," and the game stands as the first Arab video game ever published commercially. It is primitive, even by the standards of the nineties.

"There's a saying in gaming," said Radwan. "Your first ten games will suck. So I need five more games before I'm happy. But notice how you have to help people." His character takes an injured person to a Red Crescent ambulance parked, oddly, near the Dome of the Rock, which can only mean that we are in a partially liberated Jerusalem.

Radwan abruptly stopped playing and switched CDs. "This is where the trouble starts," he said, smiling wanly.

Under Siege is Afkar's signature product, downloaded by over one million people, and reaping mostly outraged press coverage for its creator. It is more sophisticated than *Under Ash*, darker, a product of the second intifada. Gaza is swathed in a terminal twilight. Backed by tanks, heavily armed, the Israelis stand in contrast to the Palestinian characters, only one of whom has access to the traditional accoutrements of the first-person shooter: guns. Radwan's Israelis rarely look Semitic: they are blond and brutish. He is disavowing any racial relationship between Arabs and Jews and drawing a strong parallel between Israelis and the popular movie image of the blond, blue-eyed American. Or Aryan. Or Nazi.

The game is divided into four chapters, each a level. There is no resolution at the end, just a message. We play either Ahmed, the resistance fighter; Mariam, the mother; Khalid, the collaborator; or Ma'an, the boy. Every level is based on an ostensibly true story. (One of the scenarios in *Under Ash* involves Baruch Goldstein, the American-born Israeli settler who shot up the Ibrahimi Mosque in Hebron in 1994, killing twenty-nine.) Contrary to what press reports suggested, there are no suicide bombing missions in either *Under Ash* or *Under Siege*. These Palestinians are always reactive, never proactive.

Radwan's fingers skittered over the keyboard, rushing through level four of *Under Siege*, hurrying to the game's grisly *coup de grâce*. There lies Ma'an, waiting for martyrdom via a concrete block to the head. Then the final message: *To harvest peace, you must see justice.* It was— even rudimentarily rendered—a ghastly image.

"Yeesh," I said.

"This is what really happened," he said quietly. "I didn't want to use real names. I respect the dead too much, and I don't want Hamas or anyone else to rely on me, to use my work. This is based on real Reuters footage."

"So, your intention is to suck your gamers in with the action, and then feed them a message?" I asked.

"Well, in a way. Remember, the only person who does not die in *Under Siege* is the old man. He is the history of Palestine. He will *never* die. I am sending a message. No matter what you do— cooperate or use your gun against the occupation—you will *still* die. This is because I don't know how to solve—I am just putting a mirror in front of events. By doing so, I'm making others understand the human point of view."

So far as I could tell, this was a depiction of what is slowly being defined as the Palestinian story: Weaponless, in the face of endless odds, they die, but die martyrs. Radwan isn't asking young Arabs to go forth as terrorists. Rather, his acquiescence to death cultism is confined to the sealed areas of Gaza and the West Bank—a place most Arabs have never visited. In the region's popular-culture narratives, the Palestinians in Occupied Palestine are always martyrs. That is their role: sacrificial lambs ennobling all Muslims through their continuous suffering.

★ ★ ★

They cannot represent themselves; they must be represented. I stood behind the Syrian programmer as she rendered a version of herself onscreen: a woman with a scarf wrapped tight around her head, tucked into a *jilbab* in accordance with the outdoor dress code for Muslim Syrian women. She moved her mouse back, and the character took a step back; she moved her hand forward, the character moved forward. The character would one day be another Mariam, in another game. A detail caught my attention. I knew that Palestinian women do not dress in the Syrian fashion. It seemed strange that there could be so simple a cultural misappropriation, given the West Bank's proximity to Damascus. Shrinking universe notwithstanding, borders are borders and walls are walls.

Radwan had already received $500,000 in funding from a Kuwaiti-based distributor called Golden Vision; the only condition, according to Radwan, was that he change a more helpful, "sharing" ending with something more resolutely downbeat. There could be no nuance; the Israeli characters had to be evil to the core. The money for the next stage of Afkar's development would come from the Gulf, as the money always does. And it, too, would come with strings.

"The Saudis want what they want," said Radwan. "But even if you make a great game, it can only be accepted by a portion of society. Saudi Arabian youths can play *Counter-Strike* until their thumbs fall off but *Quraish*—a Muslim game with Muslim teachings—has yet to be published in that country. The reason? Because there is a chance that if you play the Muslims, maybe you can lose. And in the Saudi mind, Muslims can't lose. So they will not accept the game. You can play *Under Siege* in Israel, but not in Saudi, where they refuse the fourth chapter because Palestinians lose. This is what it means to be

Arab," said Radwan. "To constantly, *constantly* negotiate with yourself. To cut yourself off at the knees."

```
<begin>
Arabia, the year 590. A grove of date trees. A
lone soldier scouts ahead. He wears a blood-red
turban, a blood-red belt. Behind him, more
soldiers in tight formation. Then, battle cries:
Jihad, jihad!
    Ten men on camelback surge ahead, lances at the
ready. These are the Muslim forces. They yell,
wave little weapons, and close upon their
Christian enemy. There is no stopping them, they
come in waves. Men fall under the blade, under the
striding camels. It is no contest.
    In minutes, the forces of Islam are victorious.
They make it look easy.
                                                <end>
```

★ ★ ★

We wound our way up the tangled hills of Jebel Ansariya, my ears popping as we rose. Low clouds rushed overhead, the sky roiling so fitfully that it was impossible to tell whether the sun had yet gone down. We circled a busy soccer field, finally making out age-charred ramparts: the Crusader castle Krak des Chevaliers.

"There she is," said Radwan. Indeed, it was hard to miss her.

"Gametime and wartime have never been far removed," writes commentator Ed Halter. "As long as humans have waged war, they've played at it." Radwan is part of that legacy. The crusades are, for him, a scar on history. This castle represents the point of division between the West, where so many of his cultural sensibilities reside, and Islam, which is where he finds his traditions, his understanding of human and divine nature.

The granite of the Krak's citadel was dark as coal. Radwan and I walked along the pathway to the entrance, battered by a wind that threatened to send us screaming into a stone village some thousand feet below. The castle's muscular haunches reared up beside us. Radwan's mood bubbled like the weather, his melancholy as impenetrable as the citadel walls.

We were out of the wind now, walking up the Krak's darkened corridors on stone so worn it felt greased underfoot, crouching as we struggled through crepuscular tunnels until we made it to the Krak's main ramparts, clouds moving fast overhead. A stage had been set up for a French/Syrian jazz concert promoting "dialogue"—a quaint, officially sanctioned piece of cultural back and forth far removed from the trenches.

"Dialogue," laughed Radwan, his mood suddenly merry. "This they call dialogue?" His laugh resounded off the top of Krak des Chevaliers and was drowned out by dueling oboes.

We drove through nightfall, twisting through a mountainous landscape toward the north. We traversed Alawi hamlets, and moved through the terrain the *Hashashinn*—the breakaway Islamic sect that became known as the Assassins—had once called home. It was an insight into Radwan's imagination, a place where video game concepts practically leap up from the pages of history.

"What are your dreams?" Radwan asked as he piloted Sara through the dark.

I was taken aback by the question. "You mean besides trying to stay sane? I'm not sure, exactly. Keep working, keep moving. How about you?"

"Me," said Radwan, "I ask only to make a difference."

"And you think you'll be doing that? I mean, with the games and the films?"

"I believe so. I have to."

"But what happens if the games and the movie just, you know, add to the shit?"

"It won't—it can't. It will at least be something to move it forward. But I'm always stuck in the shit. I get it from one side—to the British, Americans, Israelis, I am a terrorist—and I get it from the other side. In *Quraish*, I represent members of the Prophet's family: *ha'ram*. I use music: *ha'ram*. I use animations: very *ha'ram*."

We drove in silence for a few minutes, and then Radwan said, "All I ask is that people watch my work. If they don't watch it—and they comment first—that's what makes me angry."

Steep canyon walls rose up on either side of us.

"What would you advise me?" asked Radwan.

"*Advise* you? Jeez, I dunno, man."

"You're no help," said Radwan.

"Keep asking questions," I said, offering some Chicken Soup for the Video Game Developer's Soul. "And don't find any answers."

Radwan laughed. "I won't," he said. "No answers. I promise you that."

The following day, as an interregnum to our crusader-era castle whistle-stop tour, Radwan took me to a book fair. He wanted to show me that while Dar al-Fikr was far from disappointed, you couldn't say they were elated. As Radwan's publishing company, they had recently distributed an English version of *Quraish* for the U.K. market, which had quickly sold ten thousand copies; another five thousand were on order. (There are over one million people living in the United Kingdom who identify as either Middle Eastern or Arab.) Radwan was unimpressed with Dar al-Fikr's work—their version needed patches and some of the English translation verged on the absurd, suggesting that one of the Arab world's biggest publishers was not up to the job. But ten thousand copies of a Syrian PC game in a furiously competitive market without any advertising? Not too shabby.

"There is clearly a hunger for these games," Hasan Salim, the head of Dar al-Fikr, told me. He was a short man, bearded. His black suit hung like it was made of soggy paper. "Especially for the strategic games. Because there is so much reading, it is hard for Arabs to play foreign games. Make them here, and the people are happy."

Despite Radwan's claim that an "honor among thieves" mentality had saved his product from Syria's (and the Arab world's) rampant piracy, Salim was not so sanguine. "The piracy is *killing* us. And because copyright is new, there is no respect for it. The government doesn't respect, the people doesn't respect."

One of the main reasons many companies in the Middle East are so reluctant to invest in research and development or commit the effort and money necessary for building new concepts in gaming or any technology-based cultural product is that these works are not protected. There is, generally, very little advanced intellectual copyright protection in the so-called Muslim world. In a sense, this is a throwback to the socialism inherent in the early development of these societies, but it now has more to do with governmental lassitude. Or, in some cases, deliberate underhandedness. The playing of music on Syrian state radio without paying royalties (and sometimes with female vocals replacing male vocals) is hard to construe as anything but theft, and theft with the intent of breaking the back of the artistic community.

"It doesn't exactly inspire an entrepreneur to hop out of bed in the morning if he knows that he is without recourse, if his idea for the ultimate prison-break first-person shooter can, that afternoon, be ripped off by a couple of teenagers in a shack in Qatar," a prominent Lebanese businessman told me. (Something similar happened with *Under Siege*: it was cribbed for an awful first-person shooter called *Jenin: Road of Heroes* by Jordanian programmers.) Although "copy-leftists" would argue that the Arab world needs less top-down regulation, this ignores the fact that respect for content always begins with intellectual copyright protection.

"So if you ask if this market is growing, I must of course say no. This market, it is bad, because of the piracy," said Salim.

We stood talking in the midst of the annual Damascus Book Fair, which was a lesson in the stark lack of mainstream Arab ingenuity. Earlier, Radwan and I had walked through the market perusing the wares, which amounted to piles of Islamic texts differentiated not so much in content but in the shade of green of their jackets. There was ingenuity, however, in the array of anti-Semitic texts, all of which made Goebbels's publishing career seem historically incidental. There was a series of garishly illustrated retellings of the blood libel, stacks of various Jewish/Zionist 9/11 conspiracy theories replete with Stars of David superimposed over the burning World Trade Center towers.

"I don't feel comfortable with this stuff," said Radwan, showing me a copy of a comic book depicting Jews as baboons lording it over more noble members of the jungle. "It makes me feel—I dunno—odd."

We walked through the children's section and its array of "My First Qur'an" products.

"Would your daughter go for this stuff?" I asked.

"No—she'll be making up her own mind when she's ready. It's Barney for her. If I don't kill him first. We need our own versions of this stuff, man. But that's not going to happen any time soon."

Syria—along with other regimes in the Muslim world—has wiped away local creativity and ingenuity as summarily as if every artist in the region was lined up against a wall and shot. Western commentators musing on Arab backwardness and Arabs musing on American imperialism need to start with that fact before looking elsewhere.

"Come," said Radwan. "Let's get you out of here."

He didn't have to ask twice.

★ ★ ★

Salah ad-Din's castle was built by the Franks on a tall finger of escarpment that stretches into the sky. Surrounded by an expansive forest of pine that resembles the Montana backwoods, it towers over Syria, blocking off the critical pass between Aleppo and Lattakia. The walls fall away vertiginously, and while they may seem impenetrable, it took the Saracen leader only two bloody days in 1188 to wrest the castle from his crusading enemies. It has belonged to him ever since.

Except for several loud Saudi teens dressed as the Backstreet Boys, there were few people visiting on that moody afternoon, and we sat on the ramparts overlooking the inner courtyard watching clouds rush by like highway traffic. Everywhere, a sense of power, immutability. Ancient fires had blackened some of the stone, and the wind snatched words from our lips as soon as we spoke. We sat close, and shouted.

"This is where I like to come and think," yelled Radwan. "To imagine." I understood: Qala'at Salah ad-Din was where a Muslim game developer drew his inspiration. Had we shared a profession, I would have been feverishly sketching out character designs in Krak des Chevaliers. Never the twain shall meet.

"And what is it that you imagine?" I asked.

"History upon histories," he said. Then, "You know, I looked you up."

Google kept no secrets. "I see. And you found out what, exactly?"

"Your background seems interesting. When one thinks of South Africans, one does not think of your . . . situation."

"My situation?" I squinted at Radwan.

"Your situation. Your *particular* background."

"No—I suppose one doesn't." The true Syrian lingua franca is the silence between sentences: Radwan was telling me that he was a man who did his homework, and that he knew things about me one would not choose to advertise in this place, namely my Jewish background.

Why, then, was I here, sitting alongside him, the recipient of his unflagging hospitality?

The answer, I thought, lay in Radwan's office, in the great swath of American pop he owned, so much of it made by Jews (among his favorites are Jerry Seinfeld, Woody Allen, Larry David)—all of whom he had loved most of his adult life. Just as it had done for me with black people, pop had humanized the very group he was supposed to hate. Despite the Israeli occupation of Palestine and the violence it engenders, despite the virulent Jew hatred that poisons so many of the Syrian intelligentsia, Radwan was able to see me as a human being.

I didn't envy Radwan: He had to reconcile Krak des Chevaliers with Qala'at Salah ad-Din, Saudis with Syrians, *Seinfeld* with Jewish baboons, his Palestine with the real Palestine, a fantasy America with an America that rained fire upon his brothers' heads. He had to pour all this confusion into a medium he desperately loved, and try to teach his people lessons he hadn't quite learned himself. Radwan Kasmiya was, indeed, under siege.

On the drive back, as we wound down switchbacks, we listened to Johnny Cash sing about shooting a man from Reno, just to watch him die.

"Tell me this," said Radwan. "Does this song make you want to go shoot someone?"

"No more than I usually do," I said.

"Exactly. So why do they accuse me of wanting to make terrorists with my games and the movie?"

"Yeah, but isn't that what you're saying of the American games?"

"It's different. There is no context with them. No proper history."

That was true of some games, but far from all. And Radwan knew it.

"Look, I'm just trying to give us a home in the digital universe. To try to give us some . . . some digital dignity." Radwan passed me a bottle of water. "Here, drink. It was very hot up there."

I sipped from Radwan's bottle and thought of something Hasan Salim of Dar al-Fikr once said of *Under Ash* and *Under Siege*: "The child that plays these video games lives in a huge irony. On one hand he senses the anger of adults about being victims of politics, victims of mental and physical violence. And on the other side, he can sit alone on his PC and transform himself into someone with strength and able to resist U.S. forces."

I looked back at the disappearing castle and wondered if Hasan Salim had anything resembling a point. As someone who has never dealt drugs or shot a hooker, what precisely am I working through when I play *Grand Theft Auto*? Do games form some sort of advanced social evolutionary role—allowing us an outlet for violent fantasies that we'd otherwise unleash on our classmates, co-workers, fellow pimps? Are they one vast stress release valve? If that was the case, then wasn't Radwan Kasmiya's life's work merely sopping Palestinian rage and (inadvertently) propagating the Israeli cause? Or was he instead fomenting rage and rebellion, asking the same of young Arabs that the death cults do? Or was he simply developing games that gave an hour of untrammelled vicarious pleasure, and were never given another thought?

I sipped the water, and decided the only thing to do was play *Under Siege* in Palestine.

Inside the bunker-like concrete PC center in the Shu'afat refugee camp outside Jerusalem (home of hip-hoppers G-Town), I sat with Ali and Farous—both fourteen, both the perfect demographic for *Under Siege*—and had the following conversation:

Ali: Fuck this. Let's play *Gears of War*.
Richard: Hang on. Let's give this a chance. (Points to screen.) Look, the Israelis!
Ali (mocking tone): "Look, the Israelis!" If I want Israelis, I can go to the checkpoint, no?
Richard: True, but here you get to work out your frustrations—
Farous: Frustrations?

Ali: This means anger.

Farous: Man, we just want to play the good games.

Ali: *Gears of War, GTA.* Not this.

Richard: But Palestine . . . ?

(Ali pulls out the CD, slips in *Gears of War.*)

Ali: *Halas.* [Enough.]

(Conversation ends. Shooting begins.)

All the (admittedly scant) academic testimony I'd read about Arab gaming quoted articulate young Arabic men and women who had carefully thought out responses to gameplay. The summation was simple: American games = bad. Arabic games = some more, please. Indeed, many young educated Palestinians I spoke to were quick to dismiss American games like *Delta Force*, but that didn't mean they were going to embrace *Under Siege.* That game was downloaded one million times, but the digital waters move quickly. Despite the fact that Ali and Farous had lived through the second intifada and that war, to them, was not an abstraction, they were like gamers everywhere: They wanted the best graphics, the raddest physics, the finest gameplay. And who could blame them? I kept thinking back to the intrinsic, cognitive appeal of gaming—the fact that young brains are drawn to this stuff for extra-cultural reasons. By no means am I saying that many of the kids I spoke to across the Arab world weren't fully into blowing away virtual Israeli soldiers—in this, the game usually provided five minutes of vicarious thrills—but my exchange with Ali and Farous was entirely representative.

Lebanese journalist and cultural commentator Habib Battah wrote with typical insight: "It is easy to sneer at computer games as the silly embodiment of someone's teenage fantasies. Which they are. But at least in *Under Ash* the silly fantasy is not the product of someone else's teenage morality; this one's all our own." In some essential way, Radwan's Palestine was a powerful place. It conferred upon gamers who were otherwise cast as bad guys "digital dignity." It made them agents rather than corpses. It represented the very real destruction on their streets. But it didn't seem to address any specific needs.

"Look," a kid in a Ramallah gaming café said to me, his arms bearing the scars of real violence. "I'm not gonna play a game where American soldiers are blowing away dirty ragheads. Fuck that. But I'm not in this for politics, man. I'm in it for the games. If maybe your friend made games to equal the best of them, then perhaps we can talk." Whereupon we played *Grand Theft Auto* for forty-five minutes.

I left wondering if Radwan's, and perhaps gaming's, perpetual challenge, if it was to truly possess "the power of rhetoric," was matching ideology with state-of-the-art technology. That was the U.S. Army's thinking. It was Hezbollah's thinking as well. Perhaps Radwan could offer "digital dignity" to a generation of young Arabs if he had the budget and know-how. As it stood, *Under Siege*'s poor graphics and limited gameplay were another reminder of inferiority. But I wasn't convinced that there was a correlation. I'd been dealing drugs and shooting hos for the best part of an hour, and I walked the Ramallah streets feeling like I'd just left a spa. My cellphone rang. It was someone from the gaming café, with a bootleg copy of *Counter-Strike*.

"You in?" he asked.

Who was I to say no? There were aliens and Third World misfortunates to kill.

9

Book for a Nose Job

LEBANON

Muslim: No accurate census

GDP N/A

1. Talk Talk:
   Talk Talk
2. The Walkmen:
   We've Been Had
3. Public Enemy:
   Louder Than a Bomb

Pop.: **3,971,941**

Avg. age: **28.8**

Capital: **Beirut**

Independence: **Depends who you ask**

I

The Virgin Megastore in a mall on a hilltop in Beirut's Achrafiye neighborhood. A glittering CD-release party. The bash was hosted by a cosmetic dentist, who greeted me with two kisses and a coruscating smile that doubled as a commercial. Everyone had dazzlingly white ivories: each incisor, each bicuspid a star in a constellation of brilliance. Skin glowed, noses were pert, breasts stood high and proud. This part of Beirut is the Muslim world's plastic surgery polestar. "For a Saudi woman, getting plastic surgery in Beirut is like eating a Swiss roll in Switzerland—it's what they come here to do," I was told as I reached for a canapé.

Among all this reconstructed human flesh, Zaven Kouyoumdjian made an impression. He sauntered in—he always saunters—his wife, Laury, behind him. His teeth were very white, but other than that he was an Everyman: medium height, medium build, balding, spectacles. He was at once both eminently approachable and a world apart. He hugged, he kissed, he posed for a paparazzo who smelled pungently of curdled milk. Zaven placed a hand on the photographer's shoulder, knocked off a pithy quote in unaccented Arabic. Everyone shifted into his orbit.

At thirty-seven, Zaven is a phenomenon, if a fading one. He is, in his own words, "the father of reality TV in the Arab world," which is only partly an exaggeration. As the long-time host of a show called *Sire Wenfatahit*—a Lebanese slang term that means "subject open"— he is famous among Arabic speakers from Egypt to Tunisia to North Dakota. He is a voice for voiceless youth, a shining star of Generation *Al Shamshoon*.

It's a reality TV universe. Over the course of his fifteen years on television, Zaven has helped create a newly prolix Arab world. Like many observers, I couldn't help wonder if this wasn't the furnace in which democracy was being forged: a place for the vast Muslim middle ground to air their dreams, desires and fears. But I also wondered—and it was a concern I shared with Zaven himself—how difficult it would become, as this sea of prattle widened, to locate anything meaningful in it at all.

Shortly after charming everyone at or near the party, Zaven settled himself on a couch at a Starbucks, hitching up his slacks and folding his legs like Cary Grant. Laury handed me a coffee, saying, "You have to excuse me. I get a little weird when I hear him talk about himself."

Zaven grinned. "It's not so bad, my dear. Usually I'm doing the listening. This will be a nice change."

"Actually, that's not *entirely* true, *yanni*," said Laury.

He grinned again. Those teeth! "Point taken. In fact, I started talking in 1992 and I have hardly stopped to take a breath. It's okay. I have plenty to say."

Zaven was barely twenty-two when he first went on air. The Lebanese civil war had just ended and the authorities wanted to change the way television was made. From 1975 until 1990, the country was wracked by a civil war cum regional conflict that was so complicated it makes a season of *Lost* look like an episode of *Matlock*. The problems arose from Lebanon's delicate power-sharing agreement—"a house of many mansions," as historian Kamal Salibi puts it—which slightly favored the Maronite Catholic cohort among a variety of Muslim, Christian and secular factions. By the time fighting died down in 1990, over one hundred thousand people were dead. The country was in ruins.

"So there were ghosts everywhere," said Zaven. "Ghosts in the streets, ghosts on television. They decided to get rid of all the old anchors, people associated with war. They wanted a new face."

The Arab political talk show host has long been a vital part of regional political theatrics—the regime's unsmiling stooge. Until 1995, Zaven, as an anchor for the state-run Tele Liban, was essentially a version of that, albeit in a better suit with a whiter smile. If this was changing ever so slightly post-war, there still wasn't a remote control in the Arab world that could find even a broad discussion of social issues. Basically, it was swarthy Bill O'Reillys with mustaches yelling about shadowy existential threats, intercut with images of Soviet-era weaponry firing at nothing at all, crowned by forty-five-minute visual encomiums to the strong man of the minute. Zaven—and can you blame him?—wanted more.

The journey proper began in 1995, in a mid-range hotel in Washington, D.C. A TV flickered in the dark. Twenty-five-year-old Zaven sat on the bed changing channels after a long day at a Reuters conference. It had been five years since his country emerged from civil war. Someone told him to catch *The Phil Donahue Show*, the first syndicated tabloid-style talk show, which ran for twenty-six years before being cancelled in 1996. He loved it. Then someone else told him to watch Donahue's main rival.

"*Whooom!*" said Zaven. "*Boof!* I saw this emerging culture of reality TV. Oprah was in those days a genuine fat black woman who happened to have a show on TV. Then she got all skinny and started giving out handbags. I only watched Oprah three or four times, but I was caught in this fever—I really believed in it."

Zaven knew that he had found his calling. It would not be easy; he would have to break more taboos than a burlesque dancer at a Hezbollah rally. "Back in those days, everything was thought of in religious terms. You couldn't have a politician, a shaykh [religious authority], a man from the street and a chanteuse on the same show, even if their appearances were weeks apart. There was a hierarchy that had to be respected."

In official Arabic media history, Al Jazeera, based in Doha, Qatar, helped shatter the status quo. In 1996, the Qatari regime sniffed the airwaves and knew that if they didn't want their hated cousins the Saudis taking control of the airwaves, they'd need a channel of their own. They used the CNN paradigm and expertly inverted it—*The Opinion and the Other Opinion*, ran Al Jazeera's tagline. Their reporting was, for many years, an astute counterpoint to what many Arabs considered Western media hegemony, and when they covered the Clinton administration's bombing of the al-Shifa pharmaceutical plant in a suburb of Khartoum, Sudan, they earned "the trust of the Arab world." (Or sixty-nine percent of the Arab world, according to the poll numbers.)

Al Jazeera's impact on regional television cannot be overstated, but it can be misunderstood. It was a *child* of the satellite revolution, not an initiator thereof—part of a process that started with the likes of the Middle East Broadcasting Corporation (MBC) in 1991. Its international notoriety arose from two decisions: to act as Osama bin Laden's personal YouTube after 9/11, and to keep camera crews on the ground filming the horror of the Iraq invasion while most American news outlets focused on impressive computer graphics.

But in terms of the effect on political discourse, the station falls far below the lofty claims it makes for itself. Sure, if it was talk one wanted, one could do no better than Al Jazeera. There were all sorts of debate shows, all claiming to be firsts. They asked huge

questions—Why is the Arab world backward? or, Does Israel deserve
to win?—which on the surface of things looked like a huge step
forward. But Al Jazeera was never interested in, as one Lebanese
academic puts it, "broken pipes—the problems that affect us every
day. Lack of democratic process in Qatar? Forget it. It was always
about massive, insoluble issues designed to get your heart rate up." In
other words: more of the same.

"Al Jazeera's news is needed," Zaven said to me. "But their social
shows? Please. It's like the 1830s. No one is really interested in starting
a conversation."

Two years after Al Jazeera debuted, Zaven was ousted from Tele
Liban after falling afoul of Emile Lahoud, Lebanon's new Maronite
president, and thus the effective head of the station. Lahoud interpreted a signature Zaven smile, during coverage of the president's
dispute with a rival politico, as a slight. "Remove this son of a bitch,"
he reportedly said to no one in particular. No one in particular was
only too happy to oblige. Zaven spent six months alternately fearing
for his life and figuring out what kind of TV show he wanted to do
next. He knew it would have to have an Oprah-like couch: everyone
at the same level, a democratizing piece of furniture. "The shaykh
could not stare down at me. The politician must look me in the eye.
This changes television in the Muslim world."

It just so happened that Rafik al-Hariri, a billionaire Sunni former
prime minister of Lebanon, was looking for someone to do exactly
that. He had started Future TV in 1993 as a Sunni alternative to the
Maronite Catholic Lebanese Broadcast Corporation (LBC). It was an
upmarket station that depended on ratings to ensure that al-Hariri
and his fellow Sunnis had a mouthpiece in the region. (Satellite
stations in the Arab world, are often tied to a strongman and his
sectarian affiliations.) Nothing brought in eyeballs like the burgeoning genre of social programming. *Sire Wenfatahit* was born.

The job demanded the dexterity of an eleven-year-old Chinese
gymnast. The competition, women like Hala Serhan and Mona
el-Shazly, had suffered a string of controversies. (Serhan was fired

from Egypt's Dream TV for bad-mouthing Gamal Mubarak, the president's son, and for paying prostitutes to come on the show and make accusations about the Egyptian police.) The competition was fierce, but so were the strictures on what could and couldn't be said.

"One of the things you must know about me is that I'm one of the last resorts," Zaven said to me, draining his espresso. "If you want to change the world—you call Zaven. If you have nowhere else to turn—you call Zaven. If you ask an Arab where first they heard an HIV-positive person speak, they'd say Zaven. A drug addict? Zaven. And not as a victim, but telling their own story. For instance, a few weeks ago, we get a call from an Egyptian transsexual. I said to her, 'Listen, honey, you're not ready to be on my show.' And her," Zaven looked at Laury, who shrugged in confusion, "—is it *her? his?*— father was so relieved. She's not immune yet. Her community would not back her up. It would make good television, but what then? What then?"

Hamra, a neighborhood west of the Green Line, the fecund no man's land dividing Christian eastern Beirut from the Muslim sector, was a world defined by sound. The *whomph* of artillery shells hitting downtown Beirut a mile away. The *rat-a-tat* of machine-gun fire in the dawn hours after a night of silence.

While Beirut was being murdered, Hamra was gloriously alive. A boy spent his youth here, dodging between the bell-bottomed legs of men with American accents, British accents. They carried notebooks; they talked and drank in cafés that were thick with cigarette smoke. There were beautiful, sophisticated women who spoke French like Parisians. Students, journalists, intellectuals, bohemians. All of life's possibilities crammed into this warren of streets along with the cracked pavement, the hanging electrical wires, the cries of vendors.

The boy went from home to school and home again. Because of his father, he belonged to the small Armenian community in Hamra—an evangelical Christian outpost in the heart of Muslim territory. But his mother was Lebanese, and Armenians despised the Lebanese. "They are maniacs," he was told. "They kill themselves night and day. This is now in your blood."

He knew the story well: The Armenians fled the Ottoman massacres in 1915 and were taken in during the French Mandate to be resettled on the outskirts of Beirut. The Armenians worked hard; they became the merchant class. As was the way in these parts, the boy knew that the Lebanese hated the Armenians at least as much as they were in turn hated. In the civil war, the Armenians would not fight. Pigeons of Peace, they called themselves. In Arabic, "pigeon" can mean something else. Penises of Peace.

Despite this, his home was happy. He didn't know that a world could be any larger. But the Armenian community in Hamra dwindled, and the boy's father was unable to cross the Green Line. His neutrality—espoused in many spirited articles for the Armenian press—put him at odds with his co-religionists in the east. They were at once separate and at home, which is how the boy would come to feel as he left adolescence. After all, he had grown up around Muslims; their values became his values. Their rhythm, their habits were his.

The boy grew up. He studied journalism at the Lebanese American University of Beirut. His foundation as a journalist came not only from the articles his father wrote for the Armenian press, but also from the newspaper clippings he collected as a teenager during the war—photos of people who were outside his tightly prescribed life but who defined every inch of its borders. They would come to form his on-air personality. "These people, these pictures," Zaven has said, "are fragments of my soul." There is no Oprah-ish hucksterism in this statement. "That's what they are. They're my memory of the war.

"As an Armenian, with my particular background, I have been allowed a unique opportunity," Zaven once said to me. "I can say things maybe a Muslim or a Maronite could never say. I become this pan-Arab figure, even though I'm not officially an Arab. People trust me somehow. They know I'm not faking it. I don't waste this. I don't let them down. But the question is always: How far can I take it? How far can I push?"

★　★　★

I had to ask him to repeat the question.

"Are you a spy?" Zaven asked again.

My brain whirred, searching for a witty riposte, until I caught Zaven's eye and realized that he was not joking.

"Am I a *spy?*"

"That's what I asked you." Zaven took a sip of his Diet Coke. The Mediterranean lapped at the cedar boardwalk. We were at the finely appointed St. George's Yacht Club—the very spot where the patron saint of Lod purportedly slew a dragon and entered legend. We were also less than half a mile from where Zaven's boss, Rafik al-Hariri, and his convoy were annihilated by the equivalent of one thousand pounds of TNT on Valentine's Day 2005, throwing Lebanon into a fresh crisis from which it has yet to emerge. Over the fencing, I could make out the gnarled innards of surrounding buildings, still unrepaired. Beirut is riddled with such inadvertent memorials.

"You know," I said, "I can't help wonder: What would a real spy answer? What would James Bond say?"

"What's your point?"

"My point is, what is the point of the question? If I'm a trained spy, surely I'm *prepared* for this sort of thing."

Zaven's stock-in-trade is conflict. He leaned back into the wicker bar chair and gave me one of his smiles. Behind him, lying by the impossibly blue pool, were three perfectly rebuilt women in string bikinis. Given my itinerary of late, I hadn't been as excited in the presence of females since early adolescence. Zaven, however, was souring the pleasure.

"You see," he said evenly, "this is Lebanon. We have enemies. I'm not sure whether you think it is a joke, but my job is dangerous. Is it so ridiculous that you could be an Israeli spy? You tell me you're a journalist, but what a great cover story, no?"

"And now that you've asked the question?"

"I just wanted to look in your eyes when I asked it."

I felt an immense pang of sorrow for Zaven and his countrymen, who must look for clues in the irises of their club guests. "And?"

"*Halas*. I'm satisfied." He gave another signature smile, dissipating the tension as thoroughly as the women behind him had gotten rid of their cellulite, and I thought of something he'd said to me the day before. Some months after the death of his son during a battle with Israeli forces in south Lebanon, Hezbollah's secretary general, Hassan Nasrallah, had sat across from Zaven on the *Sire Wenfatahit* set. A few episodes later, Haifa Wehbe—Lebanon's most famous video-clip vixen and pop musician—tearfully insisted that she was *not* a prostitute after being swept up in a raid of an upmarket bawdy house. "A shaykh and a whore on the same show, in one month. This is Zaven," he told me.

This was the juggling act he was forced to endure: from the deadly serious to the preposterously frivolous. In the late summer of 2007, south Beirut was still rebuilding after the war with Israel in 2006. A full-blown insurgency was underway in a northern Palestinian refugee camp. The country's political leadership was frozen. There was danger everywhere. And here we were, watching three gorgeous women wearing the equivalent of dental floss dive into a pool.

"They teach us well at Mossad, no?" I said.

Zaven laughed. "Welcome to Lebanon."

"You know why I love Zaven?" Leila Obeid asked me. "Because he is not foxy. He's smart—oh, yes—but not foxy."

Leila, God bless her, is both.

I was introduced to Leila, who is a Zaven protégé, at the Starbucks at the ABC mall. She traversed the floor like an ethereal angel—resplendent in a white pantsuit, her tanned skin a perfect contrast to her attire, her considerable cleavage arranged like bouffant pillows under her jacket. She had with her a daughter of comparable beauty and refinement, whom she sent away with three alternating kisses; she greeted passers-by with two such kisses. Leila Obeid is, in a city devoted to war and plastic surgery, queen of the latter. She owns the Centre Obeid, where she has for the past fifteen years ministered to those who wish to remake themselves. She now does this on television.

"It is a pleasure [pronounced plehz-yoor] to meet you, *yanni*," said Leila, who spoke English like most middle-class Maronite Lebanese, with a Parisian accent spiced with Lebanese slang, garnished with the occasional pout of the lips and a widening of the eyes around certain words. She proffered a hand as soft as gosling down; her nails were, of course, French manicured. "I never wear makeup, *yanni*. I just do it today because I knew there would be photographers around." She wiped the gloss from her lips with a tissue. "But usually I get up and go from the house. *Halas!* This is what is best for me." She is, at fifty-two, gorgeous in an overabundant way. If she's had any work done, it's a testament to her professional abilities that I cannot tell. Most Lebanese will gladly point out any personal augmentations, but Leila claims that "this is what God gave me—this thick hair, this skin. So no work done, no."

Over her thirty years in the business Leila has quietly built a plastic surgery empire. She is nominally a consultant—and while she does perform certain aspects of the personal remodeling with her own hands ("I am the first and best with tattoo makeup—which I like to call permanent makeup"), she has a network of surgeons, dermabrasion specialists and life coaches who assist her in her makeover projects. Leila is, as she describes it, remarkably similar to a novelist: Her medium is human flesh. "I always talk about character—all these operations are to make you feel better about yourself. If I put twenty-six ladies I have worked on together, no two look alike. I am a person who knows how to read a problem. I look deep into a person's life. Sometimes, you have to *hear* their beauty. It is about finding the character, *yanni*."

What, I wondered, would Leila recommend for me.

"Well, your nose is fine, because you are an author. But if you were in music, we would have to bring down the size."

It's tempting to put Lebanon's plastic surgery obsession on the psychiatrist's couch and say that it is one of the inevitable results of living in a wartorn nation, where so much is destroyed and summarily rebuilt. But what of LA, Miami, Buenos Aires—all cities renowned for their reconstructed inhabitants? Lebanese who don't wear the veil spend a lot of time outdoors in small pieces of clothing, and for this, it's best for body parts to remain on the firmer side. What's more, Arab middle- and upper-class doyennes are no less terrified of aging than their North American counterparts. Leila is here to ensure that they age with grace. She is the host of an *Extreme Makeover*–style reality TV show. Her rise to prominence mirrors the rise of reality TV in the Arab world.

"Leila is something of a revolution in television—it is the same shock as *The Swan* in the West," Zaven told me, referring to the gruesome reality show that stunned North American audiences with its graphic portrayal of plastic surgery as a cure-all. "I said to Leila— this will *not* work. We're not ready for it here. It's impossible in the Arab world. It's premature." Nonetheless, *Beauty Clinic* had its coming-out party on *Sire Wenfatahit*.

"With Zaven, it was all him," Leila told me. "*He* chose what people would wear, *he* chose their style." Zaven discovered Leila on her twice- a-week beauty session on Future's breakfast television show, which had always enjoyed avid viewer response. He groomed her. He coached her. She is his silicon Dr. Phil.

Reality TV on Arab satellite television is one of the major cultural phenomena of the new century. The form is as old as television itself, and in its current iteration had been a fixture of European television for at least half a decade before *Survivor Borneo* debuted on CBS during the summer months of 2000 to astounding ratings. At the culmination of *Survivor*'s first season, when the clothing-averse Richard Hatch finally connived his way to a million bucks, almost fifty-two million people were watching.

Shortly thereafter, production companies like Endemol (developers of *Big Brother*, *Fear Factor* and other fan favorites) were trawling television markets, finding willing buyers everywhere. But they hit a snag with acquisitions departments in the potentially lucrative Arab market. *Bachelorette: The Burqa Years?* Not a chance.

Things, however, were changing, and that goes double for the Lebanese television industry. Each sectarian cohort enjoys its own television channel. (Even Hezbollah—ostensibly the Lebanese Shiite mouthpiece—has Al Minar, which broadcasts out of South Beirut.) LBC, the Maronite channel, was rising steadily in popularity, mainly because it was able to broadcast shows that a Muslim channel couldn't. But they had to steer away from social talk shows. Future TV, the brainchild of al-Hariri, was a different story. "For Arabs, Future was from al-Hariri, who was a good Sunni, so there is no conspiracy—it isn't someone shaking their values," one media observer told me. "But LBC, if you do a social talk show there, whatever you are saying comes from a Christian Lebanese point of view and would offend." Nonetheless, because LBC was not held to the same standards of probity as Muslim Arab stations, it was able to cast a hungry eye at the lucrative reality TV feeding frenzy. It could play with moral standards; it just couldn't talk about moral standards. ("It's not *supposed* to make sense," Zaven told me. "It's Lebanon.")

Any Arabic entertainment product with a hint of prurience is developed in Lebanon. Indeed, Arab reality TV—at least as we've come to understand the genre of late—began with a Beiruti marketing executive named Ronny Jazzar, who held the rights to the Miss Lebanon competition. In 2003, Jazzar planned to televise the lead-up to the event, rolling the cameras as contestants prepared for the big day. Although there would be no males involved (they take the "Miss" in *Miss Lebanon* pretty seriously), the show was controversial; the private space of young women would be violated. They would be filmed lounging, eating, doing their nails, and thus *Miss Lebanon* would dash any number of social taboos, making it a huge risk. And in turn making it a smash hit.

This proved too tempting for the competition. MBC—the same Saudi-backed channel that bungled the Arabic *The Simpsons*—stepped into the ring. Their *Big Brother Bahrain* proved an unequivocal disaster. Despite the fact that Bahrain is, on paper, the Persian Gulf's most liberal sheikhdom, MBC was unable to stop a raging crowd pouring forth from a large mosque, inflamed by an imam's passionate speech, converging on the *Big Brother* television studios looking to increase ratings for all the wrong reasons. "I have watched the show and it must be stopped," a placard-waving female teacher told the BBC, regardless of the fact that the contestants' sleeping quarters were segregated and that the Arab inmates of Guantanamo Bay enjoy more social leeway. "This program is a threat to Islam. This is entertainment for animals."

Our old friend Baddih Fattouh immediately shut down production, losing nine million dollars and learning a valuable lesson: Muslim channels needed to watch their step. (Recently, Saudi cleric Saleh al-Luhaidan, chairman of the Saudi Supreme Judicial Council, issued a *fatwa* against satellite stations, intimating that it is a worthy religious endeavor to slaughter those who own them.)

Ronny Jazzar, working out of Beirut, enjoyed marginally more social freedom. *American Idol* was setting unprecedented ratings records in the States, and first-season winner Kelly Clarkson was an international superstar. Talent shows have a storied history in the Arab world and Jazzar wanted to jump from the *Miss Lebanon* model to produce an Endemol-developed *Idol/Big Brother* hybrid called *Star Academy*. The idea was to bring together beautiful young guys and girls from different regions of the Arab world, put them in a compound called the "Academy" and get them to make sweet pop music for a grand prize.

"We were a little bit scared," Jazzar told me. Understandably so. Debuting in 2003, *Star Academy* became the most successful Arab television show in recent history. (Until 2007, when Abu Dhabi–financed, Egyptian-produced *Million's Poet*—in which contestants battle out their Nabati poetry skills—made it big.) The show's brilliance lay in its pan-Arabism, its embracing of text-messaging to communicate with its audience and its careful management of male/female interaction.

"The social reaction was mainly positive, if a little bit controversial," Jazzar told me. "The ratings were excellent—we were number one program that year. Boys and girls slept in the same house, yes—but separate rooms. The people participating in this kind of program are from our society and they know how to behave. We don't have to tell them not to fuck in front of the cameras."

Reality television had thus established itself in the Arab world. *Super Star*, a pan-Arab *Idol*, followed. Then *The Farm*, an Endemol product hosted by Haifa Wehbe, the inimitable video-clip vixen/alleged call girl. Then *The Perfect Bride*. All have had varying degrees of controversy and success. (LBC now has a 24-hour live-to-air reality TV channel.) Jazzar's current babies are *Mission Fashion 2* and his Leila-battling *Extreme Makeover*.

There was one further obstacle regional reality TV had to overcome. George Kordahi, host of the Arabic *Who Wants to Be a Millionaire* and a show called *Open Your Heart*, told me that "Arab culture is very discreet—there is much privacy, and privacy is something that's very important. It's fundamental. It's not easy to go into the soul of people. Western mentality—you don't care to tell problems without any shame. Here, if there is a problem, you don't talk about the problem."

The unembarrassed openness that has become a hallmark of reality TV—and one of its viler qualities—is a symptom of Western societies' long relationship with the soap box, speaker's corner and other forums for free speechifying. This made various Arab regimes uneasy. At the heart of these shows was a notion of individual aspiration translated into the imperative *Look at ME!* But when Iraqis were risking their lives in 2005 to vote in George W. Bush's Purple Revolution—a moment hailed, however briefly, as a watershed for democracy in the Middle East—Arab kids across the region were texting their preferences for *Star Academy* contestants. The SMS interaction with television—well established because of music video channels—was nothing new, but the volume was astonishing. This was actual participation. For the first time, Arab youth felt like they had a *say*.

"Imagine a young Saudi watching a Saudi guy from his own town actually going somewhere in life: That's got to have an impact on people," Habib Battah, my go-to regional cultural commentator, told me. "And it does, because it's had an impact on the religious clergy—they've thrown a fit because of these reality shows." The House of Saud brought down the cellular network on voting nights, but enterprising Saudi kids rerouted technology to vote for their candidates, texting from their computers. The entire Arab world participated. Powered by tens of millions of Saudi television viewers, Hisham Abdul Rahman, from Riyadh, won the second season of *Star Academy*. He became a bona fide regional superstar, and now hosts the MBC version of *Pimp My Ride*, called *Dallae Sayartak*.

At the time of the *Star Academy* phenomenon, there was a debate about whether reality TV would introduce the idea of democracy to Arab youth. Is voting for a reality TV contestant really voting, or has the use of the term confused some into thinking that there exists a corollary between the democratic political process and modern-day talent shows? Put another way, was Barack Obama's storied connection with young voters a result of their training at the hands of Simon Cowell's American Idols? One thing is for sure: The reality TV voting process is an attempt to introduce a participatory element into a television product—to give a viewer the notion of control, the idea that they are helping to steer events, that "I" exist as an integral part of the storyline.

"Reality television changed everything," Habib Battah told me. "And day by day maybe it changes the social aspects in Muslim countries." What shows like *Star Academy* have prompted in the Middle East is a burgeoning sense of the individual: Anybody can rise from obscurity to be a star. It's a revolutionary, if flawed, idea in cultures where social behavior is highly regulated, where the crush of the regime stifles upward mobility. And what exemplified this more than the perfectly coiffed woman who sat before me at a Beirut Starbucks?

The guests on Leila's show (just like the guests on Zaven's show), formerly anonymous Arab women, suddenly *existed*. Their problems were validated. Sure, they were exploited for entertainment, but what Western intellectuals see as a disease of our culture—this desperate need to be the centre of attention, however briefly—morphed into something else under Leila's practiced scalpel. Proof of existence. The power of one.

Leila Obeid has had an uphill battle. She is a self-made woman—her husband passed away seven years ago. To maintain the lifestyle of the Lebanese elite and educate her three daughters accordingly, she has had to work hard. The *Beauty Clinic* proposal was a big document, the most comprehensive Future had ever received for a proprietary show. It looked, on paper, like an incoming cultural Patriot missile.

Before the show was greenlit, Leila advertised for Lebanese women (she has subsequently included the UAE, Saudi and beyond) interested in appearing on a makeover show. Zaven's concerns, at least in terms of participants, proved naïve. "Night and day, they called," said Leila. "At four in the morning, they called. I was overwhelmed."

Within a matter of weeks, Leila had a season's worth of participants. She recruited an A-Team of endocrinologists, dental specialists and surgeons—practitioners she had observed over the years and whose talents she judged by asking women, "Who did your nose? Arrrgh! Who did your nose? Wow, very lovely!"—while giving each potential participant a rigorous pre-treatment checkup to see if she could sustain the abuse of a full-body makeover.

The brass at Future TV insisted that *Beauty Clinic* would have to concentrate on "'drama' . . . not just big breasts, but a lady who has lost a breast to cancer. A lady who lost all her teeth and came to be thirty kilos. A woman who is 160 kilos and can't get a job. A person whose face was kicked by her husband. Drama, drama!"

There were social challenges, like how to get an Arab housewife to show her love handles on satellite television. "I was the first person to get an Arab woman to show her body on screen. I came up with the idea that they wear only a tight-fitting one-piece with tights. This way, they are not exposing flesh." Leila told me.

When I asked Leila if in doing the show she struggled with these social conundrums, she became immediately skittish. "Please, *yanni*, we can suffer from any problem—like any person in the world—and we may wish to correct this problem. Why we must be different to you?"

But didn't the problem lie in *depicting* the fulfillment of this wish?

Leila shook her head; there was a tremor in her pout. "Why *Beauty Clinic* is accepted in the Arab world is because we are looking at drama, the beauty, the health. We were examining a woman who wanted to have her breasts bigger—and in her breasts we found a tumor. So we saved her life! We had a woman who wanted liposuction because of her weight—she was going to commit suicide. We *helped* her."

When I suggested that Leila was breaking taboos, the pout disappeared altogether. "No, no, *yanni*. Never! I will never break a taboo. For me—what is Muslim and Christian? I look at the person—each one separately. I love all, respect all. I am a simple person. I don't talk about people's country or problems. I don't show bodies. Remember, these people are in very stretchy tight swimsuits. I do not accept that we have broken a taboo. No. Never."

II

"Three, two, *wahad! Halas!*" yelled the floor director. The crowd whistled, applauded. Zaven flashed me a "holy shit!" look. The camera swept over the set. Roll tape. Action.

Sire Wenfatahit is filmed in one of three Future TV studios dotted around central Beirut. The show runs live to air every Monday night at 10 P.M. One Monday in late July, I showed up at 8:30 to watch the preparations, winding through a maze of security into a building housing all of Future's proprietary shows except for the news, which is read in an even more fortified compound near Hamra.

With its light hardwood floors and orange walls, Zaven's set reflected his image: sunny, inviting. A round table was prepared for the show's guests. (The couch was for special occasions.) Zaven's wardrobe was soft masculine: pink tie, light blue shirt, dark blue suit, frameless spectacles. After the al-Hariri bombing, the in-studio audience had been downsized for security reasons. Thirty or so enthusiastic teenagers sat in the stands. "I live in Denmark, and there he is very famous," a blond teen told me. "We *love* Zaven." She then let out an excited shriek.

When he approached me from the control room, Zaven shrugged his shoulders. "I don't know about tonight. I'm not usually nervous. Tonight, I'm a little nervous." This was a show that wouldn't merit a raised eyebrow on *Oprah*, but Zaven risked the opprobrium of many thousands. He was going after the most revered cultural figure in the Arab world: the Egyptian chanteuse Um Kalthoum, who was, from the 1930s until her death in 1975, the equivalent of Celine Dion plus Bruce Springsteen times Shania Twain.

The show opened with a clip asking folks on the street if they remembered Um Kalthoum's once-famous predecessor, Munirah al-Mahdiyyah. (Favorite lyric: "Grab the bottle/ the mezza is fresh.") "Yes, yes. They called her the Sultana," said an older woman. After the intro, Zaven made his way down the stairs to cheers from the audience. He sat at a desk behind an open Sony laptop and sipped from a coffee mug. "I was the first to do these things," Zaven said to me earlier. "No one knew what was a laptop in 1995, and the mug is not in the culture—they thought it was some weird microphone."

"The show today is odd," Zaven promised his audience, millions of Arabs watching throughout the region and beyond, "but not as weird as the situation we live with every day in the Arab world." Laughter. "I want to know: The erotic songs, the new videos, in the Arab world they are usually blamed on the Western devil, but before Um Kalthoum, singers sang very erotic songs. Are these new songs not a return to the old ways? Why must I always be making an excuse for the music I listen to nowadays—why can't I just enjoy it for its own sake? And if everything new is bad, was not Um Kalthoum a bad thing? After all, she was new once."

The previous episode of *Sire Wenfatahit* covered female circumcision in Egypt. This does not count as controversial: Rural Egypt and North Africa are easy punching bags for social programs on Arab television, and there's a broad consensus among urban television viewers the world over that female genital cutting is a bad thing. Assailing the granite edifice of Um Kalthoum's reputation? That's another story.

There is no figure in the North American pop-culture canon comparable to Um Kalthoum. Hers is the voice of a particular period in the Arab world—a genuinely pan-Arab figure who is the trill of home for four generations. She came of age as a star when pan-Arab optimism was at a high point. Her voice is an instant meme; it suggests a safer, better time, an era of (relative) innocence and optimism, when newly independent Arab nations had cast off their colonial masters and were forging their own destinies by fighting with Israel and also, occasionally, with each other. She cultivated a fusty, boyish conservatism that allowed both hardliners and liberals to embrace her. It helped that she was an exceptionally gifted singer; there has never been a voice like hers. There never will be again.

That doesn't mean, however, that her entrance onto the scene was treated with universal joy. (And it doesn't mean that legions of young Arab hipsters don't think she's a pain in the ear.) Before Um Kalthoum, in the twenties and thirties, female musicians were synonymous with prostitutes. Even if they weren't working girls, their music was spicy, sleazy, dripping with sexual allusion—from the "Oops, I Did It Again" school of pop garishness. Munirah al-Mahdiyyah was the goddess of this scene, the most powerful interpreter of the *taqtuqah* (light song) genre, ready to show a portion of fat white ankle through her skirts, ready to thrust out her prominent bosom when singing of *beautiful little birds of love flittering through my body*.

Zaven's guests were a musicologist named Elias Zahab and a singing *oud* player named Khaled Abdullah. Both men knew Um

Kalthoum's and Munirah's music well and were less than enthusiastic about comparisons to the video-clip vixens.

> Zaven to Musicologist: You're old. Maybe that's why you prefer the old singers.
> Musicologist: I will not accept the parallel between the old days and now.
> Zaven: Yes, but I will not accept the fact that the music I listen to now is a waste of time. This stuff is a part of me. How long must we be ruled by Um Kalthoum?

This was the crux of the matter—one of the quixotic cultural battles in which Zaven has now been engaged for over a decade: the tyranny of the Arabic past. "We always have The One," complained Zaven. "The One Great Leader: Nasser. The One Great Revolutionary: Abu Ammar [Yasser Arafat]. The One Great Singer: Um Kalthoum. This is the Arab way. We are ruled by these people, these dictators. And they drown our history. And we can't move forward, because they rule us still."

After the show, Zaven shrugged. "I don't know—maybe the change we're going through here isn't portrayed through music. Maybe it's portrayed through other media. Maybe our music really is a photocopy of a photocopy of a photocopy. This did not create the kind of discussion I wanted, but at least the audience knows this: that there were erotic singers around in the Arab world a hundred years ago."

The hillside satellite city of Antelias. The tires of Zaven's SUV screeched as we made our way uphill toward the apartment building he owns overlooking a valley that was not long ago unspoiled forest. It is now a quiet, parvenu-ish Armenian neighborhood.

Laury was in the kitchen making dinner. The apartment was low-lit, the dining room paneled expensively with wood, a floating ceiling

over the long table. A maid came through a sliding door from one of
the balconies carrying Zaven's younger son. "There, there," said
Zaven, patting the gurgling baby's back. "I thought I'd find fatherhood more—I don't know—natural," he told me, handing the infant
back to the maid. "Not so much."

Four years ago, Laury and Zaven embarked on the "journey," as
Zaven describes it, of parenthood. These wholesome moments in
Zaven's life—his longer than usual bachelorhood (when he was every
young woman's ideal beau), his protracted engagement, his marriage,
and now fatherhood—are key to his appeal. Impending parenthood
makes ideal television, especially in a society where family still counts,
and this was not a moment Zaven would allow to pass undocumented.
Earlier in our conversations, he had listed among his lengthy credentials
the fact that the first televised birth in the Arab world was broadcast on
his show. Tonight, the proud parents and their famous infant—a precocious kid with corkscrew curls and rapid-fire French she unleashed in
an unending stream—would join us for dinner. The couple was not as
proud of the moment as Zaven seemed to be. "I would never, never do
it again," the mother told me. She was a tall woman, with corkscrews
of her own and an abundant, high-slung bosom that could only be the
work of the white-cloaked men of Beirut's finer clinics.

"They were us on TV," said Zaven, looking to his wife.

Laury nodded her head. "There was no way I would do it, *yanni*,"
she told me. The entire nine-month "journey" was documented in
four episodes. "Four weeks of wow TV," said Zaven. "We filmed the,
how do you call it, the echoing, and we saw on TV it was a girl and
not a boy. These were great TV moments." But Zaven and Laury's
proxies ran into a snag when it came to filming the birth. "The
delivery was supposed to be on TV," says Zaven, waving an arm
toward the happy couple, "but was it ethical, wasn't it ethical, blah,
blah, blah? The family became involved. It was a fight, but in the end:
compromise. We showed photos."

I exchanged cartoon scowls with the first baby born on Arab TV,
who babbled something at me in French. She had the mien of a child

who knew she was born under special circumstances. "Let's eat," said Laury. "No more TV talk." The spread was traditional Lebanese—falafel, a meat platter, chicken shwarma, a feisty Mediterranean salad; the party had the gently frustrated aspect of a social gathering ruled by very young children. After dinner we moved through to the open lounge, Zaven flopping back on the couch and clicking on the flat screen, and we dived into his central obsession and the very thing we had been forbidden by Laury to discuss.

"Look," said Zaven. "I'm not the first one to talk about controversial issues on Arab TV, to talk about pregnancy, sex, but I was the first one to make it acceptable, to make it available to families in a non-threatening way. I was a more secular, more human approach to issues. But you must understand, I was never brash. I was always shy, always the newly married guy trying to figure things out the same as everybody. I was never the doctor, or the shaykh—the person who wanted to preach. Never. I was a journalist first, a husband second, a talk show host third."

"Here we go," said Laury.

"I wanted to do a show on how to make sex properly," Zaven told me. "The irony is that the Arab world sees a lot of porn films, but we still think it's all hit the hole, done in five minutes, and maybe a kid after. So I brought a shaykh onto the show and we started talking about the mechanism, with really strong names. I tell you, if I was on a U.S. channel, I would get hanged. But now, I have people tell me, 'Zaven, *yanni*, every time I have sex, I think of you.'" He shrugged, took a sip of his Scotch.

Did scores of Arabs really visualize Zaven when they tore each other's clothes off and did the nasty? If so, that was the power of television: It could go anywhere, even crawl into the conjugal bed to help viewers through the sticky act of lovemaking.

"No anal penetration," continued Zaven, "and no sleeping with anyone who isn't your wife. Everything else is okay: sucking, fucking, mirrors, the works. That's what a generation has taken from that show."

Sucking, fucking and mirrors aside, the hottest potato on any Arabic talk show television is homosexuality. It's a guaranteed ratings getter—the ultimate taboo—but still impossible to discuss frankly. "If there is not one Arab who is ready to talk uncovered, then I won't talk about the issue; we're *clearly* not ready. I'd love to have a guy on the show—one every girl would have an orgasm over, like Rock Hudson or that singer from Queen—and have him say that he's gay. But the Arab world is not ready for it." Zaven took another slug of Scotch. "There are, after all, no gays here, you know."

"None at all," I agreed.

"Not a one," said Zaven. "But anyway, I have other problems. Always, always competition. Here is me, considering myself the father of reality TV. Now there's *Star Academy*, and MBC's *Big Brother*, and I was like . . . well, they were taking my thunder. I said, fine! I'll be back. What can I do in the reality genre, I ask myself, not mainstream but underground?"

This led to perhaps the most significant and revolutionary of Zaven's recent projects: his *Me Now* series. He provided five kids—representatives of the panoply of Arab society—with digital video cameras and got them to film their lives over the course of a year. "This is the future," Zaven said to me. "We won't be doing the filming, our guests will be. In this way, we get *their* point of view." It's a brilliant ploy: a controlled way to integrate what's become known as "user-generated content" into the fabric of his show. It distances and in some way indemnifies Zaven from the points of view expressed. It's a backdoor approach to allowing people to speak for themselves.

Days after the kids were given their cameras, they were thrown into the maelstrom of the 2006 July War with Israel, five-hundred-pound bombs dropping within yards of their neighborhoods. The cameras became diaries—a form of communication with the outside world. Of course there were restrictions, but what Zaven did with *Me Now* was give a voice to the voiceless, reminding them that they had something to say.

Not all of these voice-giving moves work. When Zaven put out a call to the "mothers of Lebanon," asking those who opposed war to come forward and tell their stories on his show, he suffered a rare on-air embarrassment.

"I put out an open call—and only one mother showed up. I could have called a casting agency and had a hundred, but I decided to do it properly. So, I persist. Next week, two mothers came. And a week after, another mother. By then, I'd had enough. I got the message. I always felt guilty that I didn't talk more about war on my show—I thought I was too fluffy, in the clouds—but I could feel that the people weren't ready. They were not ready to talk about, or say negative things about, the war. We are still ready to fight? Fine. *Halas!*"

The frustration manifests itself in Zaven's formalistically daring annual experiments. On *Sire Wenfatahit's* birthday, he will come up with a theme for the show, find an appropriate replacement host, and either watch from the audience or from home. For one such episode— to the horror of Future management—he brought on a deaf host who communicated via sign language to deaf guests and a deaf audience.

"Jesus," I said. "That seems, I dunno, almost self-destructive."

"But it was great TV! People gave it the thumbs-up. So once a year you don't understand the TV. Big deal. My bosses said that I was breaking the TV model, which is sound married to picture. But sometimes one of the two is more than enough." This year, he will hold the show in a dying Arabic dialect called Nauri.

These experiments struck me as an unconscious reaction to being muzzled. In deliberately staging a show that is incomprehensible to most of his audience, Zaven was posing a punk-like query: *We are talking, but are we saying anything that counts?*

"Masturbation," said Hisham Musharrafieh.

"I see," I said. I was confused. "Can you give me some context?"

"You asked how we have pushed things forward. And I say masturbation."

Musharrafieh and I were jammed into his cubbyhole of an office in the heavily under-construction MBC Lebanon offices in Hamra. He had longish grey hair and deep bags under his eyes. This was the office from which he produced the talk show that had come to thrash *Sire Wenfatahit* in the ratings. It was called *Kalam Nawaem*, or *Soft Talk*.

"Five years ago, we were inspired in form, not in content, from the famous American talk show *The View*. So it was a big chance for us to get four ladies from four different countries—Egypt, Saudi, Palestine and Lebanon. These four ladies also range in their age. The main concept was to discuss the problems of the Arab women—social controversial issues. For example, masturbation."

ABC's *The View* is one of those essential shows in the evolution of talk television, a concept so simple that it's hard to believe it debuted in 1997 rather than 1957. Assemble a kaffeeklatsch of famous or semi-famous women of varying ages and political outlooks, sit them around a table, occasionally throw a famous or semi-famous guest into the muddle, roll camera. Its various hosts—Barbara Walters, Star Jones, Rosie O'Donnell, Elisabeth Hasselbeck, among others—have tickled both the tabloids and serious political punditry simply by shouting at one another. *The View* is an excellent venue for watching celebrities argue the intractable points of view that they were hired to express.

Arabized, *The View* becomes the Saudi-funded *Kalam Nawaem*. For most of its run, its principal personality has been a divorced (and recently remarried) thirty-five-year-old Saudi mother of two named Muna Abusulayman. Dark-eyed, gorgeous, Abusulayman sports a veil she refers to as "the scarf," though it is, paradoxically, a no-no for female Arabic television personalities to display their piety. Barbara Walters was once reportedly interested in having her guest on the original *The View*. The *Kalam* panel is rounded out by Farah Bseiso (the panderer), Fawziah Salameah (the matriarch) and Rania Barghout (the progressive).

"Women's sexuality is important subject to us," continued Musharrafieh, who is Charlie to these angels. "Let me show you something that can help you a lot."

My eyes widened in horror.

"Is okay, is okay—it is only document," he said. He passed me a complex chart that looked like a recent history of the global economy, in that it was moving vertiginously downward. "This was made by a doctor, who is also a shaykh, who comes on the show. On the female masturbation segment, he showed the effects on the sexual life of women when they go for masturbation. He discarded so many popular myths. For example, if they masturbate, will it affect pregnancy in the future? No. But he reminded the women that it has to do with sexual satisfaction and fantasies that may lead to perversion. The masturbating woman becomes fatigued and less energetic. She will have problems in her climax—either it will be short for her or she will have a hard time to have a sexual climax during intercourse. It was very difficult for me—usually I am a line producer on the show—to listen to this. I was very stunned—we were all stunned. Shocking? Oh, yes."

"Indeed," I said. "I find it surprising that a doctor, who is also a shaykh, is somehow a masturbation specialist. Does this stuff *have* to be vetted by a religious person?"

"Yes," Musharrafieh said simply. "They set the limits. This Muslim religious man is a true authority, a respectable authority."

"On *wanking*?" I asked.

"And why not? Having very strong, grounded beliefs, we are now simply asking questions. Leave masturbation a moment. Let's consider terrorism. This is a twist of the true Islam. Violence against women in the name of religion"—Musharrafieh shook his head—"this is a twist from true Islam. Innovating through *fatwa* new kinds of marriages that allow men to go and have multi-wives and sex in other countries? No."

"Let's talk a little about Rosie O'Donnell," I said of the hefty and outspoken lesbian, once a co-host of *The View*. "Any chance someone of her, um, persuasion could be on the show?"

Musharrafieh puffed out his cheeks, and then made the international sign of the telephone: thumb to ear, pinky to mouth. "We have had a homosexual on the phone," he said. "Oh yes! We don't believe that progress is by a hundred percent imitation. If we want to change, there must be a process. There is no on/off button. For example, saying the word 'homosexual'—*shay'th*—just to *say* it five years ago is out of the question. We were able to start building up on this issue, until we had really a homosexual on the phone. This is due to the effects of the West. The authorities do know that the people have in their homes Dr. Phil, Oprah, Springer. We think about how to adapt them to domestic cases."

"I wonder," I said, "who exactly your show is talking to? Women in the region? *Saudi* women in the region? If so, that's great. But is that really where change needs to happen? What of, for instance, Saudi men? What of challenging them?"

"I don't put it in the way that Saudis are holding us in some place," said Musharrafieh. "For sure, we are trying to make a bridge between the Arab countries in order to exchange ideas in solving social problems. I don't believe there is a show that will instantly change the values of society, but I do believe there is a show that will be a spark plug, that will encourage people to get some knowledge, and knowledge will lead to new perspectives, and new perspectives will lead to freedom. And this is our show. We are not changing, we are just enlightening. Traditions are not all of them bad, no! There is a new future coming, but we cannot be leaving our own Muslim ethics. No. That would not work."

"So, in essence, you are pushing for new values?"

"Sure. Summarized in one sentence—new values do not mean to change the good inherited values, but to change the twisted inherited values. We say on the show that when you start to speak about your problems, you are starting to solve them."

"Even when a masturbation discussion has to be vetted by a religious authority?"

"Look around you, Mr. Richard. This is Beirut. We are Arabs. Patience. Patience."

★ ★ ★

Zaven was in a reflective mood. He wanted to show me Beirut's signature Pigeon Rocks at night. We drove to the Corniche and parked on the crowded street. We bought *fuul*—boiled beans and orange slices sprinkled with spices—from a cart vendor who refused payment, insisting instead on a picture with Zaven. A Syrian tourist came up and kissed Zaven warmly on the cheeks and stared deeply into his eyes: an unspoken thank you.

"Lots of poorer tourists here, families from Syria and Egypt," said Zaven. "Also drug addicts. And this can be a gay-ish Corniche."

I speared a bean with a toothpick. "But there are no gays in the Muslim world."

"Yes. Very funny."

We stared out at the rocks, striated granite rising from the black of the sea. The tide thundered against their flanks, kicking up spray.

I asked Zaven where he thought he'd be, career-wise, eight years from now. His eyes flickered with pain, as if I'd burned him with a cigarette. It is a cruel question to ask any Lebanese, and he is a man struggling more than most with how to move forward. He is reined in by the world he works in, yet spurred on by his own restless creativity.

"The future? Strategically, I'm well established, but what should I do to make this a turning point? Is this my life? Is this it? Is there some incident that could really make me rewrite history? Or maybe this is my limit. I hate to consider that I'm at my peak now. Should I go back toward big shots, celebrities? If so, I have to remake a format that suits them. Also, I need Britney Spears, not just any time, but at the moment she cuts herself bald. Here, that can't happen, our celebrities aren't ready. But television likes celebrities."

Even for Zaven, the assailer of taboos, there is much he would never dare. His career, his livelihood, and maybe even his life, depend upon it. But one thing is for sure: Social programs like *Sire Wenfatahit* have dented a host of social taboos, especially for Arab women, and helped enlighten a generation—even if it is just to let them know that cunnilingus in the marital bed is shaykh-approved, though jerking off will kill their climax.

"There are people that would say I helped establish pop culture here, all this fluffy nonsense stuff. And I've ruined careers and I've made careers; it is often risky to be on my show. I would blame myself that sometimes I have given value to silly things. But this is me, and this is very modern, this idea of the silly having value. We can't all the time ignore 'wrong' values, sweep them under the carpet. This is what is killing us. Your values may be wrong to me, but I can't simply call it *ha'ram*. But if the people are not ready—fuck them."

I speared another couple of beans and stared out at the rocks. I had no doubt that as Zaven became more and more frustrated he would continue to play with form—perhaps he would invite a blind host for the anniversary show and film it in the dark, with no sound. He was in danger of atrophying, but to prompt further change he'd have to run great personal risks. In order to change, Zaven would have to enter the firing line. And look at all he had to lose.

"I always say—people who are not ready for change do not deserve to have a revolution. I'd say I've tried hard. I really have. But people don't want to talk about it. Homosexuality doesn't happen. The war never happened. And that's why there's never been any real reconciliation. We've buried it. That's why when bombs drop, we in Beirut call our doctor, and book for a nose job."

Part V

'ISHA

10

Full Nelson

AFGHANISTAN

Sunni Muslim: 80%

Shia Muslim: 19%

0% GDP
but have some
nifty pipelines

1. Andrew Bird:
   Scythian Empires

2. Television:
   Careful

3. Sam Roberts:
   Fixed to Ruin

Pop.: 32,738,376

Avg. age: 17.6

Capital: Kabul

Independence: Long story

"This," said the small boy, as he hurled me over his shoulder into the dust, "is body slam."

For some reason I had expected the ground to be softer, less riddled with razor-sharp pebbles. The boy did not seem so boyish when he leaped on top of me and tried to cinch my knee up to my nose.

"This," he continued, both competitor and commentator, "is half-nelson."

His WWE erudition was impressive for an eleven-year-old kid who was born under the Taliban and had lived most of his live in medieval Logar province, far outside the urban environment of Kabul. I should be clear on two things: Not every Afghan is this well versed in wrestling moves. And the part of Kabul I presently found myself in was urban in name only. There were far more goats up TV Hill than there were motor vehicles, or motors of any description. This was a mudbrick village that crawled up from the valley over which much of Kabul is dispersed, continuing up one of the ridges that cut the city into quadrants.

"Up," commanded my opponent. The wrestling sobriquet he'd accorded himself was, inexplicably, "Zach." I hypothesized that this was perhaps the most American name he had come across, but there was no way of knowing: His English was limited to Vince McMahon–approved terminology. He wore a now dust-caked *kurta* and a *weskit* (or waistcoat), while his *pakol* somehow remained on his head. His eyes were dark, close set and focused on the task at hand.

I met Zach by chance. He was shy at first—but regional hospitality had finally won over. Now, he stalked round the shabby clearing—the foundation of a mudbrick home acting as a fighting cage—and took two steps back. Then, with a "Yaheeee!" he launched himself into the air, aiming his two sandaled feet at my chest. As he sailed toward me, I had—in that frozen moment of time that tends to precede extreme discomfort—a chance to contemplate the fact that a preteen was planning to spear me, WWE style, in *Afghanistan* of all places. We were, as it happened, engaging in an activity closely akin to an ancient Persian sport—*Varzesh-e-Pahlavani*, Farsi for "sport of heroes," the wrestling discipline that helps explain the passion for WWE in Afghanistan. Persia—or Iran—is, of course, next door. But this wasn't Persian wrestling. It was American wrestling. Links. Even here.

"Hoof!" I said, as Zach's feet connected with my upper thighs, dangerously close to my groin. I helpfully dropped to the ground as a brood of children made appreciative noises. I thanked no deity in particular for the fact that Zach wasn't into Ultimate Fighting.

Hauling myself up and dusting off, I considered something my host in this country had told me that morning. "This is a pop-cultural war," said Shahir Zahine, the ex-mujahedeen, and a man who had earned the right to speak authoritatively about such things. "On one end, the pop culture of the Taliban. On the other, pop culture from elsewhere. Which one will win?" It was a question that in Afghanistan became more urgent by the day.

"This is powerbomb," said Zach, preparing for a move I was unfamiliar with. From somewhere quite far away, I heard the cackle of an AK-47. Zach paid no attention, and made for my neck.

★ ★ ★

Over the course of my travels I was always afraid I'd learn I was an intellectual anomaly, a one-of-a-kind ADD-riddled twit who found in *The Cosby Show* and *Magnum, P.I.* some sense of essential humanness where others found it in Tolstoy or the *Bhagavad Ghita* or yoga, or better yet, within themselves. That I had found like-minded people in unlikely places was itself an immense relief. But I never felt like I'd *arrived* until I met Shahir Zahine and his new wife, Melek Zimmer-Zahine. What's more, I'd never fully appreciated the larger implications—the true extent of the currents moving beneath my quest—until they took me into their world.

Shahir was born and bred in Afghanistan, while Melek was Turkish-American. I'd met her by chance some months before my arrival in Afghanistan, at breakfast in Dubai's Bastakia district. I noticed her because she was enormously pregnant while at the same time possessed of a wayward regality; the only blight on her beauty were the third-trimester bags under her eyes. She told me she was in Dubai because she had business here and decided to take of advantage of the city's superior medical care (she could just as easily have chosen Bhutan or Malawi: anywhere has superior medical care to Afghanistan). "Before considering a visit to Afghanistan, you should come by and visit me and Shahir here in Dubai," she said.

I took her up on the offer. Days later, I dropped by their rented condominium across from the Deira City Centre shopping mall. I was sitting in their pleasant living room eating from a bowl of nuts, when Melek said, "There we go. First contraction."

"First *what*?" I said. "You're in labor?"

"Seems that way," said Melek.

"Go suffer in the other room," joked Shahir, putting on the stentorian voice of the Afghani patriarch.

"This is crazy," I said. If this had been a middle-class American condominium, there would be twenty doulas hurrying around with pots of organic camomile tea and raspberry-infused hot compresses. And that's just for the expectant father. "I should go."

"Nonsense," said Shahir. He did not look like a man who spent the eighties roving Afghanistan, locked in battle with the Soviets. As a mujahedeen, Shahir had lost much of the hearing in his right ear because of a daylong firefight in an enclosed compound. His knees were destroyed from walking equine convoys through the Hindu Kush. His mouth was always upturned in a smile, but it was some time before I realized that he wore this expression to hide something essential about himself. A golf shirt and gold-rimmed spectacles removed any sense of menace about him, but there were sharp, maniacal flints in his eyes, as if they were playing short montages of all he'd seen. He pointed out a deep scar along his forehead. "I tell people this is from the Russians, and that you should have seen the other guy," he told me. "But I'm afraid it's from a benign car accident." Darn those benign car accidents.

"I'll let you know when the contractions are five minutes apart," said Melek, supporting her massive belly with a cupped arm.

"Call the doctor and see what he says," said Shahir.

"What's the doctor going to say?" she asked, brewing me a cup of tea. "I'm giving birth, no?"

I didn't know what to make of this alterna-Ozzie and Harriet exchange. The apartment was jammed with the high-end baby SUV and other hardware one finds in any Upper East Side Starbucks, but these were not your average yuppies. For one thing, they called Kabul home. For another, Melek was about to give birth and here we were drinking tea and eating olives like she was about to head off to her book club.

Shahir has four kids and Melek an eleven-year-old daughter from previous marriages. They met at a conference in Peshawar, Pakistan, shortly after 9/11. Melek was with USAID, using the region as a launch pad for post-transition reconstructive work, while Shahir was pitching a new multi-media venture called Killid Group—a news outlet, but also a means to deliver popular culture to a country long starved of it under the Taliban's iron mullahs, who ruled the country after the civil war ended in 1996 until the American-led invasion in late 2001. The Taliban's current status, thanks to an utterly botched post-conquest nation-building farce and the Obama administration's subsequent infusion of 30,000 troops, is now arguable.

"She came to fund me," said Shahir, "but instead, she fell in love and left USAID for me."

"Yeah, that's *not* what happened," said Melek, wincing at another contraction. "My job was to identify Afghans in exile in Pakistan who could play a role in influencing the society, who could open up the country to the rest of the world. The Killid idea was discussed in Peshawar, and that's how we met. Later, I became romantically interested. It wasn't a case of me falling madly in love with this guy and ditching USAID for him."

Melek's years in the U.S. State Department, working regions as action-packed as Iraq, Baluchistan and Bosnia, have given her a deep, quiet wisdom. She resigned from the U.S. government when she realized that no one was listening anymore; most of the attention was focused on the imminent invasion of Iraq. When she wasn't in the process of giving birth, Melek worked on the Killid Group, with Shahir supplying the hard-edged id, and she the nuanced ego.

That evening in Dubai, as a purple sun set over an Islamic land that couldn't be less like Afghanistan, Melek and Shahir spelled out their philosophy, which was, I felt, not only a working model for any transitional Islamic society, but the very way I viewed the world.

"I recently met a Palestinian woman," Melek said in her soft, lullaby voice. "She wanted to join Hamas and give herself up as a suicide bomber. On the face of things, this is a woman with everything— education, smarts, etcetera. She told me, though, that 'I'm hopeless. I have no more hope left.' I said to her that maybe she hadn't looked at all the possibilities. Had she done any writing, or tried to engage culturally, like Shahir and I are doing in Kabul? I told her that there is plenty she can do. And she seemed genuinely shocked, and genuinely grateful for the advice. She hadn't so much as *considered* these as options."

"It is our job," Shahir put in, "to make people consider the options."

Killid means "key" in both Farsi and Pashtu, Afghanistan's two most prominent languages, and the company comprises two radio stations run out of Kabul and the western city of Herat, along with a series of magazines, amounting to a private media empire in a country that desperately needs one. Killid contributes to the slow, meticulous work of building an Afghani fifth estate, but also a space in the public discourse where popular culture can flourish. Shahir and Melek believe this is Afghanistan's only hope of salvation.

"I've always been a firm believer, as an American and a Turk, in the power of expression," said Melek, "and I always used to say invest, invest, invest in the people's right to express themselves, regardless of what they might say. If you really are serious about democracy, let people speak. Yes, extremist voices will get through, but I'm confident that, like everywhere else, it would whittle down to lowest-common-denominator entertainment."

That's both a dreary and encouraging thought—the fact that someone with vast experience in both the region and the mechanics behind transitional societies believes that people would opt for *Transformers III* over a Taliban beard-grooming video.

"Pop culture is such a stabilizing force. I've come to learn this because of all the young people I've met—Bosnian Muslims, Iraqis, Afghanis, Lebanese—and I'll tell you why. Those that have watched MTV are not willing to strap bomb belts on and go after the seventy-two virgins. They've tasted another possibility, no matter how unreal, and they've tapped into the dream. It's the ones that don't have access to pop who are so dangerous. A lot of pop culture is about humor, and a great way to develop a sense of humor—or a sense of irony—is to watch and listen to this stuff."

Shahir nodded, popped an olive in his mouth. "I've met, oh, I'd say one or two extremists in my time. And they don't have senses of humor. In fact, you *can't* be extremist with a sense of humor."

"Right now," continued Melek, "we have a problem. Put aside for a minute the trauma and the killing. Military campaigns necessarily restrict freedom of movement, and they also restrict the space for genuine members of a civil society to do things properly. The one tool the West has for winning hearts and minds in this quote unquote War on Terror—that is culture, or popular culture—the West has not invested in properly, and the extremists are steadily taking over the public space."

At the heart of this observation, one can discern a key facet of popular culture: It creates a neutral public space. Of course, pop can be—and often is—politically or spiritually charged, but for every Toby Keith there's a Bruce Springsteen, and for every *Chronicles of Narnia* there's a *Hangover*—a push/pull between interests, because every aspect of the market needs to be serviced. A neutral public space, a place for opposing views to get a hearing, but, more than that, a place for sheer ephemera, for sitcom fluff, for chintzy pop songs.

"Bomb 'em with music videos?" I asked Shahir and Melek, as I once had Ahmad Dhani in his Jakarta compound.

"Um, that's not normally how I'd speak," said Melek, "but, yeah, that's the basic meaning. And not necessarily with pure American sensibilities, and *not* the way the Saudis do it, by watering everything down and policing it. But with genuine voices from the region, voices that have been allowed the space to develop. It needs to be able to grow."

The sun had set, and the apartment was bright with the frenzied lights of Deira. "Societies with healthy pop cultures, they tend to be more pluralistic," said Melek, leaning forward and wincing again. "This may seem optimistic, but we believe it: Pop does a funny thing, even if you don't know it's doing it—it gets into your consciousness, and you start to see yourself in others. It gives you empathy. It saves you."

I almost said "Amen" with the fervor of a born-again Midwestern Episcopalian.

"You should come to Afghanistan," said Shahir, "and see what we do."

I said that sounded like a wonderful idea.

I finished my tea and left. That night, Melek Zimmer-Zihane gave birth to a healthy boy.

Some months later, I stood on a mound of rusted anti-aircraft shells overlooking Kabul, and I thought of sharks.

It's safe to say that among the various and awful ways in which so many Afghanis have died over the course of their brutal history, not one has met with the business end of a shark. Nonetheless, in a 2004 survey conducted by the NGO Save the Children, a representative number of Afghanistan's young—my wrestling opponent Zach, perhaps, among them—were asked to name their greatest fears. Pollsters, poised to scribble "landmine" or "Spetsnaz" or "Islamofascist smack dealer," were instead asked time and time again to write "shark." Confusion abounded, until it was noted that the anniversary DVD of Steven Spielberg's masterpiece was circulating in Afghanistan's bootleg shops. Three years after the (first) fall of the Taliban, a new generation of Afghanistan's children was being introduced to a big bloodthirsty fish. They were reluctant to set foot near a river. They were afraid to bathe.

This story would not leave my mind.

I bought a bootleg copy of *Jaws* on Chicken Street, watched it in my dank hotel room, then scrambled up the west face of Kabul's so-called TV Hill, near where I'd had my ass kicked by an eleven-year-old. I walked through a mudbrick neighborhood, stepping around human excrement pouring from slate outhouses. White-shrouded widows slept in alleys like the dead, their filthy children curled alongside them, one little hand extended for alms. Bent men pushing barrows of shoes and mangoes and animal carcasses criss-crossed the streets.

Clambering up further, among the litter and tangled bracken, I came across a trail of spent anti-aircraft shells. I followed it like a child in a fairytale, slipping over loose shale, finally cresting the granite spine of the ridge. Northern Kabul appeared before me, unfurling like a dusty Persian carpet. Clear of the shit, I smelled dust and mountain air. Thousands—tens of thousands—of rusted shells, dating back to the civil war of the nineties, spilled over the lip of the mountain, where various factions had settled in to rain hellfire onto the city. Before that, the Russians. After it, the Taliban. Now, this new war. And what were Kabul's children afraid of?

Sharks.

It was the fighting season, and in the hills of the Hindu Kush, the Taliban had long since brushed the crusted ice and snow from their beards and set out to wreak their special brand of havoc upon the country, met in kind by their coalition-force enemies. Shahir and Melek Zahine seemed like crazed visionaries, destined to eat their foolish words at the barrel of a Taliban gun. But then I thought back to *Jaws*.

If, like the Taliban, you rely on terror as a central component in your business plan, and you're beaten out of top place on the Save the Children's "Most Feared List 2004" by a plastic shark, you might pause to wonder if the Zahines don't have a point.

The Killid Group hunkers behind compound walls in the raucous neighborhood of Kolola Pushta. A slow hill rises behind it, green flags crackling in the wind above lonely grave markers. During the war with the Soviets, Arab fighters financed by Saudi money tore down these flags. The Afghanis referred to the desecrators as Wahhabis and killed them for their sacrilege. But it was too late. The devil was in their house.

The devil—at least from Shahir Zahine's perspective—remains essentially unchanged, even if, with the emergence of the Taliban, the fundamentalists have become authentically Afghan. "There's a notion in Islam of *itijihad*—the responsibility to question—but that's been thrown aside," said Shahir as we drove toward the Killid compound in his dirty white Land Rover. It was several months since the birth of his son in Dubai, and both Shahir and Melek had returned to manage Killid through this critical time in Afghanistan's history, a period of relative—and I use the following term loosely—peace.

The Land Rover bounced up and down over rutted roads like a dinghy in high seas. We passed schoolboys, their backpacks hanging low over their buttocks, yelling at each other as they made their way through knots of scooter traffic. We clunked over deep sluices running with what looked to be—but smelled nothing like—chocolate-marshmallow pudding. As we drove, Shahir waved his hand over the destruction and conjured the future from the rubble: "I see here a discotheque, with some restaurants and some shopping," he said, turning bomb sites into neighborhoods, ruins into entertainment complexes.

"Modernization, and by extension popular culture, is like *itijihad*, a constant questioning of the status quo," continued Shahir, "and once the young people sink their teeth into it, it's so dangerous, because it involves questioning. Ask a cleric here about *itijihad*. They consider it a sin!"

And that's the Killid Group in the eyes of Afghanistan's bad guys: *itijihad*, sin incarnate. Past a reception area flanked by a resource center, one enters a large courtyard dominated by a cherry tree. The low, two-story compound is divided into departments. Inside the newsroom: a series of ancient PCs. Around a sagging boardroom table, thirty men dressed in varying degrees of Kabul smart/casual and six women with chadors are engaged in a story meeting. In a side room, a desultory radio set-up is arranged around a dining-room table—two microphones, a ten-track mixing board and a PC.

This ain't Al Jazeera—there is no government or clerical involvement—which is partly what makes Killid so encouraging. While Killid relied on initial start-up funding from the EU and USAID, it now operates on its own revenue. Shahir's business acumen has ensured that it remains an independent media company, owned and operated by Afghanis, for Afghanis. The operation is divided simply: there's *Killid*, the weekly current affairs magazine; *Mursal*, the family weekly; and Radio Killid, in Kabul, Herat and soon Jalalabad (along with the thirty partner stations across the country).

"Seven years ago—you wouldn't show a woman on the front of a magazine, if there were any magazines," Shahir told me, after we had eaten afternoon cookies with his crew. "Now, we do that all the time. But it's a war. Many of the mujahedeen I knew, including my commanders, now work for me. They went from working AK-47s to Microsoft Word. We have transformed combat routes into routes of independent media. Everything is backward to forward. This is creating a very interesting form of popular culture."

"Right," I said. "So how do you define *Afghani* popular culture?"

I knew that conditions had changed immeasurably since the fall of the Taliban—Zach's wrestling moves, among other things, proved it. Televisions, formerly banned, were now bolted to the walls of pokey restaurants around the country. Men clustered around greasy tables watching Al Jazeera or Bollywood soaps or DVDs of action films. Satellite dishes allowed wealthier villagers to bring the entire world into their compounds. The studied moans of hardcore porn were background noise in Kabul's Internet cafés. But pockets of the country were untouched by any of this, hunched under forbidding peaks, enveloped in tribal customs unchanged for centuries. "Television has made us more aware, and better informed," an Afghani villager, in a moment of charming frankness, told BBC.com during my stay. "When we see TV, we realize how backward we are. At the same time, we want to preserve our Islamic values."

Shahir smiled his upturned smile. "Almost nothing is produced in this country except poppies. And the best hashish. And very rough toilet paper. Films are very popular, music is very popular. We do have bootleg movie industries, and bootleg music industries. So, like everything, pop culture is still an import. It comes from Tajikistan, Uzbekistan, Pakistan, India. And the United States of America. I see it as my job to coalesce all this, to make sense of it, to make it less dangerous."

To understand how Shahir is doing this, one need only listen to Killid's signature late-night radio show, Radio-e-Dunya. It is programmed by an emaciated French musicologist named Jerome

Louis, and four times a week he meticulously illuminates the branches of a great musical tree linking Tajiki pop to four-bar blues to Bach to Ravi Shankar to A Tribe Called Quest. He asks Afghanis to step back and look at this structure from afar, and reminds them that nothing is truly foreign.

But the boughs head off in some strange directions. That evening, as Shahir and I drove back to the Zahines' home, I looked across the Shar-e-Now public park and stared, with the same astonishment that must have stricken the Save the Children pollsters, at a painted sign above a curtained doorway. The muscled figure of Arnold Schwarzenegger—once the Terminator, now the Gubernator—stared back at me. There was almost no signage in Kabul, except for the odd cellular phone billboard. So this came as a surprise.

I looked back at Shahir, google-eyed. "Arnie," I said, slackly.

Shahir nodded. "Arnie," he said. "You will see him everywhere."

Sitting under a dripping chinar tree in the Zahines' garden, ten or so city blocks from the Killid Group compound, I listened to Shahir and Melek argue over a small but telling point, one which went a long way to defining an existential problem at the heart of their mission: Pop was well and good, but what pop? Where, and when, and for whom? Should the great glut of everything be dumped on the Afghan doorstep to be sorted through in the messy process of modernization, or should it be meted out in increments? And who got to be the arbiter of Afghani taste? The iron mullahs? Sufi mystics? Or Shahir and Melek Zahine?

Melek had just finished nursing her son; Shahir's three boys were sprawled out on the day bed in the family room, watching bootleg DVDs. The house is a Kabul original, a two-story structure with rich cedar door and window frames, dark wood furnishings, whitewashed walls. Light crawled through it languidly. The yard was a firefight of flowering pink rosebushes and cherry trees, with knotted vines forming a bower above the entrance. From beyond the compound's thick mudbrick walls: the furious bleating of Kabul's traffic.

"Recently," said Melek, waving away the first of the evening's mosquitoes, "we argued over whether to profile an Afghan rapper named DJ Diamond."

"I hate rap," said Shahir, "and I didn't like his rap."

"That's not the point," said Melek. "This is a guy who is making history, so that makes him a relevant cultural item. It's not our choice whether we like what he sounds like."

"I don't know. The station manager and I—we didn't like the music."

"You were out of touch," said Melek gently. "The sad thing is: There aren't enough examples of Afghan artists influenced by Western pop producing in the country—that crossover isn't happening yet. But what you do have is many Western products coming into the country. There's not much innovative stuff happening."

"Evolution takes time," said Shahir. "We work slow—we may have been very critical on the political side, but on the social side we are slow. We've tried the last seven years to influence society, but not by running too far ahead of the mainstream. I am not," he added, "a sensationalist."

But pop often *depended* on sensationalism, didn't it?

"We will go slow," he continued. "Others have chosen to do differently. That is their choice."

One learns that it is a choice with deadly consequences. The murder, depending on whom one asks, was either an honor killing of the standard variety or a direct result of Afghani media's headlong rush into the future. All anyone knows for sure is that on May 18, 2005, a young woman named Shaima Rezayee was killed in her Kabul home by one or more male members of her family, who are fiercely traditional Shia Hozara. She had recently been fired as a presenter

for the music-clip television show *Hop*, because she had become—
to borrow an Afghan neo-Orwellianism—"incompatible." Rezayee
wore jeans, hats and not a full-length blue *burqa*. She engaged with
her male co-hosts in the kind of on-air banter that would have been
typical in the West if TV had existed in 1843. Ask anyone at Tolo
TV—*Hop's* home—and they'll tell you Rezayee had gone off the
rails and was killed by her enraged kin because of her drinking. If
you ask Shahir and Melek, her crime was her behavior on national
television.

Though Tolo TV's owners, Moby Group, is Afghanistan's highest
profile media empire—a flashier, if that's the word, version of Killid—
the compound feels like a base Pablo Escobar would have used to
move crates of cocaine out of Medellin: shabby armed men, barbed
wire, trailers, frenzied activity. Moby, owned by the Mohseni brothers,
Afghan nationals late of Melbourne, was started in 2002 with capital
from the brothers' stock brokerage in Australia. Security was tight:
They receive *fatwas* like HBO gets Golden Globes. Tolo TV, Arman
FM 98.1 and other Moby outfits are, despite what management
would say, targets.

In five years they had "changed the taste of the people for music,"
Massood Sanjer, the voice of Arman FM and one of the more famous
men in Afghanistan, told me the day I paid a visit. "Now, they want
Afghan and Tajiki pop, and also Shakira, and Enrique Iglesias and
J.Lo and Arabic—everything. This after no music with the Taliban!

"Jennifer Lopez is a little bit popular here," Sanjer added. We
stood before a bank of old monitors and watched one of her videos
play on *Hop*. The extra-governmental Religious Council complained
after *Hop* ran her clip for "Ain't It Funny," in which the chanteuse in
question writhes around on ten million thread-count bedsheets
wearing fancy underwear. "We receive lots of pressure after this song,"
he said. J.Lo's cleavage, along with her highly regarded rear end, were
summarily obscured with big blocks of digital fuzz. It was like
watching TV with glaucoma.

"Meanwhile," said Sanjer, "they watch porno film at home on

satellite. Two years ago, things were better, but the media has come under increasing pressure by the government. Day by day the pressure is increasing. Day by day."

Killid and Moby had almost identical aims and business models—a vertically integrated approach to media that saw popular culture not just as a weapon against extremism, but also as a means to bring the outside world into Afghanistan. To present another version of reality. But it was a question of pace. Had Moby not moved too fast?

"But what must we do?" asked Sanjer rhetorically. "Leave TV and radio for government or the Talib? We need the free market system here. It can't just be NGOs using and spending all the money. And if we are a little bit controversial, so be it. But look—*just look*—how we change things."

"But what if I like to listen to *suras* around the clock?"

"There are many stations for you. Just change the dial."

It was exactly that simple: The essence of a civil society is conceding that you can just change the dial, and, by doing so, refrain from suicide-bombing the offending station. But Shaima Rezayee's family wouldn't change the dial. There will always be martyrs for the cause of change, and in Afghanistan, they are too often young women.

Kabul in the early morning is a city of smoke. We drove north, while myriad wood fires buried the city under striations of fragrant white haze. Before us, the Hindu Kush. Once we passed the military bases, the road evened out and we wound our way alongside the Mahipar Valley, following the Kabul River as it cut a jagged Joker's smile through the Surobi Mountains.

Shahir was furious with me. The previous evening, during a dinner party at his house, I'd overindulged in his Johnny Walker, and when his driver was returning me to the hotel, I hopped out of the truck early and strolled back in the quiet of the night. That this was a bad idea occurred to me about five minutes into the walk. Nonetheless, the air was clearing my head, and as I sang a Nirvana medley and became increasingly lost, Shahir called me on my mobile and informed me, in no uncertain terms, that what I was doing was beyond the realm of stupid.

Even before this incident, my relationship with Shahir was fraying. I was another North American, digging for edification through the rubble of his ruined land—effete, naïve, dead to the real dangers of his world. And life in Kabul—even for the upper middle class—is no picnic. The Zahine clan was jammed into the compound. There was no public space for the kids, few sporting activities, fewer places—outside of a restaurant—to spend time as a family. The baby was fussy. Kidnappings were a constant concern.

So the fellow-feeling in the Land Rover that morning was less than salutary. The landscape struggled mightily to make up for it. Morning sun dissolved the smoke, hitting the higher parts of the snow-encrusted peaks. It was through these passes that British troops retreated from Kabul after the so-called Auckland's Folly—the attack and occupation of the country in the 1840s. Ghilzai warriors descended, slaughtering thousands, leaving trails of gore through two feet of snow all the way to Jalalabad.

"Why didn't you tell me Afghanistan was so beautiful?" I asked Shahir, trying to massage my way through the tension.

"That's because I forget it's beautiful," he said. He was looking out the window, suddenly a tourist in a land he had spilled blood for.

This was Afghanistan as it was a hundred years ago: We stopped for goats, dodged braying mules, gave alms to roadside beggars. We entered a fecund delta along the Kabul River that, with its palm trees and wavering poplars and bulrushes and rudimentary river craft, looked like the Hollywood set for a Moses movie. But the future was on its way, and the people here will meet the twenty-first century with a mixture of bafflement and desire and fear. It is these poor souls who will be asked to reconcile their deep Muslim and traditional values with J-Lo, when they do not possess the faculties to engage in such a negotiation.

Two hours later: the city of Jalalabad. Smuggler's paradise, drug dealer's lair, terrorist hot spot. Warlords' wedding-cake cribs intermingled with mudbrick houses and stretches of swooning, blackened stalls where all manner of iron-age industry was for sale. Any creature short of a pig that could be hacked up and flayed was available for dinner.

"My God, they're paving the sidewalks," said Shahir as we drove by workmen laying interlocking brick. "My, oh my, a real city!"

The Jalalabad Killid complex is a concrete building off a deeply pitted dirt road running with sewage. It was cool despite the heat outside, and we sank into a lounge-set in a room with the curtains drawn, the *thwock thwock* of a fan the only sound in the deep stillness of the exhausted afternoon. Over what is technically known as a feast—heaped platters that would have fed half of Jalalabad for a week—Shahir started talking.

"There is one golden condition of Afghans: It's our tiredness, our fatigue of fighting against the current. There is no real investment from this generation to fight. Second, there is no real, fixed ideology behind anything. There is no real intellectual position. They will leave Islam for pop, or pop for Islam. One of the two. It could go either way. If you ask them if they believe in Islam, they will tell you that they are afraid of God. They are Muslim, why? Because they are insecure. They have no ideology. No one thinks."

Out of this, Shahir believes, pop can become what it once was for me—a refuge. Pop was a dreamland where my dim understanding of the world I lived in was washed aside and a new universe was constructed with a different set of rules. But no matter how distant and apart we were as Apartheid-era South Africans, we were still—at least in our own estimation—"European." Without connecting roots, however, without context, without the faintest of cultural links, pop becomes easy to demonize, the work of some maniac machine, infused with subliminal power—a force from afar come to conquer, to own.

★ ★ ★

Later that day, I ventured into town—with Shahir's bodyguard, a giant named Dawlat Khan. I led us into an underground plaza, the very bowels of this teeming city. We walked down broken stairs into a swarm of bodies, the heat so severe it was like being sucked into the backdraft of a blaze. Young men, hundreds of them. Some leaned against cracked walls lined with faded posters, their kurta pajamas hanging limp with sweat. Others flicked through video-clips on PCs, sound tearing through speakers. Young imams screamed *suras*. Others just screamed.

I saw a clip of *Friends*. I saw images of Jean-Claude Van Damme. I heard Schwarzenegger bellow, *If it bleeds, we can kill it!* I heard Bollywood tunes. I heard Akon. The plaza was a smoldering hell of DVDs, cheap mobile phones, MP3 players. Posted on a wall was an advert in Pashtu for a bodybuilding scheme of the old Charles Atlas variety: *Don't stay puny! Become a man!*

It felt like a medieval torture chamber outfitted with the pain-inflicting tools of the future, which made me think Afghan society—like many Muslim societies—was being ripped apart as men were once drawn and quartered. They were tethered to the four raging mares of technology, culture, the generation gap and their traditional values. The psychic tearing never stops.

This plaza contained the resultant morass of desire, conservatism, progressivism, loathing of the old, fear of the new, with no oasis of cultural calm where a weary mind could rest and find its bearings. It was a collective psychological and cultural assault that has no precedent in history, mostly because technology has never delivered content with such speed and force and in such tasty packaging. Once you're online, there are no longer tiers of availability. One day there is nothing, and the next there is everything. But my hosts in this country believed that the clamorous mess in this plaza could be used as a weapon for good. And they had built an independent Afghan media empire in their attempt to prove it.

Dawlat Khan, my protector, placed a hand on my shoulder. His face was drenched in sweat; he was wincing from the noise. It was time to go up. A big man among big men, he hunched down, put forward a granite shoulder, and opened a gap in the crowd.

In the truck driving back to Kabul, under the flickering shadows of the Surobi Mountains, Shahir placed something on my lap. I looked down at a nine-millimeter handgun in a leather holster.

"I thought you were done with guns," I said.

"Yes, but guns aren't done with me."

"Whatever it takes, right?"

"No, no. But sometimes, on the road back from Jalalabad, this is the tool you need."

I thought back to the plaza—a crazed vision of Afghanistan's ungovernable future—and sank low in my seat, trying to stave off the despairing notion that Shahir Zahine made Don Quixote look like General George C. Marshall.

Don't stay puny! Become a man!

The signs were everywhere: flexing muscle-bound men, veins throbbing through sun-browned skin, many of whom were Arnold Schwarzenegger. The burgeoning Afghan obsession with wrestling was also an obsession with getting pumped.

I should, in the interest of full disclosure, reveal that it is an obsession that I once shared. I learned the art at Brian's Gym in Norwood, Johannesburg, and I wanted to look like Sylvester Stallone. I would stand in front of the gym's many mirrors and "hit the light," which is the technical term for flexing and getting the right balance of shadow to most flatter the musculature. I wanted pecs, delts, tris to burst forth from my puny body, stretching the material of my T-shirts to reveal the work of masculine art beneath. Bodybuilding is alchemy: The pupa bursts forth from the cocoon to become a vein-rippled monster.

"You can become the person you dream of being, bodybuilders say. You can defy both nurture and nature and transform yourself," wrote Samuel W. Fussell in *Muscle: Confessions of an Unlikely Bodybuilder*. I supposed the same applied to a nation.

I did not enter the Omid Gym, on the outskirts of the 10th Municipality, Kabul's Shia district, rippling with muscle—mostly because my serious bodybuilding career ended around the same time it began. The long room, separated from the world by a paradoxically dainty lace curtain, faded to murk the further one stood from the grimy window. The machines shrieked like souls in pain and the place reeked like snake vomit. Pages ripped from bodybuilding magazines papered the walls. Over the small counter, there were the *hadiths* of the Prophet alongside the sayings of Arnie. Two heavily muscled young men sucked back cans of Red Bull. I introduced myself.

"To be honest," said Bashir, the bigger of the two, wearing a Jägermeister T-shirt and jeans, "this is not about being a health complex. Afghans, compared to other nations, we are small. We see the movies and we see the bigger men, and we want to be like this."

The heroes of American popular culture are men and women in dazzling physical condition—animatronic versions of Michelangelo's *David* in furious motion, either kicking ass, making love or solving complex intellectual problems, all with their deltoids. Anyone who has ordered the Denny's Lumberjack Slam breakfast in, say, Rochester, New York, would allow that the reality is otherwise. But it is safe to assume that Bashir will never enjoy such an opportunity.

The bodybuilding movement, which existed during the especially lean days of the Taliban, became more of a phenomenon when big American soldiers and their attendant culture poured into the country. This was a reaction to the epicene ideal of feminized masculinity that reigned during the Taliban era. With no place for women in public life, men were expected to present both sides—the masculine and the feminine. Hard-boiled killers were photographed with heavy kohl and lipstick, staring coquettishly into space, images as lurid as Ted Turner colorizations. But there was nothing feminine about Stallone in *Rambo III* when, double-fisting M60s, he single-handedly mowed down a Red Army battalion. And there was nothing feminine about Arnie in *Terminator II*, a movie that landed Bashir in the notorious Pul-e-Charkhi prison, which broods on the outskirts of Kabul on the Jalalabad road.

"They catch me in Shar-e-Now park with the video in my pants. Two weeks in Pul-e-Charkhi. Then another time, they catch me with short beard. The same again."

So when the Taliban raided a gym that was packed during noontime prayer, Bashir wasn't having it. He leaped from the second-floor window, and ran. Under the Taliban there were no posters on the gym wall, no music. "There wasn't much to eat to make up for the energy you lost—I was around sixty-two kilograms. Now I'm eighty-four kilos." Young men used and abused knocked-off equipment, their bones aching, weak with hunger, getting further from the Schwarzeneggian ideal with every lat pull-down and bicep curl. Once a year, in the ill-lit and underused Shar-e-Now cinema, there would be a show. Participants were allowed to display the upper half of their body, and they had to keep their beards regulation length. When these men hit the light—intermittent, considering Kabul's capricious electricity system—their ribs were as prominent as their abs.

"Our muscles were small," Bashir told me. "We could bench-press very little, and there were no magazines on how to do proper training." Sometimes a magazine would drift in from Peshawar and the pages would be neatly torn out and circulated around town, young men crowding over them to glean some of the wisdom contained therein. "We tried," said Bashir, "but we could not be like our heroes." There was no hint of irony in his words, just a deep bitterness. He returned to his Red Bull. We were done talking.

Later that day, I met with Ahmad Yasin Qaderi, leaning in his office chair at the reception desk of the remarkably clean Champions Gym in the Qall-e-Fatullah district. Behind him, glowing under pot lights, was a veritable gallery of Myoplex product. This was more health club than stinking muscle shop, and men hit the light with remarkable aplomb. Qaderi is a minor celebrity, and the decor in Champions is an ode to his body: pictures of him everywhere, veins snaking around his massive quads. There is even an *Eid* greeting card depicting our hero with a Taliban-style beard. Qaderi was Mr. Kabul 1385 (or 2006) in the eighty-kilogram category. Akon was serenading him over the PA.

"I am twenty-two, and have loved bodybuilding since I was a child," Qaderi informed me. He has an older brother in the Netherlands who sent magazines during the final days of the Taliban, which is when Qaderi started pumping iron in earnest. He beat out ninety-four other men for the Mr. Kabul title.

Still, Qaderi didn't have the money to continue his professional career. "I spend eleven thousand dollars on myself to win Mr. Kabul. To win Mr. Afghanistan, I must spend fifteen thousand dollars. I don't have such money. There is no sponsor, and no government support." And indeed, his body is a sign of class, a status symbol. It's an upwardly mobile body. An American body.

And in Afghanistan, few have as American a body as the humble proprietor of Kabul's most famous workout emporium: Gold Gym.

"I do two dips, I talk to you," said Bawar Hotak when I paid him a visit one gloomy Kabul afternoon. Also chief of the Afghanistan National Bodybuilding Federation, Hotak is one of the biggest men I have ever encountered. Like the equipment Afghani bodybuilders once used, Hotak himself seemed knocked together from machine parts—his back was as broad and curved as a bulldozer scoop, his wrists as thick as jet engine pistons, his chest as wide as a truck grille. His long nose sloped downward, culminating in an edifice of a chin that projected above the vastness of his torso. There was a long scar snaking around his wrist—the result of a car accident. Between dips, he removed his shirt and donned a military vest. "*Commando*," I said, referring to the Schwarzenegger film that made the look famous. He smiled happily, wiping away sweat with his discarded shirt. We ambled outside for a juice.

The dusty parking lot outside Gold (note, not "Gold's"; the name is in homage to Arnie's famous Venice Beach institution, not an attempt to infringe copyright) was busy with street kids carrying tin cans of burning incense and selling all manner of baubles. The crowd opened as Hotak strode out. His credibility comes in part from his father's business—farming and trucking—which has allowed him the financial independence to pursue bodybuilding in earnest.

Hotak mixed a cherry-red protein supplement concoction, street kids looking on in wonder, and told me that there are over one thousand gyms in Afghanistan, an astonishing figure when one considers how much of the country is a) uninhabitable and b) Stone Age. Gold itself is not a profitable business—Hotak takes in just enough membership fees to keep things going (he doesn't charge the poor, doesn't charge the police, and other members pay fees on a pro rata basis).

In his youth, he was a wrestler, but he found that he put on muscle like most of us gain extra chins and decided to concentrate on bodybuilding. He spent the Taliban years in Peshawar. During the first year of the regime, he visited Kabul to participate in a competition, and when he showed too much leg, three Taliban—in a stroke of bravery that can only be explained by the promise of those seventy-two heavenly virgins—leapt from the audience and beat him with sticks.

"They were lucky you didn't kill them," I said.

"No—I was sort of a guest. I could not kill them." Hotak spent his requisite time in jail, then made his way back to Peshawar. He had already decided to build the first modern gym in Afghanistan. "They used to make the equipment from an old gearbox, some old tank parts. They would make the weights from cement—one side maybe five kilos, the other side maybe four. Not good. Many injuries." Within months of the Taliban's fall, Hotak was importing equipment from Iran and Pakistan. Future plans include inviting foreign champions, men whose pictures hang in the entrance to the gym like yearbook photos from Thug High, to come in and help train his trainers: Arnie, Ronnie Coleman and Jay Cutler. "These three heroes have not yet visited Afghanistan," said Hotak. "Everyone here loves these guys. Maybe if they knew how much Afghanistan loved them, they would come." He stopped suddenly, midstream. His eyes moistened, and he took my hand in his great, gnarled mitt.

"We just want to *live*," he told me. It was an awkward moment, like watching Dolph Lundgren struggle to emote opposite Kate Winslet in a handsome romantic period epic. Still, I felt a lump of emotion in my own throat.

I nodded. "I can understand that," I said. Hotak's granite face had turned to trembling jelly. He was like a boy—or maybe an old man—who has come to a first, or a final, understanding of how harsh the world is.

"But then why no support? *Why doesn't anyone care?*"

I got a momentary sense of what it must be like to live in Kabul, or any place like it. You could only snatch at your dreams, never able to take the whole sensual mess in hand. There was, despite all that Shahir and Melek (and, indeed, I) believed, an inherent cruelty in living under the thrall of American pop culture. It gave you but the slightest of tastes, just enough to let you know you were starving.

Returning to Gold so I could pick up my bag, I dodged newcomers flooding in, greeted by Hotak with a kiss on the cheek. The floor was laid with Persian carpets, while the ceiling crumbled from accumulated moisture. It was evening, and as the world outside darkened, the fluorescents flickered on. Gold Gym members flocked toward the mirror, and hit the light.

"If you one day go to California . . ." Hotak said.

"I'll be sure to tell Arnie about Gold," I finished.

He smiled, knowing how silly that sounded, and strode through his gym, unembarrassed by the tears drying on his face.

We ate a simple breakfast under the chinar tree, the madness of Kabul braying on the other side of the mudbrick wall. Melek had of late been insensible with the strain of motherhood. It was all she could do to keep her eyes open.

"There are still so many taboos in this part of the world," she said through a sigh. "I remember growing up in America with TV shows that were really out there—that framed my outlook at a young age: *M*A*S*H*, *The Jeffersons*, *All in the Family*—all shows that questioned authority, looked at racism." These shows were America's version of commercial, mass *itijihad* during a critical period of the country's history, and helped work through the knots of the civil rights debate. A few decades later, a black dude is running the whole shebang. *Amen* if you will.

"That's what I want for Afghanistan," Melek said. "And let me give you an example of how not to do it: The States developed Alhurra, the satellite radio and television station, and broadcast it to the Iraqi and North African populations. The people know it is U.S. propaganda, they know it is psychological games. The administration would get more bang for their buck if they supported a real initiative in the region, not just some 501(c)(3) tax credit in Washington. The public knows when something is wrong."

"If we lose," said Shahir, "it's because we were not given the space—because the U.S. and NATO and all that are kissing the ass of the fundamentalists, making deals with the devil and taking up too much damn room."

Shahir looked at me. The maniacal flittering in his eyes had died down, which made him truly menacing. "This is our *life* and our money. We could have a much bigger impact if people looked to us as a test case in the region. Pop culture and the development of open societies don't have huge lobbies. Who is defending progressive values? Does the U.S. even put a fraction—a *fraction*—of the billions they've spent in Afghanistan towards the media—the free, local media? And it's not just the funding we need, but the political will. Funding is one part of it, but to buy into the idea that culture can help win this? That would be a different story."

★ ★ ★

Shahir piloted his Land Rover through dust and traffic north of Kabul toward the Shomali plain. The city felt mean and hungry, as if we were weaving through the teeth of a snapping mouth. Shahir was silent until we were on the outskirts of town.

"This Arabization of *The Simpsons*—this *Al Shamshoon* that you told me about," said Shahir. "To turn *The Simpsons* into Arabic is a courageous step. If they did it right, that would have been a great thing—the satire, the humor, the humanness. If the spirit was kept— this would be the true changing. If it worked, it could mean something big. If it worked . . ."

We turned off the main road, and into a *National Geographic* special. Half-naked boys made way for us; girls in colorful veils stopped to stare as we passed. After ten minutes, we arrived at Shahir's family *qala*, or what was left of it. It had been bombed by the Russians and many died, but what remained looked like a crumbling colony for giant termites. The surrounding land was stupidly beautiful: forty acres of peach trees and apple trees and pink roses growing from the cracked mud. There were waves and waves of bulrushes, walnut trees and mulberry trees centuries old. Water gurgled through an intricate system of sluices. The property was ringed by the Hindu Kush, which reared up starkly some ten kilometers away, backlit by a fading sun. From the underbrush, I saw three magpies take wing, startled by our footfalls.

"I think I understand why you fought," I said, as we strolled through the ruined *qala*. He answered "yes" in the way the Pashtu sometimes do, by sucking in his breath. Minutes later, we rounded into a clearing and encountered an old man, his face rutted with deep crags, only eye teeth remaining in his mouth. Shahir pulled on the elder's beard twice, like a bell ringer, then kissed his hand—a beautiful and intimate gesture of respect.

"This man has been on this land forever," said Shahir, "as has his family."

We made our way to two wicker daybeds, and a servant brought us candy-sweet mulberries in deep wooden bowls, which we washed down with peppery *lassi*. I felt as if we had been removed from the flow of time, the very opposite of that Jalalabad underworld.

"I came here to regenerate during the fighting," said Shahir, "although at the time the land was in very poor condition. Before that, I spent the weekends and my childhood summers here, getting fat in the mulberry trees. When I was boy, in the winter, every night, I was here in my dreams. And then—*poof!*—I'd wake up in Kabul."

He lay back on his daybed, his hands behind his head, and looked up through the branches of the mulberry tree into the clear blue of the gloaming. A muezzin cried in the distance. "This would be perfect," said Shahir, "if someone would only shut him up."

It was becoming increasingly difficult to believe—this being our second title fight—that Zach wasn't *aiming* for my balls, rather than hitting them accidentally. I had taken to stalking the ring with one hand acting as a jockstrap, which made me move with the loping awkwardness of a baboon. This caused much laughter from the audience, most of them decidedly in Zach's camp.

In the shadow of a mudbrick house, swathed in a *burqa*, Zach's mother—at least I assumed it was his mother—stared out at the melee, keeping watch. She said nothing, did nothing, but kept an eye on her brood.

The day before, on the drive back from the *qala*, Shahir had said, "I think one day, eventually, pop culture will win. The extremists know that pop has roots outside their little box. It has links to the U.S. and Europe and Asia, and links to other ideas and other futures. It will start to free our people. It will start to free our women. It will change things."

Was it possible for someone like Zach—who had now raised his arms in the air, inciting his fans to cheer him on in his *coup de grâce*—to become an extremist? Was it possible for his mother to become a feminist? Had his wrestling jones, as Shahir and Melek believed, forever differentiated him—and perhaps those around him—from the likes of the Taliban? Zach would—could—never live a life that approached anything resembling an American suburban existence. Afghanistan was too far away from that. His traditional upbringing would not allow for it, nor would the corruption and poverty and violence that have poisoned this country for generations. But when it came down to the choice as Shahir and Melek defined it—Taliban vs. *Transformers*—did the WWE prevent him from even considering filling out a Taliban employment form? Did the dumbest professional sport of them all have the means to enlighten Zach and his crew of fellow fanboys, to get his mother reading Germaine Greer, and to keep extremism at bay, all the while inventing awesomer wrestling holds and wickeder Spandex costumes?

"*Yaheeee!*" yelled Zach.

"Ah, fuck," I said, and braced myself.

11

This Melting Town

IRAN

Shia Muslim: 89%

Sunni Muslim: 9%

35% GDP

1. Farzad:
   14

2. Blind Gary Davis:
   Pure Religion

3. Django Reinhardt:
   Farewell Blues

Pop.: 65,875,226

Avg. age: 26.4

Capital: Tehran

Independence: April 1,1979
(Islamic Republic of Iran)

I awoke looking down upon a stretch of water so blue it mocked even the idea of another color. The plane banked; my stomach churned. The first officer babbled into the PA system, informing us that we were minutes away from landing at the island of Qeshm, separated from the Iranian mainland by the frothy ribbon of the legendary Strait of Hormuz.

I swallowed dryly and thought: Last stop.

Iran's Qeshm has just about seen it all. A quarter of the size of Rhode Island, it has ten thousand times the history—Umayyads, Abbasids, Portuguese, British, you name it have left their fingerprints on the joint. It is entirely incidental, but not historically inappropriate, that when the USS *Vincennes* shot down an Iranian passenger airliner in 1988, the wreckage landed a mile or so off the southern shore of the island. One day soon, the malls and business parks the Iranian government is encouraging here will pull in millions of visitors a year. Now, tourists must make do with an array of natural attractions—rock sculpted by eons of saltwater pouring into the peculiar limestone of the island's valleys, sunken mangrove forests, birdlife great of variety and hearty of voice.

I deplaned, and purchased something to eat at an airport stall. Scarfing it down, I hailed a rusted cab from the small taxi rank. I showed the cabbie an image from the insleeve of a CD. He looked nonplussed. I pointed and made guttural noises. He rattled his prayer beads. I pleaded. He shrugged. We negotiated an exorbitant there-'n'-back price, I mimed the importance of speedy driving, and off we went.

Lying back against the springs of the little Paykan's busted back-bench, I allowed that I was becoming emotional. In fact, I'd been a little *verklempt* since arriving in Iran. My visa was valid for a scant nine days. Not enough time to pronounce confidently on a country as dazzlingly complex as this one. So, after a year on the road, I figured I'd take something of a vacation. Treat my time in a country that was perhaps the most feared and loathed, as far as Western interests go, as a pop-cultural theme park ride. In other words, I wanted to confirm that even in America's number one *bête noire*, there were links. Axis of Evil or no, I was here to get my heart warmed.

The heartless cabbie shook me awake forty or so kilometers later, at the mouth of the village of Laaft. I had learned of this place from the owner of the Iranian fusion music label Hermes, who has traveled his country looking for hundreds of examples of what I now hoped to encounter. The music of Qeshm told the story of Qeshm—an island that has played host to the entire world. This place found its rhythm from fishing, date harvesting, salt mining and Islam, and it interpreted that rhythm through thousands of ancient voices from far away. And it is the lament of Qeshm's oarsmen during the *rezif* ceremonies that had so fascinated Hermes and the label's attendant musicians and musicologists.

It sounds eerily like the blues.

A week or so before my flight to Qeshm, early on in my Iranian peregrinations, I stared at the enormous swastika flag and thought, "Here we go."

Alongside it, sculptures of the Third Reich eagle. Also: daggers and swords emblazoned with same, SS leathers, a replica Luger. I looked at the heavy metal musician I'll call Slash on account of his resemblance to Guns N' Roses' famous axeman, and said, "Oy!"

"Yes. I don't know why I keep this stuff. But I do. I hide it when foreigners come, because my friends tell me it will make many people scared or angry."

"That it may."

"Still, I am obsessed with war," said Slash. "I know every tank battle, every infantry move of World War II." Indeed, the rest of Slash's otherwise meticulously kept apartment looked like a small armory circa the Spanish Civil War—replica guns, obscure signal flags, tank shells—with a Megadeth banner for good measure. There are a number of metal heads the world over hewing dangerously close to National Socialism in both outlook and aesthetics, but it was nonetheless strange to encounter the phenomenon here in Iran, in the home of one of the country's better-known metal musicians. In Iran, after all, it isn't necessary to dabble with Nazism in order to tap a rich and prodigious vein of anti-semitism.

Links. The vaunted bridge. If this was one of the possible outcomes—an Iranian metal musician with a Nazi jones—what did it all amount to? If I was told that Ayatollah Khomeini was an X-Men superfan and dressed up as Wolverine for *Eid*, was this supposed to ease my mind? If Mahmoud Ahmadinejad—president of Iran, one of the most loathed men in the West and one of the more beloved in the developing world for his strident Fuck-You-Zionist-America posturing—donned Donald Duck pajamas at bedtime, would that undermine the threat of a nuclear-armed theocracy? Europe had plenty of cultural links and still managed to tear itself apart on a number of memorable occasions, as Slash could no doubt confirm.

And where, after all, were the links in the Muslim world? Even though Iran and Afghanistan shared a rather lengthy border, a religion, many episodes of history, several flatbread recipes and a language, one couldn't exactly confuse the two countries. Both were subject to the vicissitudes of culture and circumstance, and were thus utterly different. And yet . . .

Iran was an intellectually dangerous choice for a last stop, because even the most careful of cultural theories is likely to unravel in the tumult of Tehran. Slash, by way of example. President Ahmadinejad seems to glory in what, by all rights, sounds like neo-Nazi rhetoric: We will wipe Israel off the map! What Holocaust? The world is run by a Jewish cabal! But Slash was not a neo-Nazi, at least not in the conventional sense. (Insofar as there is a neo-Nazi "conventional sense.") Like almost all of the young Iranian artists I'd encountered, he looked for inspiration both far back in Persian history and far away in the West. Buried in his quest—just to make things a tad *more* confusing—is resentment at the Arab conquering of Persia shortly after the dawn of Islam, and an implicit criticism of the religion they brought along with them.

"The name of our band, Kahtmayan, was the twenty-sixth day of the month during the era of the Sassanids," he told me. "When the Arabs came, they gave us the moon calendar, and so we lost this day, and this word. Me and my band, we found a dead word—we found it on the Internet. And we made it alive. We play very old Eastern melodies very fast, in a Western style. So it becomes metal, which is the son of rock. It is both Western and Eastern."

"That all sounds very nice," I said. "Where does the Nazi accessorizing come in?"

"I do not hate Jews. I do not believe in Hitler. It is powerful—the images, the red on black. Just *look* at this stuff! It says something to me. It is a huge image. It seduces me."

Tehran does not have architecture. It has buildings. These structures—concrete monuments to conformity—reveal nothing. Outside, traffic rages. Hidden inside, fourteen million lives unfold. One experiences the city either in a wide shot or in extreme close-up—no in-betweens. That night in Tehran, I sat with a heavy metal musician who, pleasantly, wasn't an SS fanboy. Farzad Golpayegani leaned back in an office chair in his fastidiously neat room and pressed play.

The first twelve bars were gentle, an Eastern plaint. Then, a roar of intensity obliterated any sense of place: This was an indefinable musical geography. A breath, then fingers rushed up a fret-board until there were no more notes, and we again fell away into a furious but controlled dissonance: hammering bass, screaming guitars. I now knew *exactly* where we were.

This was the sound of Tehran.

Farzad's grasp of Persian traditional music is clearly in evidence. But slowly the wails, the noise, the anger found a way in. In "9," the first track on his album *Two*, the screams were downright ghostly. The numerical assignations—this demure mathematics—is Farzad's way of assuring the authorities that he does not compose dangerous music. Not at all, sir, it is merely an aggregation of notes on a modal scale that happen to sound this way due to Pythagorean principles. Yes, sir, I'm aware that Pythagoras was not a Muslim. No, sir, guitar is not a traditional Persian instrument. And yes, sir, I will cut my hair as soon as I get home.

Farzad shared his otherwise quiet south-Tehran apartment with his widowed mother. Around the corner loomed a series of brutish government complexes, evoking Dickens's Department of Circumlocutions from *Little Dorrit*: people entered, but did they ever leave? There were four of us sprawled on various surfaces in Farzad's room, listening to the measured fury of his music.

Farzad was stooped and kindly: Gregory Peck as Atticus Finch, with a long black ponytail and a black T-shirt. In addition to his musical accomplishments, he is a graphic designer and painter, as was his father. Golpayegani Senior's paintings hung on the walls of the apartment: blocky, abstract affairs. Farzad's own works feature eyeballs, melting bodies, lean twisted figures.

Over the past ten years, Farzad has created a meticulous body of work: three albums and several recorded improvisational sessions. He calls his work a "culture jam." He is a member of an Iranian hard rock and metal scene that is complex, varied and dates back decades. The "jam" was partly invented by a band called O-Hum that married hard rock with the words of the ancient Persian poet Hafez. The scene has grown since then, and it is subject to the vibrations of the times.

Farzad is, after all, one of many in this city who believe U.S. Patriot missiles are gassed up and ready to make the trip over from aircraft carriers skulking in the Persian Gulf. Meanwhile, his government, at war with many of those it professes to serve, threatens to move the country into the nuclear family. His latest work, *Three*, is as a result some of the more unsettling avant-rock I'd heard since early, atom-bomb-war jittery Pink Floyd. Farzad's music is created under the threat of annihilation from forces abroad and forces within. To say that he has merely appropriated metal and hard rock—a sentiment with which your average mullah would most certainly agree—is to suggest that his music is far less subversive than it actually is. There is more to *Three* than a mere conjoining of cultures. Farzad and his peers are painstakingly inventing a new musical language, forging a new means of cultural reconciliation.

"If I have an aim," said Farzad, "it has always been to mix Iranian traditional with heavy metal music." He slopped some arak into my glass and picked up a seven-string acoustic guitar. He tunes it "wrong," which makes it sound like a setar, the three-stringed Persian lute, not to be confused with the sub-continental sitar of Ravi Shankar. "You may think it's an Eastern instrument, but it's not. I try to make sure that the music has an Iranian spirit," said Farzad.

"Which means?"

"Well, I don't know the exact Iranian notes, and I don't even know complete Iranian musical theory, but sometimes it can happen that by changing tuning or using certain scales you will sound closer to the Iranian. But it is a complete invention, these methods. I have come up with them myself."

Properly, there are no scales in traditional Persian music. Furthermore, there is no written musical language, so music has always passed orally through generations of masters and students by means of the *radif*, or "order." The melodies of the *radif* are formulated upon an ancient modal system called *dastgah*. Without the master/student continuum and the years of study this demands, the *radif* evaporates, as does the traditional Persian repertoire. While there is no immediate threat of this, Farzad is an example of how official post-revolutionary Iran's subjugation of musicians—banning their work, imposing restrictions on where and how they can play—is far more of a threat to Persian culture than is Iron Maiden.

"Oh, folkloric music is changing," said Farzad. "For sure. The kids no longer care. This is why I am putting together a manual for the old tunings and the old styles that the kids can do on an acoustic guitar." The guitar, at least among the heavy metal and rock set, is wiping out the old string instruments like the setar, which are comparatively difficult to play. The acoustic guitar you can learn online. The setar, no chance.

"We can't learn these old ways," Farzad told me. "There isn't the time anymore, the support. So we must find them with our own methods. The government doesn't like this mixing. Fine. We go underground, and we do it anyway."

As I sat listening to Farzad's music, I was suddenly hit with the notion that *this* was what the links could amount to: deep, buried, fused marriages of cultural complicity. It couldn't solve all of the world's problems—or perhaps any of them—but popular culture could do something both more and less than that. Slowly, through an onslaught of industrial popular culture from a country called America, we were forging cultural relationships that, over time, would become more apparent and more coherent. What's the flipside to the homogenizing effects of globalized popular culture? We unite under a series of common idioms. Farzad's manual, I thought, could also be construed as a gentle universal directive.

★ ★ ★

"If you want to know us," Ayatollah Rafsanjani, one-time president of the Islamic Republic, apparently said of his countrymen, "become a Shia first." I am not a Shia, and have no immediate plans to become one. But, short of religious conversion, the dizzying nature of Iran's cultural complicity with and hostility toward the West becomes simultaneously clearer and dimmer by reading one Jalal Al Ahmad. He is the author of the infamous indictment of Western influence called *Gharbzadegi*, or "West-struck-ness." Like most screeds, *Gharbzadegi* is hard reading, but Ayatollah Khomeini slogged through it, placing it in his grab bag of secular and religious ideologies justifying the Islamic Revolution of 1979. For his part, Al Ahmad denounced his religious Shiite family and affiliated himself with the Iranian communist party in the fifties. He supported democratically elected Prime Minister Dr. Mohammad Mosaddeq's nationalization of the country's oil industry in 1951 (as did most Iranians). The Americans and the Brits, duly freaked, engineered a coup and handed power back to the Shah—one of those dumb-ass acts of Cold War expediency remembered in these parts as an unforgivable betrayal.

Al Ahmad believed that Iranians were struck stupid by the razzle-dazzle of the West and posited that the decline of everything authentically Iranian—like carpet weaving, lute playing and, if I read him correctly, Marxist-Leninism—was the result of a series of Western "economic and existential victories over the East." Al Ahmad failed, however, to provide a convincing summation of what being an Iranian was, as opposed to what it *wasn't*. By locating Iran on a map one comes to understand how Persian culture can *only* be a bulk bag of Liquorice Allsorts, plonked as it is in the middle of the world, a vast compound of East, West and everything in between. I met Iranians, like Slash, who are still resentful of the Arabic influence that came with the defeat of the Sassanids in the early Islamic era. There are those that look back to the French influence on the Qajar dynasty in the eighteenth century as the beginning of the end. But the truth is, by dint of geography and the poor manners of those who have stormed its borders on the way to somewhere else, Iran has always been a hodgepodge.

In the sixties and early seventies—during the Shah's waning days—there were robust rock and pop scenes in Iran. Indeed, Western pop culture, indigenous or otherwise, was readily available. This resulted in a reflexive backlash: State-run television and a number of musical luminaries agitated for the creation of the Center for Preservation and Propagation of Iranian Music. The search for an identity became a conservative cultural rummaging through the Iranian past, which contributed to the Islamo-Puritanism of the Revolution. What was Iran's identity? The Ayatollah suggested—rather forcefully—that it was Shia Islam. The Revolution did not create these impulses. It merely set them in stone. This is, to no small degree, the story of many of the countries I visited, Islamic Revolution or no.

What's the net result of all this? Nothing American is unworthy of suspicion. The Middle East Media Research Institute recently posted a report by Iranian state television that concluded, "Zionism is not restricted to the capitalistic weapons companies, such as Lockheed and the banks that support it. Cinema is considered another, subtle, weapon in the hands of those who support this corrupt ideology. In Hollywood, Disney is the manufacturer of this weapon, and *Pirates of the Caribbean* is its newest ammunition."

Jack Sparrow—pirate, fop, Zionist marauder. Hilarious, until you remember that the Islamic Republic of Iran wants the bomb. Proxy Iranian armies are in open conflict with Western interests all over the world. This is a very real war. And at least one side believes that it is being waged through pop. President Ahmadinejad, visiting New York in late 2007 to address the United Nations and to remind Columbia University students that Iran is, among other things, homo-free, held an *iftar* meet 'n' greet at the Uptown Hilton for the city's Iranian luminaries. He spoke of the movie *300*—the tale of several hundred gym-buffed Spartans in leather Speedos soundly thrashing zillions of effete Persians at the Battle of Thermopylae—which most Iranians interpret as a vicious cultural attack, not realizing that only about five non-Iranian people in North America would connect "Persia" with "Iran," and I'd hesitate to include the film's director in that number. "That film claimed that under Darius the Great twenty-seven nations paid tribute to Iran," said Ahmadinejad. "But, in a meeting . . . I corrected that impression. 'No,' I said, 'under Darius *forty-two* nations paid tribute to Iran.'" That clears that up.

The power of pop shakes the foundations built by the Ayatollahs. But pulling quotes at random from the annals of Ahmadinejad and his cronies makes them sound loonier than they actually are. There is a cold logic to these words. Laid on top of each other, they are the grey concrete bricks that make up the edifice of Iran. It is one that seems all but immutable, the mass protests following 2009's disputed general election notwithstanding.

Where, then, the bridge?

I stood in the kitchen of a sad apartment in central Tehran speaking to Mamak Khadem, a woman whose band, Axiom of Choice, had rejigged my understanding of what is, often derisively, called "world music." It had been suggested to me that if I wasn't up for conversion to Shia Islam, Axiom's music was an excellent alternative. Mamak's voice weaves through millennia of Persian-influenced music, everything from the traditional lovelorn laments of the great Persian poets Hafez and Rumi to the seventies synth rock of Fleetwood Mac. This is Big Gesture music—a cultural trope shared with Arabs—that is, apparently, central to Shia culture. Tears are art's WD-40; melancholy is a muse. As the primary example, Mamak pointed to the Shia holy day of *Ashura*—the commemoration of the betrayal and murder of Husayn ibn Ali, grandson of the Prophet, who Shiites believe was in line for the caliphate. It is a day of mourning, culminating in *Ta'zieh*, or passion plays that re-enact the betrayal, and lengthy, highly stylized retellings of the tragedy that bring hardened warriors to tears. But these lachrymose, if beautiful, histrionics exact an enormous psychological toll.

"We are trained to be sad," Mamak told me. "We need it. We must always be mourning. And wherever we are, we can't get this place out of our blood."

For the past several hours, Mamak's apartment had doubled as a sound studio. I'd been recording a radio show with a representative coterie of Iran's fusion music royalty, including the head of the record label Hermes, Ramin Sadighi, who would inadvertently send me to Qeshm.

As the designated on-air personality, I was made comfortable on a cream-colored leather couch and then read—into a microphone covered with a tea towel—a summation of what music meant in Iran. I told the microphone that there are but eight concert halls in this megalopolis of fourteen million plus. There is a Public Space Office, a branch of law enforcement that exercises strict controls over musical activities. There is a Ministry of Culture that presides over the issuance of musical permits for live performances or for the release of albums. Satellite and the Internet are among the very few ways for the people to listen to non-official music. But there is yet another unofficial channel: the street, with many vendors of CDs and DVDs, which you can purchase for less than two dollars apiece.

I told the microphone that Iran is a crossroads; it connects the East to the West, the North to the South. The Iranian plateau is famous for accepting, and of course transforming, traditions that have passed through it: "The musical being of Iranian music . . . has lived on the streets, and influenced the way people see and hear things, for many thousands of years," said I, with uncharacteristic poetry.

The apartment was large and airy, but reflected the gray of the day. On the table before me were dates, dried raspberries, pistachios, a layer cake.

"Sometimes I wonder, how can such terrible things continue to happen to a people?" said Mamak when I had finished being Casey Kasem. "The Shah, the Revolution, the Iran-Iraq war, and then all these small, everyday tragedies that it seems happen with every Iranian family here." Mamak told me how she was sent to America to live with relatives when she was sixteen, while the war raged and her brother succumbed to cancer instead of dying on the front with the young *basaji*—frontline shock troops given one-way tickets into martyrdom by acting as human mine sweeps or cannon fodder.

Throughout the recording of the show, I had this feeling that the government of Iran was engaged in the creation of a great national tragedy, an act of self-abnegation, a denial of the principles of the great love poets Hafez and Rumi, a crushing of the frivolous under the sandal of the Ayatollah. How different was this from Saudi Arabia, or Syria, or Lebanon? What were the artists I'd met over the course of my travels doing but *fighting* that impulse? And if this crushing of the cultural spirit was one of the purposes of Saudi or Egyptian or Iranian authoritarianism—and, surely, it was—then were not these artists engaged in *social* transformation as well as cultural transformation? Were they not, to a greater or lesser degree, revolutionaries?

"By doing what we do," said Mamak, "I guess we fight the status quo. Maybe even without knowing it we do it. But inside our work, there is a code: *freedom*. You wish to pray five times a day, please, be our guest. Do what you have to do. But please, we ask, *leave us alone*."

Every morning, I'd stroll north along Ferdosi Street. After twenty minutes of dodging men who looked at the ground as they hurried on, I'd encounter a small fellow with but one item for sale. He stood perilously close to the traffic that tore along Ferdosi with a ferocity that is rarely encountered outside of open warfare, and said nothing. He wore a cardigan and creased slacks. His face had the rumpled look of a newborn Shar-Pei pup with manic depression—he was, basically, the Bob Newhart of Iran, without being funny. And his only ware was an ancient record player, a different one each day.

It was never a traditional turntable. One morning it was a Fisher Price portable unit. The following day it was a player built into an old briefcase. Then a turntable set inside a plastic bubble. He sold old platters to go along with them—Shah-era Iranian disco-pop by Googoosh or Vigen Derderian or Hayedeh. Pure, sugary nostalgia—a fact he underscored by keeping the sugar cubes for his tea spinning on the turntable, which was plugged into a nearby generator.

On my second morning, and for the next several days, I drank tea with him, thumbing through the several records that were, apparently, gratis with the player. And I thought of something I had read in *Shah of Shahs*, an account of the Revolution by the great Polish journalist Ryszard Kapuscinski. The author becomes subject to a wonderful rhetorical disquisition from a carpet merchant, who states, "What have we [Iranians] given the world? We have given poetry, the miniature [painting] and carpets. As you can see, these are useless things from the productive viewpoint. But it is through such things that we have expressed our true selves. We have given the world this miraculous, unique uselessness." It took an Iranian carpet merchant to deliver a superb description of my obsession with pop. The fellow goes on to describe the carpet as a vessel of transportation—in a desert, it is an imaginary garden, a vista "from which color or freshness never fades."

That, I thought, is what I'd been chasing for more than two years. To find a metaphor for it here on Ferdosi Street, the axis of Tehran, and therefore the axis of the Axis of Evil, seemed perfect.

My final night in Tehran. At the beginning of the evening, the place is tidy and buttoned down—an average middle-class apartment. Now, cigarette butts sizzle alongside chicken bones in Styrofoam cartons, bodies are slouched on couches, moonshine pools on a coffee table. There is a synthesizer, a *darbuka* drum, a musician hunched over a guitar, eyes red, strumming furiously. I had come to hear him play flamenco. Now I heard a fearsome combination of blues, jazz and a music that is native to this land—a mash-up of half-tones, quarter-tones and twelve-bar blues.

Alongside me, a big man with an unruly ponytail drinks arak and orange juice. He has the frame of an ex-athlete, thick body, big hands. His name is Arash Jafari and he is a self-proclaimed "heavy metal percussionist." He takes his motto from Turkish *darbuka* master Misirli Ahmet: *You must lose the rhythm to find it.* Earlier he told me, "CNN stated that in Iran, they treat metal heads and homosexuals the same way. Ho! I feel sorry for the homosexuals." Arash once wrote a song with the following lyrics:

> Don't need the flared hand
> To know where I am
> Can't see the dark side of who I am
> What I need is the end
> It's the time to hide in the river as I'm drowned
> Another wicked wave
> This choking is not a dying cause
> No one's gonna take our souls out this town
> I'm out this Melting Town
> I'm out this Melting Town

"Years on the road," I kept saying. "Two years!" I recalled—almost tearfully, thanks to the arak—young Misha bidding me farewell with raised devil horns as I drove out onto the Kazakh steppes.

"To Misha," I yelled, raising my glass.

"To Misha," agreed my companions, random toasts having become a loose theme of the evening.

Later that night, Arash and I careened through the city toward the airport in his Peugeot 306. An empty highway: lines and lines of concrete towers. Traffic lights flashed on slick asphalt. Tupac spurred us on, spitting out rhymes as we tore through intersections, screeched around corners, laughed like lunatics. Huge murals of Ayatollahs, eyebrows raised, watched us contravene every last one of their edicts. "Ghosts, ghosts—jump out of the way, ghosts!" yelled Arash as the airport control tower blinked at us.

Qeshm-bound, I pulled my backpack from the car.

"I hope you get what you look for," said Arash.

"I hope so too," said I.

"Keep it metal, my brother."

"Keep it metal," I said. But then again, what choice did he have?

Half a day later, employing a series of remarkably evocative gesticulations, I made it understood that the cabbie should wait for me until I had done what I planned to do. Having nothing planned, I walked toward the Persian Gulf along a dirt laneway. The inhabitants of Laaft were uniformly old—or looked that way. Their cheeks had caved in, their eyes were sunken. It was clear from their expressions that they had no earthly idea what I was doing in their village. And I realized there would be no way to get across my intention to meet some musicians and listen to them jam. What had seemed perfectly reasonable at four in the morning in Tehran now seemed idiotic.

It wasn't brutally hot, but the atmosphere threatened a strangulating ferocity—a hundred desert winds blowing in from all the Middle East. Laaft's humble mudbrick homes were dominated by towers that channeled those winds into damp rooms moaning with afternoon prayers. I walked through streets that smelled of boiled dust and sea, over to the Gulf, which was still and silent, as if it was playing dead. Palm trees creaked in the breeze, and it was all I could do not to rest against a trunk and sleep for the next hundred years.

What, I wondered, would I wake up to find? A post-apocalyptic Iranian Mad Max leaning over me about to nick a kidney? Or a McDonald's serving Halal Big Macs? Were those the only two possible outcomes? Or was there a third way, a means of cultural conciliation that was already very much underway, thanks to *Freej* and *Under Siege*, Farzad and Zaven, Tamer Nafar and Ahmad Dhani, Zach the

Wrestler and Wayne Stewart the muscle car builder? As a North American, I didn't always agree with what they had to say. They saw things right to left, I saw them left to right: We looked up from the page and subjectively disagreed. But the idiom—and everything buried within it—had become our connection.

I stood at a crossroads, as Robert Johnson once did when he met the devil and made a pact. And while this was a different crossroads, it seemed that the devil presented no less confounding a choice. We could live in ignorance of how much the cultures of the Muslim world share with America, or we could choose to explore those links. Or perhaps it was just enough to know how much we shared, to know how much intersects, to know that what Ahmadinejad and his kind are doing is denying vital parts of their *own* culture, as much as they were anything from the West.

Did one really have to be Shia to understand Iran, or just a bluesman? Being neither, I couldn't say. But to cast this as a clash of civilizations? This was not Mordor vs. Middle Earth; there is no ring to throw into Sauron's flaming eye. No hobbits would be jumping about in slow motion on a downy bed when this was done with. No, nothing so grand at all.

iPod earbuds inserted, I cued up the Hermes Qeshm compilation. The opening twangs of an *oud*. Then, the unmistakable *junk-a-junk* of a blues riff. I stared out over the water. This wasn't properly blues—it didn't come from precisely the same impetus—but its provenance was undoubtedly African, it was most certainly devotional, motivated also by forced labor and a sense of loneliness and displacement. In other words, it was blues. Hard-drinking the people of Qeshm were not. Islamic they most certainly were. But it is the way of our species that we have shared cultures since the moment that one of our hirsute monkey ancestors first started banging a bone against a rock, and have done so ever since.

I stumbled back down the pitted street, and it was a testament to the power of the music that the following unlikely scenario took shape in my head:

An Iranian/American delegation, however low-level, however secret. Severe men and women in gray suits sit across from one another in an airport Sheraton in, say, Dusseldorf—one of those airless, windowless sub-level conference chambers where half the world's troubles begin, and the other half are exacerbated.

Mr. Ahmadi slides across a CD to Ms. Thompson. *Please, pass this on to your sons, with my compliments. It contains the heavy metal shenanigans of one Farzad, a young Tehranian with an immeasurably long ponytail. I would go so far as to say that it rocks the pants off Tool, or even Iron Maiden. I'd say Farzad will rock their pants off.*

Ms. Thompson smiles—not realizing she is supposed to engage in the elaborate ritual of refusals of the Persian *ta'araf*—grabs the CD and slides across one of her own. In fact, Ms. Thompson knows jack about Persian culture, or at least she did until these exchanges with Mr. Ahmadi. *Why, that's so kind, Mr. Ahmadi. Given how low my sons wear their pants, I shouldn't be surprised if they are indeed rocked off. In kind, please accept these Blind Reverend Gary Davis blues recordings. Just picked 'em up off iTunes, and they sound awfully like the stuff you gave me last year in Amman. So similar it's creepy. It sounds like it comes from the same darn place.*

Mr. Ahmadi, who has already forgiven Ms. Thompson for ignoring the intricacies of *ta'araf*, forgoes the same. And over bad coffee and donut holes, the two parties get down to the minutiae of deflecting a massive, apocalyptic war.

"We must love one another or die," wrote Auden in his lament "September 1, 1939." He later disavowed the poem because of that line. I could understand both why he wrote it, and why he excised it from his oeuvre. Far be it for me to fiddle with genius, but what if he had penned, "We must *understand* one another or die." Or would that still have seemed a paltry sentiment to him after the unimaginable atrocities of the Second World War? It depends, I suppose, on the day. In Qeshm, during a lightly chilled war, it didn't seem so paltry to me.

In the dying light, off a body of water where the East has met the West in battle for as long as there have been battleships, my imagined scenario in the Dusseldorf Sheraton seemed at once awfully naïve and utterly, completely necessary. Auden, in the same poem, called the 1930s "a low dishonest decade." Having just lived through one, I can understand why the bard considered it such a bummer. After all, the stakes quickly become so very, very high.

The cabbie honked, breaking my reverie. It was time to go home.

Oh, one last thing. Shortly after the Iranian elections in June of 2009, when the world watched—or rather, read Tweets—of mass protests on the streets of Tehran and other major cities, I received an email. I cannot reveal who sent it, but suffice to say he wears a black T-shirt to bed at night. The individual in question was not political, but he took his metal seriously, and he wanted the government and the religious authorities off his fret board. "I want them to leave me the fuck alone," he wrote.

I was worried about my long-haired pals in Tehran, and I was right to be. Every night, they were risking their lives by joining protests calling for a review of the election results that favored the incumbent Ahmadinejad, when they believed that the opposition candidate Mir-Hossein Mousavi had won fair and square. The country was divided, as split down the middle as, say, America. The only recourse was to take to the streets, which they did in numbers that rattled the very last mullah in the squalid regime.

Late at night, when Ahmadinejad and his Revolutionary Guard cronies had locked down the cities, Iranians would take to the rooftops and yell out "Allah Akbar"—God is great—reclaiming the cry of the Islamic revolution that was supposed to lead to an era of freedom under the banner of Islam. But if God was so great, wondered my friend in his email, why were they in this mess in the first place?

Instead, on the rooftop of his Tehran building, among satellite dishes and laundry lines, my friend and *his* cronies raised the sign of the devil horns, the heavy metal salutation born of the seventies. This they did, night after night, for months. Instead of invocations to a God they did not believe in, they yelled something closer to their hearts, as essential to their identities as Iran itself.

"Death to fake metal," they screamed.

SELECTED BIBLIOGRAPHY AND
SUGGESTED EXPLORATIONS

WaWaWeeWa: An Introduction

Read

Adorno, Theodor W. *Critical Models: Interventions and Catchwords.* Translated by Henry W. Pickford. New York: Columbia University Press, 1998.

Cowen, Tyler. *Creative Destruction: How Globalization Is Changing the World's Cultures.* Princeton, NJ: Princeton University Press, 2002.

Ellabbad, Mohieddin. *The Illustrator's Notebook.* Toronto: Groundwood Books, 2006.

Huntington, Samuel P. *The Clash of Civilizations and the Remaking of World Order.* New York: Touchstone, 1997.

Lewis, Bernard. *The Middle East: A Brief History of the Last 2,000 Years.* New York: Scribner, 2003, c1995.

Marozzi, Justin. *Tamerlane: Sword of Islam, Conquerer of the World.* Cambridge, MA: Da Capo Press, 2006.

Qutb, Sayyid. Signposts, quoted in Coll, Steve. *Ghost Wars: The Secret History of the CIA, Afghanistan, and Bin Laden, from the Soviet Invasion to September 10, 2001.* New York: Penguin, 2005.

Said, Edward W. *Culture and Imperialism.* New York: Vintage Books, 1994.

Shaheen, Jack. *Reel Bad Arabs: How Hollywood Vilifies a People*. New York: Olive Branch Press, 2001.

Listen

Nirvana. *Nevermind*. Vinyl recording. Produced and engineered by Butch Vg. Los Angeles, CA: Geffen Records, 1991.

View

Borat: Cultural Learnings of America for Make Benefit Glorious Nation of Kazakhstan. Motion picture. Directed by Larry Charles. Los Angeles: Twentieth Century Fox Film Corporation and Dune Entertainment, 2006.

Reel Bad Arabs: How Hollywood Vilifies a People. DVD. Directed by Sut Jhally. Northampton, MA: Media Education Foundation, 2006.

Surf

CIA. "The World Factbook—Kazakhstan." https://www.cia.gov/library/publications/the-world-factbook/geos/kz.html.

Freud, Sigmund. *The Interpretation of Dreams*. Preface to the Third German Edition. Psych Web. www.psywww.com/books/interp/preface.htm.

"Germans Urged Not to Laugh at Borat." *The Independent*, London. November 2, 2006. FindArticles.com. findarticles.com/p/articles/mi_qn4158/is_/ai_n16824452.

Chapter 1: How Do You Know?

Read

Anderson, Jon Lee. *The Fall of Baghdad*. New York: Penguin Press, 2004.

Auden, W.H. "To My Pupils." In *The Orators*. 1931. *Selected Poems: New Edition*. Edited by Edward Mendelson. New York: Vintage Books, 1979.

Corsello, Andrew. "Lionel of Arabia." *GQ*, December 2006.

Lambert, Frank. *The Barbary Wars: American Independence in the Atlantic World*. New York: Hill and Wang, 2005.

Levitan, Daniel J. *The World in Six Songs: How the Musical Brain Created Human Nature.* New York: Dutton, 2008.

Oren, Michael B. *Power, Faith and Fantasy: America in the Middle East, 1776 to the Present.* New York: W.W. Norton, 2007.

Sha'ban, Fuad. *Islam and Arabs in Early American Thought: The Roots of Orientalism in America.* Durham, NC: Acorn Press, 1991.

Wilson, Carl. *Let's Talk About Love: A Journey to the End of Taste.* New York: Continuum, 2007.

Listen

Richie, Lionel. *Can't Slow Down.* Vinyl recording. Hollywood, CA: Motown, 1983.

———. *Dancing on the Ceiling.* Vinyl recording. Hollywood, CA: Motown, 1986.

Women of Egypt 1924–1931: Pioneers of Stardom and Fame. CD. Compilation and text by Amira Mitchell. London: Topic Records, 2006.

View

Bennett Powell, Jane. "Watch the Anniversary Events in Tripoli." BBC. April 15, 2006.
news.bbc.co.uk/media/avdb/news_web/video/9012da68003f490/nb/09012da68003f65e_16x9_nb.asx.

Top Gun. Motion picture. Directed by Tony Scott and produced by Don Simpson and Jerry Bruckheimer. Hollywood, CA: Paramount Pictures, 1986.

Surf

Boyne, Walter J. "El Dorado Canyon." *Journal of the Airforce Association.* 82, no. 3 (March 1999). http://www.afa.org/magazine/march1999/0399canyon.asp.

CBC Arts. "Lionel Richie Rocks Libya in Peace Concert." CBC.ca. April 15, 2006. www.cbc.ca/arts/story/2006/04/15/ritchie-libya.html.

Keller, Nuh Ha Mim. "The Concept of Bid'a in the Islamic Shari'a." 1995. www.masud.co.uk/ISLAM/nuh/bida.htm.

Pesca, Mike. "Lionel Richie: The Key to Peace in the Middle East." NPR online interview with Andrew Corsello. December 4, 2006. www.npr.org/templates/story/story.php?storyId=6576395.

Reagan, Ronald. "National Defense—Libya." www.ronaldreagan. com/libya.html.

"Targeting Gaddafi." *Time*. April 21, 1986. www.time.com/time/ magazine/article/0,9171,961140,00.html.

Chapter 2: The Sheikh's Batmobile

Read

Aboushakra, Eyad. *Driving Arabia: The History of the Automobile in the Middle East*. Dubai: Explorer Publishing, 2006.

Boym, Svetlana. *The Future of Nostalgia*. New York: Basic Books, 2001.

Coll, Steve. *The Bin Ladens: An Arabian Family in the American Century*. New York: Penguin Press, 2008.

Connerton, Paul. *How Societies Remember*. Cambridge [England]: Cambridge University Press, 1989.

Huyssen, Andreas. *Twilight Memories: Marking Time in a Culture of Amnesia*. New York: Routledge, 1955.

Petrusich, Amanda. *It Still Moves: Lost Songs, Lost Highways, and the Search for the Next American Music*. New York: Faber and Faber, 2008.

Surf

Anderson, John. "Wolverine's Claws . . . SOLD to the Highest Bidder!" Comics Alliance. April 15, 2007. www.comicsalliance. com/2007/04/15/wolverines-claws-sold-to-the-highest-bidder.

"The History of the Batmobile." www.batmobilehistory.com.

Chapter 3: So You Can Watch What They Watch

Read

Abu-Lughod, Lila. *Local Contexts of Islamism in Popular Media*. Leiden: Amsterdam University Press, 2006.

Ali, Tariq. "In Princes' Pockets." *London Review of Books.* July 19, 2007.

Coll, Steve. *Ghost Wars: The Secret History of the CIA, Afghanistan, and Bin Laden, from the Soviet Invasion to September 10, 2001.* New York: Penguin, 2005.

Irwin, Robert. *For Lust of Knowing: The Orientalists and Their Enemies.* London: Penguin, 2007.

Irwin, William, Mark T. Conard and Aeon J. Skoble, eds. *The Simpsons and Philosophy: The D'Oh of Homer.* Chicago, IL: Open Court, 2001.

Lynch, Marc. *Voices of the New Arab Public: Iraq, Al-Jazeera, and Middle East Politics Today.* New York: Columbia University Press, 2006.

Said, Edward W. *Orientalism.* New York: Vintage Books, 1979.

Sakr, Naomi, ed. *Arab Media and Political Renewal: Community, Legitimacy and Public Life.* London: I.B. Tauris, 2007.

Siddiqui, Haroon. *Being Muslim.* Toronto: Groundwood Books, 2006.

Surf

CIA. "The World Factbook—Saudi Arabia." https://www.cia.gov/library/publications/the-world-factbook/geos/sa.html#People.

Cochrane, Paul. "Saudi Arabia's Media Influence." Arab Media & Society. October, 2007. www.arabmediasociety.com/countries/index.php?c_article=122.

El-Rashidi, Yasmine. "D'oh! Arabized Simpsons Aren't Getting Many Laughs." *The Wall Street Journal.* October 14, 2005. online.wsj.com/article_email/SB112925107943268353-lMyQjAxMDE1MjE5NDIxNTQxWj.html.

Freej. www.freej.ae/#.

Malik, Talal. "Power 100: The World's Most Powerful Arabs." Arabian Business.com. March 30, 2008. www.arabianbusiness.com/power100/list.php.

Roberts, Genevieve. "Homer Becomes Omar for Arab Makeover of Simpsons." *The Independent.* October 23, 2005. www. independent.

co.uk/news/media/homer-becomes-omar-for-arab-makeover-of-simpsons-511733.html.

Shavit, Uriya. "Al-Qaeda's Saudi Origins: Islamist Ideology." *Middle East Quarterly* 13, no. 4 (Fall 2006). www.meforum.org/article/999.

Tatweer. Leisure & Entertainment. www.tatweerdubai.com/En/tc-1-Leisure-&-Entertainment.

—. "Press Release: Tatweer to Transform Award Winning Cartoon Series—'Freej'—into Major Theme Park in Dubailand." April 30, 2008. www.freejdubailand.ae/english.pdf.

Chapter 4: The Genie Leaves the Bottle

Read

Abu-Lughod, Lila. *Local Contexts of Islamism in Popular Media*. Leiden: Amsterdam University Press, 2006.

Coll, Steve. *The Bin Ladens: An Arabian Family in the American Century*. New York: Penguin Press, 2008.

Giroux, Henry A. *The Mouse That Roared: Disney and the End of Innocence*. Lanham, MD: Rowman & Littlefield, 1999.

Hiaasen, Carl. *Team Rodent: How Disney Devours the World*. New York: Ballantine Publishing Group, 1998.

Lewis, Bernard. *The Political Language of Islam*. Chicago: University of Chicago Press, 1988.

Mahfouz, Naguib. *The Cairo Trilogy*. London: Everyman's Library, 2001.

Oren, Michael B. *Six Days of War: June 1967 and the Making of the Modern Middle East*. Oxford: Oxford University Press, 2002.

Sammond, Nicholas. *Babes in Tomorrowland: Walt Disney and the Making of the American Child*, 1930-1960. Durham, NC: Duke University Press, 2005.

St. John, Robert. *Tongue of the Prophets: The Life Story of Eliezer Ben Yehuda*. Westport, CT: Greenwood Press, [1972, (c)1952].

View

Aladdin. DVD. Directed and produced by John Musker and Ron Clements. Burbank, CA: Walt Disney Pictures, 1992.

Brother Bear. DVD. Directed by Aaron Blaise and Robert Walker. Burbank, CA: Walt Disney Pictures, 2003.

Lion King. Special edition DVD. Directed by Roger Allers and Rob Minkoff and produced by Don Hahn. Burbank, CA: Walt Disney Pictures, 1994.

Little Mermaid. DVD. Directed and written by John Musker and Ron Clements. Burbank, CA: Walt Disney Pictures,1989.

Surf's Up. DVD. Directed by Ash Brannon and Chris Buch. N.p.: Sony Pictures Animation, 2007.

Chapter 5: Turn Up the Noise, Turn Down the Suck

Read

Arnett, Jeffrey Jensen. *Metalheads: Heavy Metal Music and Adolescent Alienation.* Boulder: Westview Press, 1996.

LeVine, Mark. *Heavy Metal Islam: Rock, Resistance, and the Struggle for the Soul of Islam.* New York: Three Rivers Press, 2008.

Listen

Odious. "Invitation to Chaotic Revelation" from the album *Mirror of Vibration.* CD. 2007.

View

Global Metal. DVD. Directed by Sam Dunn and Scot McFadyen. Toronto: Global Banger Productions Inc., 2007.

Heavy Metal in Baghdad. DVD. Directed by Suroosh Alvi and Eddy Moretti. VBS.TV, 2007.

Metal: A Headbanger's Journey. DVD. Directed by Sam Dunn and Scot McFadyen. Toronto: Global Banger Productions Inc., 2005.

Surf

Encyclopaedia Metallum: The Metal Archives. www.metalarchives.com.

Hampton, Howard. "Rock the Casbah." *New York Times: Sunday Book Review.* July 20, 2008. www.nytimes.com/2008/07/20/books/review/Hampton-t.html?ref=review.

MPACUK—Muslim Discussion Forum. forum.mpacuk.org/showthread.php?t=9139&page=31.

Napoli, James J. "A Satanic Khamsiin Blows Through Egypt." *Washington Report on Middle East Affairs.* April/May 1997. www.wrmea.com/backissues/0497/9704088.htm.

Sabri, Mustafa. "A Topic of Dispute in Islam: Music." *Beyan-ul-Haq,* 3, issue 63 (1910). Reprinted in *Anadolu,* 5, no. 4 (Winter 1995). www.wakeup.org/anadolu/05/4/mustafa_sabri_en.html.

Whitaker, Brian. "Highway to Hell." guardian.co.uk. June 2, 2003. http://www.guardian.co.uk/world/2003/jun/02/worlddispatch.brianwhitaker.

"Paul Wilson—the Impact of the Plastic People on a Communist Universe." Interview with Jan Velinger. Radio Czech. May 31, 2005. www.radio.cz/en/article/67064.

Chapter 6: Ain't Nobody's Bitch

Read

Colegrave, Stephen, and Chris Sullivan. *Punk: The Definitive Record of a Revolution.* New York: Thunders Mouth Press, 2005.

Marcus, Greil. *Lipstick Traces: A Secret History of the Twentieth Century.* Cambridge, MA: Harvard University Press, 1990.

McNeil, Legs, and Gillian McCain. *Please Kill Me: The Uncensored Oral History of Punk.* New York: Penguin, 1997.

Listen

Brandals. *The Brandals.* CD. N.p.: Sirkus Records, 2003.

Dewa. *Laskar Cinta.* CD. Jakarta: EMI Indonesia, 2004.

JKT: SKRG. CD. Jakarta: Aksara Records, 2004.

Teenage Death Star. *Longway to Nowhere.* CD. N.p.: FF CUTS Records, 2008.

White Shoes & The Couples Company. *White Shoes & The Couples Company.* CD. Jakarta: Aksara Records, 2005.

View

Garasi. DVD. Directed by Agung Sentausa and produced by Mira Lesmana. Jakarta, Miles Films, 2006.

Janji Joni. DVD. Directed by Joko Anwar. Jakarta: Kalyana Shira Films, 2005.

Surf

Barker, Thomas. "Ahmadiyah and Crisis of Indonesian Islam." The Jakarta Post. July 11, 2008. www.thejakartapost.com/news/2008/07/11/ahmadiyah-and-crisis-indonesian-islam.html.

PBS Frontline. "The Crash: Timeline of the Panic." www.pbs.org/wgbh/pages/frontline/shows/crash/etc/cron.html.

Tedjasukmana, Jason. "Can Dhani Dewa Rock the Casbah?" *Time World.* June 20, 2007. www.time.com/time/world/article/0,8599,1635351,00.html.

Chapter 7: You're the Terrorist

Read

Aslan, Reza. *No God but God: The Origins, Evolution, and Future of Islam.* New York: Random House, 2006.

Bascunan, Rodrigo, and Christian Pearce. *Enter The Babylon System: Unpacking Gun Culture from Samuel Colt to 50 Cent.* Toronto: Vintage Canada, 2008.

Chang, Jeff. *Can't Stop, Won't Stop: A History of the Hip-Hop Generation.* New York: Picador, 2005.

Lawrence, Bruce. *The Qur'an: A Biography.* London: Atlantic Books, 2006.

Watkins, S. Craig. *Hip Hop Matters: Politics, Pop Culture, and the Struggle for the Soul of a Movement.* Boston: Beacon Press, 2005.

View

Arotzim Shel Za'am. (Channels of Rage.) Documentary. Directed by Anat Halachmi. Tel Aviv: Anat Halachmi Productions, 2003.

DAM. "Innocent Criminals." www.youtube.com/watch?v=Dz3TxIes6mM.

Surf

DAM official website. www.dampalestine.com.

Gray/Brooklyn, Madison. "How Phat Conquered Palestine." *Time Entertainment*. December 5, 2007. www.time.com/time/arts/article/0,8599,1691246,00.html.

Katz, Jonathan M. "Zionist Rapper Wins Fans and Angers Critics." *AP Worldstream*. December 5, 2003. www.highbeam.com/doc/1P1-88054423.html.

Khazzoom, Loolwa. "The Arts: Hip-Hop Conquers Israel." *Hadassah Magazine*. 86, no. 8 (April 2005). www.hadassah.org/news/content/per_hadassah/archive/2005/05_April/art.asp.

McGirk, Tim. "Taking the Rap." *Time World*. February 22, 2007. www.time.com/time/magazine/article/0,9171,1592612,00.html?iid=digg_share.

"Palestine: Angry Islamists Break up Hip-Hop Concert with Kalashnikovs." *Freemuse*. October 6, 2005. www.freemuse.org/sw10796.asp.

Ramallah Underground website. www.ramallahunderground.com.

Subliminal website. http://www.tact-records.com/en.

Chapter 8: Stop Watching the News and Get in the Game

Read

Gee, James Paul. In *Gaming Lives in the Twenty-first Century: Literate Connections*, by Cynthia L. Selfe and Gail E. Hawisher, eds. New York: Palgrave, 2007.

——. *Good Video Games and Good Learning: Collected Essays on Video Games, Learning and Literacy*. New York: P. Lang, 2007.

Halter, Ed. *From Sun Tzu to Xbox: War and Video Games*. New York: Thunder's Mouth Press, 2006.

Johnson, Steven. *Everything Bad Is Good For You: How Today's Popular Culture Is Actually Making Us Smarter*. New York: Riverhead Books, 2006.

Lessig, Lawrence. *Free Culture: How Big Media Uses Technology and the Law to Lock Down and Control Creativity*. New York: Penguin Press, 2004.

Poole, Steven. *Trigger Happy: Videogames and the Entertainment Revolution*. New York: Arcade Publishing, 2004.

Surf

Afkar Media website. http://www.afkarmedia.com/.

Blakeslee, Sandra. "Video-Game Killing Builds Visual Skills, Researchers Report." *The New York Times: Technology*. May 29, 2003. query.nytimes.com/gst/fullpage.html?res=9E00E1D61E31 F93AA15756COA9659C8B63.

Friedman, Thomas L. "Giving the Hatemongers No Place to Hide." *The New York Times*. July 22, 2005. www.nytimes.com/2005 /07/22/opinion/22friedman.html.

"Islamogaming—Looking for Videogames in the Muslim World." 1UP.com. September 24, 2006. www.quraishgame.com/press/ islamogaming_cgw_2.pdf.

Riddell, Rob. "Doom Goes To War: The Marines Are Looking for a Few Good Games." *Wired*. April 1997. www.wired.com/wired/ archive/5.04/ff_doom.html.

Suellentrop, Chris. "The Evildoers Do Super Mario Bros.: The War on Terror's Least-Frightening Video Games." *Slate: Gaming: The Art of Play*. August 12, 2005. www.slate.com/id/2124363/.

"The Terrorists' Network: An Analysis of 'Pro-Arab' Video Games." *Allacademic Research*. www.allacademic.com/meta/p_mla_apa_ research_citation/1/6/9/0/5/pages169050/p169050-28.php.

Vargas, Jose Antonio. "Way Radical, Dude: Now Playing: Video Games with an Islamist Twist." *Washington Post: Arts & Living*. October 9, 2006. www.washingtonpost.com/wp-dyn/content/ article/2006/10/08/AR2006100800931.html.

"What is KUMA\WAR?" www.kumawar.com.

Play

Quraish. Video game. Created by Radwan Kasmiya and developed by Afkar Media. Syria: Dar al-Fikr, 2006.

Under Ash. Video game. Developed by Afkar Media. Syria: Dar al-Fikr, 2002.

Under Siege. Video game. Designed by Radwan Kasmiya. Syria: Dar al-Fikr, 2005.

Chapter 9: Book for a Nose Job

Read

Lynch, Marc. *Voices of the New Arab Public: Iraq, Al-Jazeera, and Middle East Politics Today.* New York: Columbia University Press, 2006.

Norton, Augustus Richard. *Hezbollah: A Short History.* Princeton, NJ: Princeton University Press, 2007.

Salibi, Kamal. *A House of Many Mansions: The History of Lebanon Reconsidered.* Berkeley: University of California Press, 1988.

Surf

"Al Jazeera Viewers Base in Saudi Arabia Is 5 Times Larger Than United States Sponsored AlHurra's Audience." September 5, 2004. www.ameinfo.com/56546.html.

Allied Media Corp. "Al Jazeera TV Viewer Demographic: Who Watches Al Jazeera?" 2007. www.allied-media.com/aljazeera/JAZdemog.html.

"Arab Big Brother Show Suspended." *BBC News.* March 1, 2004. news.bbc.co.uk/2/hi/middle_east/3522897.stm.

Aspden, Rachel. "Middle East: Of Poetry and Princes." *Newstatesman.* March 5, 2007. www.newstatesman.com/middle-east/2007/ 03/poetry-achievement-pinnacle.

www.economist.com/world/mideast-africa/displaystory.cfm?story_id=12267354&fsrc=rss.

Leila Obeid website. http://www.leilaobeid.com.

"The Power of Soft Talk." *MEB Journal.* March-April 2008. www.mebjournal.com/content/view/390/212.

"Saudi Arabia: Death to the Media Moguls!" *The Economist.* September 18, 2008.

Stigset, Marianne. "Reality TV Hits the Jackpot." Zawya. February

2005. www.zawya.com/story.cfm/sidZAWYA20050207113840/ Reality%20TV%20hits%20the%20jackpot%20.

Zaven Online.com. www.zavenonline.com.

Chapter 10: Full Nelson

Read

Ewans, Martin. *Afghanistan: A Short History of Its People and Politics.* New York: HarperCollins, 2002.

Fussell, Samuel Wilson. *Muscle: Confessions of an Unlikely Bodybuilder.* New York: Avon Books, 1992.

Surf

"Afghan Villagers Answer Your Questions." *BBC News.* June 19, 2007. news.bbc.co.uk/2/hi/south_asia/6763865.stm.

MOBY website. mobygroup.com/index.php.

Philp, Catherine. "The Woman Killed for Pop Music: Bright and Modern, She Hosted a Music Show in Afghanistan. It Drove Extremists to Murder Her." *The Times.* May 20, 2005. www.timesonline.co.uk/tol/news/world/article524399.ece.

"Premiere: Arman FM, Afghanistan." *Monocle.* monocle.com/sections/culture/Web-Articles/Arman-FM-Afghanistan.

Qarizadah, Daud. "Obituary: Shaima Rezayee." June 15, 2005. www.guardian.co.uk/news/2005/jun/15/guardianobituaries.media.

The Killid Group website. www.thekillidgroup.com.

Chapter 11: This Melting Town

Read

Bowden, Mark. *Guests of the Ayatollah: The First Battle in America's War with Militant Islam.* New York: Atlantic Monthly Press, 2006.

De Bellaigue, Christopher. *In the Rose Garden of the Martyrs: A Memoir of Iran.* New York: HarperCollins, 2005.

Kapuscinski, Ryszard. *Shah of Shahs.* 1982. Translated from the Polish by William R. Brand and Katarzyna Mroczkowska-Brand. New York: Vintage International, 1992, (c)1985.

Majd, Hooman. *The Ayatollah Begs to Differ: The Paradox of Modern Iran.* New York: Doubleday, 2008.

Varzi, Roxanne. *Warring Souls: Youth, Media, and Martyrdom in Post-Revolution Iran.* Durham, NC: Duke University Press, 2006.

Listen

Farzad Golpayegani's Official Website. http://www.farzadonline.com.

Qeshm Island. CD. Tehran: Hermes Records, 2003.

Surf

"Iran's Ahmadinejad: Movie '300' Vilifies Islam." March 21, 2007. archive.newsmax.com/archives/ic/2007/3/21/93653.shtml.

Majd, Hooman. "Visiting Dignitaries: Iftar." *The New Yorker.* October 8, 2007. www.newyorker.com/talk/2007/10/08/071008ta_talk_majd.

Middle East Media Research Institute. "Iranian TV: Disney's 'Pirates of the Caribbean—Dead Man's Chest' Is a Pawn of the Zionist Lobby to Gain Cultural Control." Special Dispatch no. 1302. September 27, 2006. www.memri.org/bin/articles.cgi?Page=subjects&Area=antisemitism&ID=SP130206.

ACKNOWLEDGMENTS

If I screwed up this book, I have only myself to blame. But if it is at all a workable piece of prose, I must attribute much of its success to an astonishing array of individuals, dotted as they are all over the planet.

Lorna Poplak has scoured countless versions of the manuscript. She did her damnedest to iron out the rough patches and has been instrumental in making sure that not only are the facts correct, but that they come in the right order. Any mistakes can safely be ascribed to me, but she made sure there were fewer of them. I cannot thank her enough.

Kevin Bloom was there from the beginning, with his usual mixture of insight and tough love. He helped get me started in Johannesburg in 2006, and he has seen me through the whole process. Ian Pearson, patron saint of Canadian literary non-fiction, went through the entire manuscript, bettering it immeasurably, proving that an alarming knowledge of both junk-culture and grammar can come in handy simultaneously. Nick Fairhead read an early draft of the introduction and helped steer me away from the rocks. Hosannas all.

Branko Brkic of the late and thoroughly lamented *Maverick Magazine* published a number of the raw ideas that took further shape herein. He was the rudder on my *dhow* during my research in the Gulf. Lisa Godfrey and the good folks at *Q*, CBC, constantly checked in with me on the road. Greig Dymond and Andre Meyer at CBC.ca were also early supporters, as was Pat Fothergill, late of *The Walrus*.

On the road, the full list is too long to include, but the major players who pitched in with advice, warm meals and stern lectures are Mitch Prothero, Habib Battah and Fatima Reda in Lebanon; Amy Mina in Jordan; Claudia Maedler, John MacDonald and Aspen Aman in Dubai; Michael Metrinko and Amanda Lindhout in Afghanistan; Hanin Sidharta and Jason Tedjasukmana in Indonesia; Aysha Selim in Egypt; Tim Mackintosh-Smith in Yemen; Kerry Suek in Qatar; Arash Jafari in Iran; Liz Taylor-Edmonds and Hanne Foighel in Israel.

David Tarigan, Zavan Kouyoumjian, Radwan Kasmiya, and Shahir and Melek Zahine were more than interview subjects. They took me into their lives and their homes, and treated my work as seriously as if it were their own. Their hospitality is an example that I hope one day to emulate, if ever I should get the chance.

On the Canadian front, my agents Don Sedgwick and Shaun Bradley kept the home fires burning. Nahayat Tizhoosh came onto the project early and remains a steadfast Sheikh's Batmobiler. Valda Poplak did fine work in compiling the bibliography. At Penguin Canada, Helen Reeves was the first person to hop inside the Batmobile and drove it through a sludge of early drafts, leaving the muck of later drafts for Alex Schultz, who has done a marvelous job of editing the manuscript. Jennifer Notman wrote epistles to Hamas and Hezbollah, Lisa Rundle made fancy documents out of Excel. Eleanor Gasparik went way beyond the call of duty in copy editing and fact checking, while David Ross kept a fierce hand on a hectic final few months of production. Thanks also to my *boetie* Stephen Myers.

The Toronto Writers' Centre, under the steadfast stewardship of Mitch Kowalski, remains the kernel of my writing cosmos. The trio of Giles Blunt, Andrew Westoll and Jonathan Hayes are the stars of that particular constellation. Cheers to Josh Knelman, who checked in with late advice and suggestions.

The Banff Centre was kind enough to provide food and accommodation for a time, and there I found Marni Jackson and Moira Farr who further kicked the manuscript's ass. Jeff Warren kicked my ass at mountain squash and subtly reminded me that lazy prose gets no one anywhere.

Kevin McLean has been a mentor, friend and cycling partner for the duration of this project. Without his sound counsel and generosity, this would have been a much lonelier process. For this, he has earned the right for me to drop him on the hills on our daily summer training sessions. Lindsay Page provided comedy, my family provided solace, my father provided bread. David Stephen, First Officer and great friend, gritted his teeth and made me his life partner so that I could avail myself of free air travel. My research would be paltrier were it not for his help. Bob R. in New York City did an Arabic check-through, which has hopefully kept me out of linguistic hot water.

In closing, I would like to mention the journalists working in the region who shall not leave as I did: fatter, smugger, with an excellent tan. Over the course of the two-plus years I was working on my book, a number of journalists have been kidnapped or otherwise incarcerated. As I write this, Canadian freelance writer and photographer Amanda Lindhout, Australian Nigel Brennan and their driver and fixer are still the reluctant guests of Somali kidnappers outside of Mogadishu. It happened to CBC-TV reporter Mellissa Fung in Afghanistan, BBC journalist Alan Johnson in the Gaza Strip and hundreds of others across the region. A general lack of respect for journalists has prevailed on every side of the so-called War on Terror. I offer no solutions. I just ask that we get pissed off every time it happens.